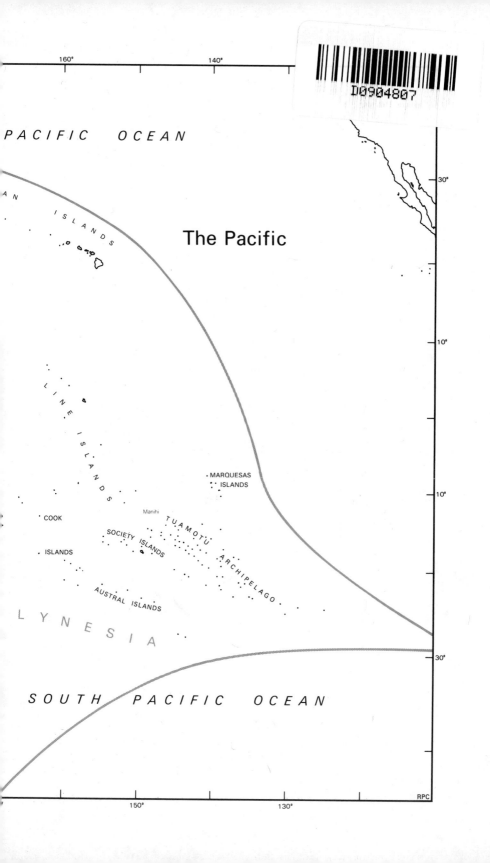

160°   140°

PACIFIC   OCEAN

30°

The Pacific

A N

I S L A N D S

L
I
N
E

I
S
L
A
N
D
S

· MARQUESAS
: · ISLANDS

10°

· COOK   Manihi

T U A M O T U

SOCIETY   ISLANDS

A
R
C
H
I
P
E
L
A
G
O

· ISLANDS

AUSTRAL   ISLANDS

L   Y   N   E   S   I   A

30°

SOUTH   PACIFIC   OCEAN

150°   130°

10°

10°

TRANSACTIONS
IN KINSHIP

*ASSOCIATION FOR SOCIAL
ANTHROPOLOGY IN OCEANIA*
Monograph Series

Mac Marshall, Series Editor
Everett A. Wingert, Associate Editor for Cartography

Other books in this series:
No. 1 *Adoption in Eastern Oceania*, edited by Vern Carroll
No. 2 *Land Tenure in Oceania*, edited by Henry P. Lundsgaarde
No. 3 *Pacific Atoll Populations*, edited by Vern Carroll

The ASAO Monograph Series was founded with the help of the
Wenner-Gren Foundation for Anthropological Research.

ASAO Monograph No. 4

TRANSACTIONS IN KINSHIP
Adoption and Fosterage in Oceania

Edited by Ivan Brady

THE UNIVERSITY PRESS OF HAWAII
Honolulu

Manufactured in the United States of America.
Composition by Asco Trade Typesetting Limited, Hong Kong

Library of Congress Cataloging in Publication Data
Main entry under title:

Transactions in kinship.

(ASAO monograph; no. 4)
Bibliography: p.
1. Kinship—Oceanica—Addresses, essays, lec-
tures. 2. Adoption—Oceanica—Addresses, essays,
lectures. I. Brady, Ivan A. II. Series:
Association for Social Anthropology in Oceania.
ASAO monograph; no. 4.
GN663.T72   301.42'1'099   76-10342
ISBN 0-8248-0478-3

GN
663
T72

595474

CONTENTS

FIGURES

TABLES

EDITOR'S PREFACE

In a recent "state of the art" review, Eggan (1972) notes that despite a century or more of substantial progress in the study of kinship since Morgan's pioneering efforts, we are still at a rather indeterminate state in our understanding of what kinship is, how it ought to be studied, and how it relates to other aspects of society and culture. We have never been more prepared for achieving a major synthesis of the diverse methods and theories used in kinship analyses than we are at present, but the indications are that such a synthesis will not be achieved quickly (see Barnes 1971; Eggan 1972; Schneider 1972). These circumstances demand a departure from methods and theories that obscure important data and incline the observer toward "simple models of complexity" (see Keesing 1972); they also invite an expanded probe of the meaning and scope of kinship phenomena generally, including adoption and fosterage.

A rigorous pursuit of the problems of describing and explaining adoption and related practices may contribute to resolving some of the larger problems that continue to confront us in attempts to understand kinship and social organization. From careful analysis of the social relations and cultural content that people conceptualize and put into practice when they 'make kinship' or rearrange their domestic organization through adoption, we may gain a better notion of how kinship systems generally are conceived and transformed into enduring and adaptive patterns (see Weckler 1953:555; Keesing 1970:991; Carroll 1970b:15). This volume has been assembled with these problems in mind. In focusing specifically on the nature of adoption and fosterage in Oceania, in some cases from divergent theoretical perspectives, we have necessarily engaged a dialogue concerning both the place of adoption in kinship studies and the nature of kinship itself. What remains to be determined is just how far these lines of inquiry will take us toward improving our understanding of the larger issues.

Published information on Oceanic adoption has increased steadily since Firth's description of adoption among the Maori in 1929. His famous Tikopia ethnography of 1936 includes a pioneering review of adoption on Tikopia and elsewhere in Polynesia (1936:588–596). Hogbin's work on Wogeo provides some interesting data on Melanesian adoption from about the same time period (1935, 1936). Weckler's (1953) study on Mokil is the first systematic attempt to describe adoption in a Micronesian culture. More recent accounts, such as those by Lambert (1964), Monberg (1970), and Keesing (1970), complement the systematic coverage provided by Vern Carroll's *Adoption in Eastern Oceania*— the first monograph in the ASAO Series. More than any work preceding it, Carroll's volume documents adoption as a widespread practice in Oceania that is comparable in complexity and importance to marriage as a domain of inquiry in kinship studies (see Hogbin 1971; Metge 1971; Wilson 1971; Foster 1972; Brady 1973; McKinley 1973 for reviews of this volume).

The idea of producing a second volume on adoption in the ASAO Series was suggested by Carroll in 1971, on the premise that additional ethnographic and theoretical coverage would be useful in attempting to solve some of the problems illuminated by the first volume. Several persons actively engaged in Oceanic research at the time, most of whom are represented here as authors, responded favorably to the idea. A symposium that clarified many of the existing issues and framed the content of the present work was organized and presented at the First Annual ASAO Meeting at Orcas Island, Washington, in 1972.

In addition to the contributors to this volume, the ethnographers attending the Orcas Island symposium included Charles Urbano-wicz and Marion Kelly. John Kirkpatrick and Charles Broder did not participate in the symposium, but they added substantially to the diversity and quality of the project by submitting a chapter in 1973. Rusiate Nayacakalou of Fiji, had plans for a chapter but passed away before they could be fulfilled. His contribution is conspicuously absent, and his presence is deeply missed. Another friend and colleague, Scott Wilson, whose chapter is included, died in late 1975. We dedicate this volume to their memory.

As in most projects of this kind, the path from conceptualization to press is often long and dotted with people who share with the authors the burden of evaluation and production. For stimulating and substantial intellectual commentary, we wish to acknowledge a large debt to Harold Scheffler and David Schneider. Their views, although often opposed and not necessarily represented in singular fashion in any of the following chapters, have contributed effectively to the merit of this project. Professor Schneider, in particular, generously diverted his energies through various stages of ill health to careful considerations of this work as it developed. Mac Marshall's careful reading and commentary helped immeasurably in bringing the final draft to fruition. Among the many other persons who have provided vital suggestions and encouragement, we wish to thank Janie Brady, Vern Carroll, Beth Dillingham, Barry Isaac, Bernd Lambert, and Carol Stack. A special note of appreciation is owed our typists, Jackie Bisaillon, Gloria Bowman, Margaret Heisel, and Helen Raby.

Finally, a brief note on chapter organization may be useful here. Rather than cluster the chapters by geographic region, the sequence has been ordered to maximize subtopic continuity. The chapters dealing primarily with adoption and land tenure and those concerned with alliance and social mobility, for example, occur in sequence. The societies described by Marshall, Wilson, Rynkiewich, Smith, and Kirkpatrick and Broder are in Micronesia; those covered by Brooks, Morton, Brady and Shore are in Polynesia; and Tonkinson's contribution concerns adoption in a Melanesian group. Carroll's (1970a) volume also includes descriptions of adoption in each of these areas, allowing considerable control in comparisons beyond the scope of the present work.

IVAN BRADY

TRANSACTIONS
IN KINSHIP

NOTES

Single quotes are used consistently throughout this book for glosses of native words, concepts, and conventional phrases.

The following standard abbreviations are used in this volume: F—father; M—mother; C—child; Ch—children; S—son; D—daughter; B—brother; Z—sister; H—husband; W—wife.

PROBLEMS OF DESCRIPTION AND EXPLANATION IN THE STUDY OF ADOPTION

Ivan Brady

INTRODUCTION

This chapter provides a summary of the main problems en-
countered to date in describing and explaining adoption in
Oceania. Most of the issues outlined below are pursued in specific
ethnographic contexts in the succeeding chapters, so this discourse
also serves as a general introduction to the volume. The most
immediate task is to narrow the scope of inquiry by providing
some definitions of adoption in relation to parenthood, siblingship,
marriage, and formal friendship. A review of existing explanations
of Oceanic adoption is undertaken in conclusion. The precedent
set for this discussion by Vern Carroll's *Adoption in Eastern
Oceania* (1970a) is evident throughout.

PRELIMINARY DEFINITIONS

Carroll suggests that we begin our analyses of adoption with
culturally specific and lexically labeled categories from each
society studied, thereby insuring "... our consideration of the full
range of information relevant to what the natives themselves
consider 'adoption'" (1970b:11). However, he sees as "hopeless"
even the most careful efforts "... to provide ethnographic
definitions of customary practices in terms of their 'essential
features' or in terms of a 'lowest common denominator' of at-

tributes . . ." (1970b:7). He then rejects any attempt to achieve a rigorously substantive definition of adoption in advance of an analytical reference point that offers a "coherent motivation" for assembling data pertinent to adoption. In this case, such a reference point ". . . can be provided only by a general theory of kinship" (1970b:8). The point in beginning the inquiry with culturally specific semantic data, therefore, is primarily to develop a data base with the least possible distortion of empirical reality for subsequent theory construction (cf. Atkins 1974), rather than to produce substantive definitions as ends in themselves (see also Goodenough 1965, 1970a).[1]

Nevertheless, Carroll recognizes the need for a "working" definition of adoption for preliminary focus. The contributors to his volume are careful to specify as clearly as possible what 'adoption' means in the cultural context of each society studied, and Carroll provides the following construct against which these data may be weighed: "*Adoption* [is] *any customary and optional procedure for taking as one's own a child of other parents*" (1970b:3). He discusses some of the difficulties inherent in operationalizing this definition, such as the meaning of "taking as one's own" where a child does not relinquish all claims to his former identity, and the contributors to that volume document several ways in which it is possible to qualify as a 'parent' or a 'child'. A further distinction is drawn in most of these societies between 'fosterage' as a temporary kinship obligation to take care of other peoples' children, and 'adoption' as a transaction in parenthood involving permanent assumption of the major responsibilities of jural parenthood (1970b:7). Transforming these concepts into strong analytic tools that allow an observer to distinguish one practice from another without ambiguity has proved to be a task with definite limitations. However, the issues involved are crucial to the study of adoption generally, and it is instructive to elaborate on them in terms of Ward Goodenough's contribution to Carroll's volume.

TRANSACTIONS IN PARENTHOOD

Goodenough (1970b) suggests that adoption and fosterage might usefully be analyzed as transactions in parenthood, primarily because adoption and fosterage entail a reallocation of parental rights and duties (as if they were property) to persons other than a child's natural parents. He states further that the study of adoption and fosterage can help to clarify the social and cultural structure of parenthood in fact and theory (1970b: 392; see also Weckler 1953: 555) and that a thorough ethnography of parenthood is prerequisite to a satisfactory assessment of adoption (1970b: 409), if not to an understanding of kinship in general. Underlying this thesis is the premise that all kin relationships ". . . in one way or another derive from a chain of parent-child connections" (1970b: 391; see also Goodenough 1970a: 23; Scheffler and Lounsbury 1972; Atkins 1974).

Laying a foundation for a thorough ethnography of parenthood, Goodenough suggests that a minimal analytic distinction be drawn among three forms: (1) *jural parenthood*, which is functionally derived from ". . . the social necessity to order human relations according to a code of rules in which social relationships are categorized and differently assigned rights and duties" (1970b: 391); (2) *psychic parenthood*, which is functionally derived from ". . . the human capacity to form emotional attachments" (1970b: 391); and, (3) *natural parenthood*, which is functionally derived from ". . . the human process of procreation" (1970b: 391; see also Atkins 1974: 2). These forms are defined differently for the two sexes primarily because of the difference between the natural associations children have with adult men and women (Goodenough 1970b: 392). Furthermore, noting that children have a more direct relationship with women because of the nature of parturition relative to biological paternity and because women usually provide the initial nurturance given to infants, Goodenough suggests that motherhood is the more basic of the two primary parental roles (1970b: 392). In view of this, and given that jural rather than psychic or natural parenthood is the primary dimension at stake in adoption transactions (see Goody 1969), let us consider jural motherhood specifically as an example from Goodenough's conceptual scheme.

In general, a jural relationship ". . . is one in which one party can make a demand upon another and there is public agreement that the other is obligated to comply with the demand" (Goodenough 1970b: 410). In this sense, jural motherhood is ". . . a social role that is culturally delimited and publicly sanctioned" (1970b: 394). Rather than define jural motherhood specifically by the content of the role itself, however, Goodenough does so in terms of a "... constant among the otherwise variable criteria by which women are entitled to the role." The constant in this case is parturition: "... jural motherhood consists of the rights and duties in relation to a child to which a woman has claim by virtue of her having borne it, provided she is eligible to bear it and provided no other disqualifying circumstances attend its birth" (1970b:394). Jural motherhood thereby is limited, at least initially, to claims based on coincidence with biological motherhood, and the analytic distinction drawn above between jural and natural parenthood is operationally merged to that extent. But the actual assignment of jural motherhood is still negotiable: "These rights may be delegated to other women in fosterage, they may be transferred to someone else in adoption, they may be forfeited in case of ineligibility, or they may be surrendered in the event of a divorce" (1970b:394), among other possibilities.

One such possibility that this definition obscures is that jural motherhood may be shared with persons other than the biological mother at a child's birth. That is, sharing of jural rights and duties may exist exclusive of special delegation through adoption or fosterage, declarations of ineligibility, and divorce transactions. A similar pattern may apply to jural fatherhood, which Goodenough defines narrowly as the rights and duties "... in relation to a child to which a person has claim by virtue of his being married or having been most immediately married to the woman who bore the child, provided he is otherwise eligible and provided no disqualifying circumstances attend the child's birth" (1970b:396). These entitlements may be renegotiated through adoption or fosterage, but their existence as features of jural parenthood is not predicated on such arrangements. Shared jural parenthood thus may be a structural feature of the kinship system itself. This means that jural parenthood is necessarily a matter of degree in such systems, and that it is *not* limited initially to claims based on coincidence with biological parenthood made by the woman who bore the child and by the man who has priority rights in the mother's sexuality (cf. Goodenough 1970b:394ff).

The Oceanic data at hand suggest that all persons classified as 'parents' acquire certain rights in and jural obligations toward a 'child' at the time of his birth by virtue of their identity as 'siblings' of the child's natural parents. The extent to which these widespread jural ties are activated depends in part on the history of personal adherence by the principals to the code for conduct governing 'parental' relations and 'siblingship' in that society. This pattern, in turn, helps determine the frequency and scope of adoption and fosterage (see especially Kirkpatrick and Broder, chapter 9). But the structural network into which the child is born is one of shared jural parenthood at the outset. Similar patterns may obtain in other societies where classificatory parental terminology predominates.

Recognizing that jural parenthood may be a matter of degree, exclusive of adoption and fosterage transactions, means that what Goodenough has defined as jural parenthood per se may be viewed more accurately as *primary* jural parenthood in Oceanic systems (see also Howard et al. 1970). Goodenough has implied as much in his discussion of persons in kinship networks who hold *existing* but perhaps latent entitlements to the children of other parents (1970b:388ff). However, since these entitlements need not be latent, and given that "the rights of the jural parents in relation to their own child may even be fewer than the rights of their own parents or of their older siblings" (1970b:404), the concept of primary jural parenthood requires additional qualifications to be unambiguous.

In general, *primary jural parenthood* may be said to exist *where one or more persons have assumed the greatest responsibility to nurture a child, to look after his interests, and to defend his rights according to the rules of that society.* This alignment may be generated either by birth or by adoption.[2] *Secondary jural parenthood* would then be present *wherever persons other than the primary jural parents are formally obligated to share the responsibility of the primary jural parents for their 'children', whether or not that responsibility is ever actually assumed.*[3] The result is a complex network of parenthood that can be described in terms of its jural structure, its cultural identity assignments, and the sociocultural transformations that affect the distribution of each of these components in adoption and fosterage transactions.

The basic issues at stake in adoption and fosterage transactions involving children, then, are how, to what extent, under what conditions, and to whom *primary* jural parenthood is to be transferred. Determining these patterns relative to the distribution of psychic parenthood and the biogenetic constructs attributed to parenthood in particular societies is crucial for understanding adoption from Goodenough's transactional perspective. Furthermore, recognizing that jural parenthood may be a matter of degree exclusive of adoption and fosterage may help clarify what is meant by "taking a child as one's own" in certain contexts, and thereby illuminate with less risk of empirical distortion the nature of succession to primary jural parenthood by persons with existing but latent entitlements to children. This is especially pertinent to the study of adoption in Oceania since most such arrangements are negotiated among close kinsmen who may already stand in a relationship of classificatory 'parent' or 'grandparent' to their adoptees.

Whether or not succession to primary jural parenthood and related transactions constitute "adoption" in any useful analytic sense is another matter. Goodenough notes that: "The term 'adoption' has been applied indiscriminately to what appear to be instances of succession and of the exercise of overriding grandparental rights, as well as to instances of sharing and of outright transfer of jural parenthood" (1970b:409), leaving the issue of whether these phenomena ought to be identified analytically as "adoption" unresolved. Carroll suggests that: "As an analytic tool the term 'adoption' may prove to be quite useless; as a descriptive term it appears to be quite indispensable" (1970b:11).

In the interest of proper description and in keeping with the precedent set for delimiting the subject matter in Carroll's volume, the contributors to this volume have been careful to specify as accurately as possible what 'adoption' means in the societies they have studied. The empirical range of what has been identified as 'adoption' in this manner covers each of the contingencies enumerated by Goodenough as transactions in parenthood in a variety of ethnographic contexts. Careful consideration of these data suggests that if we are to show some fidelity to culturally specific paradigms in our analyses, then the notion of adoption as transactions in parenthood is too restrictive.

SIBLING ADOPTIONS

While most transactions ordinarily identified as 'adoption' are in fact 'parent-child' relations of one kind or another, other transactions that are classified generically by the same term involve the adoption of persons as 'siblings' (see Firth 1965:191; Silverman 1970, 1971; Lambert 1970). The adoptee in these instances becomes an adoptive 'sibling' rather than a 'child', and the sponsor's role is that of 'sibling' rather than 'parent'. It is analytically possible, of course, to derive siblingship from parent-child connections and to treat the analysis of adoptive siblingship arbitrarily in this context. But adoptive 'siblingship' appears to be distinguished clearly from adoptive 'parenthood' by the people themselves, and there is no reason to suspect that all adoptive sibling transactions are either conducted in the language of parent-child relations or that they necessarily involve 'parents' as principals in any direct way.[4] It makes little sense, therefore, to translate such relations into parent-child terms, or to conceive of them primarily as transactions in parenthood.

Although Goodenough does not suggest explicitly that adoptive siblingship should be subsumed under transactions in parenthood, his model fails to take adoptive siblingship into account as a category in itself and as it relates to adoption practices generally. As Fortes' (1969) intensive analysis of filiation and siblingship suggests, and as the data in Carroll's volume illustrate, siblingship and parenthood are cultural constructs and social roles that may be subject to independent manipulation in adoption transactions. Carroll (1970b:10) submits that the construction of any general theory of kinship will have to take such practices as adoptive siblingship into account.

Goodenough is careful to stress that adoption and fosterage viewed as transactions in parenthood are "... only part of a more general phenomenon," and that a broader view of the field of kinship transactions "... could well change our perspective on adoption as it is dealt with in [Carroll's 1970a] volume" (1970b: 395). In light of the above discussion, it seems useful to revise adoption as transactions in parenthood. The broader category of "transactions in kinship" would include both transactions in parenthood and adoptive siblingship. Moreover, on this broader level of analysis, the problems of differentiating adoption from similar transactions such as birth, formal friendship, and marriage come to the fore (see Carroll 1970b:10–11; Brady 1973:438).

ADOPTION AND FOSTERAGE REDEFINED

Emphasizing the importance of adoption as a sociocultural process of recruitment to kinship identities, a new definition may be formulated as follows: *Adoption is any positive and formal transaction in kinship, other than birth or marriage, that creates new or revises existing kinship bonds to bring them into accordance with any other kinship identity set customarily occupied by two or more persons in that society.* To be of any use as an analytic construct against which concrete and culturally specific data may be evaluated, the terms of this definition and the premises underlying it must be made clear.

Use of the phrases "transactions in kinship" and "kinship identity set" presumes that there is something we can confidently and realistically identify as "kinship" relative to all other aspects of society and culture. The literature on this topic is voluminous and often contradictory, a major part of the problem being the search for a common analytic reference language for describing kinship on a comparative basis (see Gellner 1957, 1960; Leach 1958; Beattie 1964; Schneider 1964, 1965a, 1968a, 1969, 1972; Lévi-Strauss 1967a, 1969; Buchler and Selby 1968; Goodenough 1970a; Barnes 1971; Scheffler 1966, 1970, 1973; Chock 1974; Keesing 1975). Rather than attempt an extended review of these issues here, it is sufficient for present purposes to compare what is meant by consanguinity and adoption as kinship identity constructs.

Consanguineal kinship can be defined in terms of parenthood and genealogical connectedness.[5] Scheffler and Lounsbury, for example, use genealogical connection "... as a cover term for a wide variety of culturally postulated forms of congenital relatedness between persons" (1972:38). More specifically, genealogical connection designates "... those *culturally posited* forms of interpersonal connectedness that are held to be direct consequences of processes of engendering and bearing children that have the property of indissolubility" (1972:37–38). On the other hand,

"The *social* relations normatively entailed by [consanguineal] kinship are not conceived as congenital or indissoluble, no matter how binding they may be in law or morality . . ." (1972:39). Furthermore, ". . . one *cannot* choose his [consanguineal] kinsmen whereas he *may or may not* choose to fulfill the duties and obligations of being a kinsman or a particular kind of kinsman" (1972:39; see also Schneider 1968a:24; Fortes 1969:16–18). Thus, when the code for conduct that governs behavior among consanguineal kin is ruptured through inappropriate behavior or is realigned in adoption or related transactions, the underlying 'natural' construct ideally endures in local theory.[6]

Adoptive kinship lacks a culturally posited construct that is 'congenital' or 'natural' in the same substantive sense generally assigned to relationships by birth. Following Schneider's (1968a, 1970) useful analysis of American kinship, and applying it to this broader definitional context, birth can be viewed as a construct that obtains "in nature." Legitimate births obtain "in nature" as well as "in law." Adoption and marriage are relationships that obtain "in law" or "in custom" only. Subtracting the normative or "code" features from a step, affinal, or adoptive kinship identity theoretically dissolves the relationship entirely.[7] Persons who do share culturally posited heredity may be assigned a high priority as candidates for adoption, and adoptive kinship identities may be designed to emulate as closely as possible those that are derived from or normally assigned to 'congenital relatedness', such as 'parent', 'child', or 'sibling' (see Freed 1963; Goody 1969).[8] Adoption emerges in this light as one method of recruiting people to fill these identities in the social system; birth is another. But noting the parallel of these two as modes of recruitment is not to say that adoptive kinship and consanguinity are ultimately the same thing. Aside from its lacking a purely 'congenital' construct on the order of birth, adoption is more or less volitional as an act, and it is terminable as a relationship. Consanguinity is not volitional, and it is theoretically not terminable as a 'congenital' or 'natural' construct.

What *is* overtly alterable in the consanguineal case is the normative and nominal content of the relationship, as Scheffler and Lounsbury assert by noting the lack of "indissolubility" in social relations entailed by consanguinity. As a result of a quarrel or some perceived breach in the code for conduct governing relation-ships among consanguines in American kinship, for example, kinship identities may be denied voluntarily and social relation-ships severed to the point of rendering the 'congenital' ties normatively and nominally ineffective (see Schneider 1968a). More formal yet is the well-known custom of *ambil-anak* in Indonesia. The spouse of a 'real' child is socially and jurally redefined as a 'consanguine' relative to his marital group, kin terms are reassigned in the process, and the inheritance profile of the principals is altered accordingly. The intention is to maintain descent and property group continuity in favor of the proper sex (see Kennedy 1937:291; Murdock 1949:21). Similarly, the custom known as *ko motu te ngafa* 'breaking the [ramage] family' in the Ellice Islands is a process whereby consanguines who are too closely related to marry each other (closer than fourth cousins) can be socially and jurally redefined as more 'distant' relatives in order to accommodate the marriage (see Brady 1975:116). Beattie (1971) makes a similar point with reference to 'cutting kinship' in Bunyoro. Under certain circumstances, then, a relation-ship based on 'congenital' ties and expressed as a 'consanguineal' identity may be denied voluntarily or otherwise be effectively reassigned through social and jural processes. It is precisely this culturally specific capability to manipulate and change kinship identities that makes adoption possible.

The definition of adoption presented here is phrased in terms of kinship identity change processes rather than in terms of specific kinship identities or sociocultural content. As such, it can accom-modate any kinship identity set (M–C, F–C, B–Z, etc.) that may be subject to realignment or transfer in adoption, whatever the sociocultural content of that set happens to be in particular societies. But the actual content of the set must be specified, of course, in order to operationalize the definition. This requires a delineation of the necessary and sufficient conditions that con-stitute 'kinship' in particular societies, including the criteria used in those societies for allocating and distributing the various specific identities represented by the category 'kinsmen'. Further-more, these facts should be described relative to the minimal substantive, normative, terminological, and symbolic dimensions of the whole paradigm glossed as 'kinship', rather than being arbitrarily restricted in focus to criteria phrased only in geneal-ogical terms. Changes in any of these dimensions may represent formal or effective changes in a person's kinship identity and thereby are pertinent to an understanding of adoptive processes.

In some Pacific societies, for example, shared land may con-stitute a sufficient condition for identifying a person as a 'kinsman', in conjunction with or exclusive of the presence of shared 'blood' as a cultural construct (see Silverman 1970, 1971; Lundsgaarde and Silverman 1972; Brady, chapter 7). Adoption events and adoptive kinship identities also depend on land tenure considera-tions in these societies. The formal allocation of land rights to an adoptee by the sponsors concretizes and validates the event for the principals and their fellow kinsmen; it also changes the kinship identity of the adoptee to one that is socially, jurally, and symbolic-ally closer in relative kinship distance to the sponsors than before. Whether or not such identity assignments are simply normative entailments and metaphoric extensions of genealogical criteria (see Scheffler 1972a, 1972b; cf. Silverman 1971) is an important problem but not the main concern here. The important point is that formally shared land is comparable to shared 'blood' at *some* level of sociocultural reality as an element for conceptually grounding kinship identities and relationships in these societies and, presumably, elsewhere. Shared land must be taken into account, therefore, as one of several possible 'kinship' dimensions that are susceptible to manipulation and reassignment in adoption transactions (but cf. Tonkinson, chapter 10).

Similarly, kin terms are not the only features through which kinship classification is established (see Schneider 1972:49; Chock 1974), and they are not the only features subject to negotiation and transfer in adoption. All adoptive identities have a nominal component that is expressed through kin-term assignments, but the notion that adoption involves a change in primary kin-term assignments must be given careful consideration relative to other kinds of changes possible. Some Oceanic 'adoption' events entail more extensive kin-term changes than others, depending largely upon the context of recruitment from which the adoptee is drawn. In instances where the adoptee is recruited from 'outside' the sponsor's existing kinship network, the adoptee acquires a new kinship identity in his adoptive context, and kin terms are assigned accordingly to cover his adoptive position. The change in kinship identity in such cases is conspicuous and easily identified by the assignment of primary kin terms where they would otherwise be inappropriate.

In 'adoption' transactions involving succession to primary jural parenthood by persons who already stand in the relationship of classificatory 'parent' or 'grandparent' to the adoptee, the reassignment of kin terminology may be nothing more extensive than adding a secondary or derivative meaning to specify the 'adoptive' relation in a kinship network where the primary kin-term allocations remain unchanged. The distinctive features of 'adoption' in these cases may thus be rooted more conspicuously in sociological or jural criteria, such as residential realignments and formal changes in property group affiliation or inheritance profiles, than in terminological changes. A satisfactory account of adoption must reconcile these differences with respect to primary kin-term allocations, especially where the observer's definition of adoption depends on validating an actual change in "genealogical position" for the adoptee (see Howard et al. 1970:21).

The stipulation in the definition presented above that adoption be a "formal" transaction means that the change in kinship identity must be jurally binding (see Goodenough 1970b:409, quoted above) for at least the principal negotiators and the adoptees. Such relationships are also ideally intended to endure indefinitely. It is rare in some societies for adoptions to endure for long periods of time (see Carroll 1970c), but, as in American marriages, the actual endurance of an adoption relationship is a performance or situational feature rather than a structural one. It is thereby isolable from the structural criterion of "permanence" implied or stated at the time of the negotiations. Knowledge that the arrangement *can be* terminated and the relationship discharged by mutual consent or default may be taken into account at the outset by the principals as part of their decision to negotiate the transaction. This may be important as surety for the adoptee in the event of unforeseen complications that adversely affect his welfare, or as protection for the adopters in the event the adoptee's performance fails to meet their expectations. This does not mean, however, that the relationship *will be* terminated necessarily, and adoptions generally are *negotiated* on the premise that they will endure indefinitely.[9]

Termination of the relationship is a separate transaction, if and when it becomes pertinent as an issue.

The criterion of permanence or intended duration also appears to be a significant point of contrast between adoption and fosterage, as suggested at the beginning of this chapter. Fosterage can be defined relative to adoption as *a temporary change in kinship identity through kin group and perhaps residential realignment where no permanent arrangement is either negotiated or intended* (see also Goody 1969:75; Marshall, chapter 2; Smith, chapter 11). Foster relationships thus are engineered more or less explicitly on the premise that they will *not* endure indefinitely. Fosterage is a jural transaction insofar as there is customary agreement concerning the rights and duties of the principals, but the kinship identity changes involved are not generally conceived of as jurally binding on other than a temporary or de facto basis.

Where dependent children are involved, as is the usual case,[10] fosterage represents the temporary sharing of primary jural parenthood with persons who would otherwise not be entitled to do so, or the simple activation of latent obligations among 'classificatory' kin to 'care for' a child for a short time (cf. Goodenough 1970b:409). The latter cases occasionally phase neatly into formal 'adoption' transactions as instances of succession to primary jural parenthood. The empirical range of 'adoption' is thus likely to include some transactions that begin as simple 'fosterage' and are transformed into more formal and enduring relationships in the long run (see Lambert 1970; Brady, chapter 7). Similarly, some transactions ambiguously identified as 'adoption' at the outset may fail to manifest themselves as formal transactions altogether in the long run—that is, they may effectively dissolve without further consideration by any of the original principals (see Carroll 1970c; Lieber 1970). Furthermore, the distinction between 'adoption' and 'fosterage' is not made in some societies (see Howard 1970:368) and is fundamentally irrelevant in others, so it is possible for an observer to distort the reality of the situation by insisting on an absolute distinction where none in fact exists (see also Kirkpatrick and Broder, chapter 9).

None of this poses any serious difficulties for the definitions presented here. Adoption and fosterage have been defined analytically as different aspects of the same phenomenon—that is, as isolable points on a continuum of kinship identity change processes. It may be expected that some transactions will be more explicit than others (see Carroll 1970c), that some will be more formal than others, and that events structured one way at the time of negotiations may be transformed into other patterns in the long run. If the observer specifies the nature of the event in terms of intended duration and the level of formality relative to the kinship identity features reallocated or reassigned, the results can be placed at some point on the continuum between absolutely formal adoptions and absolutely minimal and informal fosterage, or at two different points at different times (see figure 1).

The third dimension shown in figure 1 is the degree to which an adoption transaction is jurally exclusive or inclusive of the adoptee's previous identity. As intimated above in the section on kin-term changes, some events glossed as 'adoption' involve a formal and more or less complete substitution of one set of kinsmen for another. The identification of the adoptee with his natal group is severed socially and jurally to the extent that all previously existing rights and duties are forfeited indefinitely in exchange for a formal assumption of new ones appropriate to the adoptive identity (see Firth 1959: 126–127). This is the *jurally exclusive* extreme, and it is comparatively rare in Oceania. The *jurally inclusive* extreme, on the other hand, involves only a partial or perhaps no significant

FIGURE 1.   An Analytic Continuum of Adoption and Fosterage.

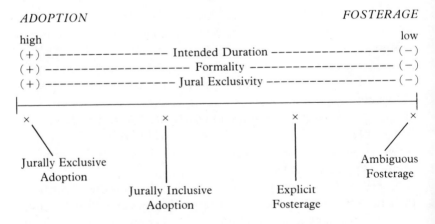

forfeiture of the adoptee's existing kinship identity and con-comitant rights and duties in his natal group. The adoptee simply adds a new set of relatives he either did not have before or to whom he stood in a different relationship before (see Ottino 1970; Carroll 1970c).[11] Most Oceanic 'adoptions' incline toward this extreme and, as such, may imply (if not precipitate) a lesser degree of permanence than is suggested by the more complete changes in kinship identity associated with jurally exclusive transactions. Fosterage, of course, is, by definition, jurally inclusive of the adoptee's previous kinship identity. Ultimate responsibility for a foster child's welfare remains with the child's primary jural parents despite some delegation of that responsibility to the foster parents on a temporary basis. For these reasons, some jurally inclusive adoptions may be more difficult to differentiate from explicit fosterage transactions than from their jurally exclusive counterparts.

Furthermore, since some components of an adoptee's previous identity and relationships with his parents or siblings can be transferred or shared with his adopters while others remain intact, it follows that not all adoption events are necessarily inclusive or exclusive of the same components. A transaction that is jurally exclusive with respect to inheritance rights, for example, may be jurally inclusive with respect to incest taboo parameters and so on. Another separable component in the Gilbert Islands and other Pacific societies is the primary right or responsibility for "bringing up" a child. It may be transferred in adoption without depriving the child's previous jural parents of their authority to decide on the child's marriage or place of residence, for example, and the transaction is jurally inclusive to that extent. The Gilbertese, in fact, make a triple distinction among formally 'adopted' children, 'foster' children who are expected to spend most of their time in the home of their guardians, and children who are simply staying with relatives for a short period (Lambert, personal communication). However refractory to analysis this sort of shared jural parenthood may be, it is incumbent on the observer to specify as clearly as possible both the sociocultural terms and the degree of exclusive-ness in each case pertinent to temporary or enduring changes in kinship identities.

MECHANICAL DIMENSIONS OF ADOPTION

The stipulation of a paired relationship in the phrase "kinship identity set" in the definition above is meant to indicate a minimal mechanical dimension of adoption transactions, rather than to pass judgment a priori on the overall scope of relationships that may be affected. The focus in each transaction is placed at a minimum on two individuals or groups as principals. Some diagrams may help to illustrate these points.

All of the individual units in figure 2 represent principals in the sense that default by any one of them may invalidate the arrangement as negotiated and thereby force termination. Their relationships, therefore, are governed by mutual interest or reciprocity. Three dyads cover these fundamental relationships: *adopter* ⟶ *adoptee*, *adoptee* ⟶ *primary jural parents*, and *adopter* ⟶ *adoptee's primary jural parents* (cf. Ottino 1970:105).

As a transaction in parenthood between two adults on behalf of a dependent child, the primary responsibility for negotiating the arrangement lies as a general rule with the child's primary jural parents and the prospective adopter (figure 2a). The child C, as adoptee, is the third party and serves as the definitive link in any wider alliance and exchange relationships that may result from the transaction. The principals labeled A and B in this figure may or may not be 'congenital' kinsmen (as indicated by the parentheses), and they may or may not establish a formal relationship as 'siblings' as a result of the transaction (see Rynkiewich, chapter 6). But B has the primary responsibility as jural parent over C and is the source of that responsibility for A. B's responsibility may be delegated in advance to another person or agency who then acts as principal negotiator on C's behalf, as is commonplace in American adoption. The person B then is phased out and the result may be a transaction that is jurally exclusive of the adoptee's former kinship identity, although it need not be in all cases.

If A and B are 'congenital' kinsmen, B's responsibility may be shared in advance on a latent or secondary priority basis with A as a structural feature of the kinship system. The transaction in this case is not exclusive of the adoptee's former kinship identity, and the event may be focused as much on engineering or increasing solidarity between A and B as it is concerned with the adoptee per se. The wider contextual features must be determined empirically and specified by the observer in each case, for there is much variation in this regard.[12] Irrespective of variations in these wider features, however, events represented by figure 2a are the most frequent type reported in the literature from Oceania.

In events identified as 'parental' adoptions (figure 2b), the responsibility for negotiations and effective sponsorship of the arrangement lies for the most part with the adoptive 'child' (see Silverman 1970:214ff; Rynkiewich, chapter 6). These cases are unusual in that the 'child' as a subordinate in the adoptive relationship assumes (or perhaps acquires through the death of his primary jural parents) a prerogative to act on his own behalf in obtaining an adoptive 'parent'. The outcome is still a transaction in parenthood, similar to those represented by figure 2a. But the focus on principal negotiators is placed most directly in a vertical rather than a horizontal kinship context in this case, and the importance of a third party as subject is peripheral or is eliminated entirely.

The context of negotiations in sibling adoptions (figure 2c) is horizontal (as in 2a), but the importance of a third party subject is eliminated (as in 2b). The key feature is that the principals negotiate approximately equal positions for themselves as adoptive 'siblings', irrespective of third party subjects. Other combinations are possible, of course, as in the adoption of persons as 'grandchildren'. The three forms illustrated here are intended to represent only the core or elementary features from which more complex relationships may be built.

FIGURE 2.   Three Types of Adoption.

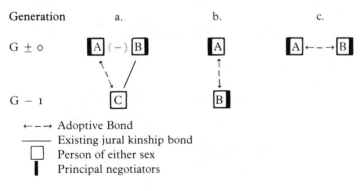

Generation   a.   b.   c.

G ± 0   A (−) B   A   A ←－→ B

G − 1   C   B

←－→ Adoptive Bond
───── Existing jural kinship bond
☐   Person of either sex
▌   Principal negotiators

ADOPTION, MARRIAGE, AND POSITIVE TRANSFORMATIONS

The stipulation that adoption is a transaction in kinship "other than marriage" is important but problematic insofar as marriage itself has proved difficult to define satisfactorily (cf. Leach 1955; Gough 1959; Goodenough 1970a; Dillingham and Isaac 1975). Both adoption and marriage create relatives "in custom only," regardless of any preexisting consanguineal ties; both may function as important devices for achieving diffuse and enduring solidarity where none exists beforehand, thereby promoting sociability and alliance (see Schneider 1968a). Each links at least two people in a manner that they were not linked before (see Goodenough 1970a:121; Fortes 1962, 1969). One basic and apparently crucial difference, however, has to do with the differential allocation of priority rights of sexual access to other persons or groups. Marriage generally promotes sexuality between the principals in each transaction, whereas adoption prohibits sexuality on a similar scale. In adoption, the principals are either bound by existing incest taboo parameters, as in the jurally inclusive adoption of consanguineal kin, or else new parameters are set as part of the transaction.[13]

The definitional stipulation that adoption is a "positive" transaction means that it is akin to birth and marriage insofar as all three represent transactions in kinship that bring people together in new and structurally solidary relationships. Death, divorce, "disowning" a son, and 'cutting kinship' in the ways previously outlined are also transactions in kinship in that they involve an alteration of kinship identities. But the change in these instances is negative. Negative transactions undermine rather than contribute to structural solidarity for the persons involved.

ADOPTION AND FORMAL FRIENDSHIP

What has been called 'formal friendship' and 'blood brotherhood' in the ethnographic literature from Oceania and beyond also poses some considerations that need at least minimal clarification relative to adoption. The common denominator of adoptive siblingship, blood brotherhood, and formal friendship appears to be mainly an extension of the normative and nominal content of 'congenital' (and usually same-sex) siblingship to other persons. Each of these customs qualifies as adoption in the analytic sense employed here to the extent that individuals are formally recruited to fill a kinship identity as 'siblings' (see Evans-Pritchard 1962; Wolf 1966; Marshall, chapter 2; Morton, chapter 4; Rynkiewich, chapter 6; Brady, chapter 7).[14]

Whether it will ultimately prove useful to differentiate among these customs as special types of adoption, or to disqualify them as adoption altogether on the basis of criteria not considered here, remains to be determined. But it is evident that the sociocultural processes underlying blood brotherhood and formal friendship are those of adoption generally, and a thorough analysis of these practices may further aid our discovery of new facts about kinship, how it is defined in particular societies, and how it can be manipulated as a sociocultural system to accommodate cultural persistence and population survival.

EXPLANATIONS, FUNCTIONS, AND PROCESSES

Carroll (1970c) advances the argument that adoption on Nukuoro can be explained as part of a larger pattern of sharing resources among kinsmen. By emphasizing 'parent-child' bonds in particular and by being restricted almost exclusively to relations among consanguines, Nukuoro adoption reiterates the nominal, normative, and symbolic content of close kinship and results in relations that actualize or reinforce kin-group solidarity. Consanguineal kin are viable 'relatives' only to the extent that they follow the code for conduct governing such relationships, and the code in this case includes a fundamental norm for sharing strategic resources widely (Carroll 1970c: 147; see also Schneider 1970: 377; Silverman 1971). Sharing children as 'adoptees' activates this norm and further communicates the message that all relatives are necessarily interdependent. This thesis clearly represents the major features underlying parental succession and other types of 'adoption' on Nukuoro; it also appears to be generally applicable to other Oceanic societies that have a high frequency of adoption and fosterage (see Carroll 1970b: 13).

Marshall (chapter 2) deals with Carroll's thesis along with other issues that are essentially demographic. He suggests that the high rates of adoption and fosterage in greater Trukese society cannot be explained exclusively as a response to demographic and domestic cycle imbalances caused by infertility (see Ruth Goodenough 1970; Fischer 1963) or by random irregularities in the birth cycles of small populations (see Fischer 1970). Structural compulsions for sharing children as 'adoptees' may promote adoption transactions even in the absence of demographic imbalances and therefore must be included as either complementary or independent considerations in explaining adoption and fosterage rates in these communities.

According to Levy (1970), Tahitian adoption communicates a psychological message to participants that all social relationships are conditional. This means that children, as highly valued assets to parents and community, nevertheless have a contingent relationship with their parents that is subject to manipulation through adoption. Brooks (chapter 3) adds another, more positive side to this message in the occasionally hostile climate of the Tuamotus: lost kinsmen are replaceable. Adoption thereby serves a basic ecological as well as a social and psychological function in this context (see also Alkire 1965).

Kirkpatrick and Broder (chapter 9) pick up the theme of conditionality once again and discuss its relevance to explanations of adoption and parenthood on Yap. They isolate the significance of long-term nurturance and cumulative 'work' or 'service' relationships for validating both consanguineal and adoptive kinship identities and for binding parents to children as members of the same estate. They note that Yapese adoption cannot be described or explained realistically without taking into account the system of symbols and meanings that frame for individuals the nature of social action in kinship networks (see also Schneider 1968a; Silverman 1971), and they pose some intriguing questions concerning the cultural possibilities for reallocating rights and duties in adoption and related transactions. Shore (chapter 8) asserts a similar thesis in his evaluation of adoption for both domestic and political alliance purposes in Samoa. He adds children as adoptees to Lévi-Strauss' list of women and goods as exchange media between groups,[15] and he stresses the importance of naming as a symbolic and normative feature of adoption transactions in the context of both descent and alliance theory.

The functional importance of conditionality in parent-child relations and of the focus on sociocultural aspects of kinship in adoption transactions is summed up succinctly by Lieber in his review of adoption on Kapingamarangi: "The cultural models of kinship relations and behavior in general and of adoption in particular afford an ideal framework within which, and by means of which, people can manipulate their social relationships to their immediate or future advantage" (1970:203). Morton (chapter 4) musters additional support for this generalization in his analysis of Tongan adoption as a kinship goal management and achievement system. Wilson (chapter 5), Rynkiewich (chapter 6), and Brady (chapter 7) document the use of adoptive kinship as a means of gaining access to strategic resources such as land in two Micronesian cultures and in a Polynesian culture, respectively. Tonkinson (chapter 10) illustrates the management of social relations and the reallocation of kinship identities through adoption in support of marital exchange and alliance needs in a New Hebridean community. Smith (chapter 11) focuses on the comparatively low rate of fosterage on Rota and a correspondingly wide range of functional alternatives to the practice. His analysis also reveals the importance of fosterage as an adaptive strategy through which people continue to manipulate social relationships to their advantage in the face of dramatic culture change (see also Howard et al. 1970).

In even more particular terms, adoption and fosterage have been posited in this and in Carroll's (1970a) volume as sociocultural means for: (1) assisting indigent persons or groups by placing disadvantaged individuals in more advantageous socioeconomic positions within their kin groups and communities; (2) providing childless couples with social offspring, thereby at least partially validating their adult statuses; (3) insuring estate and descent group continuity by providing formal heirs; (4) filling vacant domestic work roles in households; (5) satisfying strong affective demands for close association among persons who would otherwise remain more distant; (6) absorbing 'outsiders' into local kin groups and communities; (7) extending the range of hospitality and general kinship obligations as survival insurance among persons and groups who would otherwise be classified as 'non-kinsmen'; and, (8) consolidating and actualizing existing kinship obligations for sharing resources and providing mutual assistance in times of need. The motivations cited by the participants in adoption are equally varied and often disparate from the standpoint of each person involved. Similarly, the reasons for maintaining an adoptive bond may change radically in the course of a lifetime (see Carroll 1970b: 12–13; Lieber 1970), thereby posing further problems for analysis and placing considerable emphasis on the need for processual or developmental models in descriptions and explanations of adoption and related practices.

Most accounts of Oceanic adoption to date have been cast in a structural rather than a processual analytic frame (see Brown 1963; Barnett 1965; Schneider 1972:61); that is, they have been concerned primarily with the relationships among adoption, fosterage, and other aspects of society and culture under given conditions, rather than with the interrelationships of these elements in the context·of change and realignment over time (but see Ottino 1970; Tonkinson, chapter 10). In other than an approximate sense, viable explanations of these customs must necessarily hinge on more than functional propositions that pertain to the internal structuring of culture (see Goodenough 1970a: 122ff). In addition to a powerful theory of contextualization (Keesing 1972) and a careful mapping of the "purely cultural" or symbolic domain underlying adoption and parenthood in particular societies (see Schneider 1968a; Hooper 1970; Silverman 1970), there is a need to identify and specify the various combinations of cognitive, sociocultural, and ecological processes that generate adoptive kinship. Process identification in this sense represents a sufficient level of explanation (Barnett 1965; Barth 1966).

In sum, a rigorously comprehensive and integrative theory of kinship is needed, one that delineates and explains variable form, function, meaning, context, and process with equal facility and with the least possible distortion of empirical reality. Such a theory must also explain, of course, the nature of adoption and fosterage and related practices that have until recently occupied the periphery of kinship studies. On the other hand, as Carroll (1970b) points out, answers to questions about adoption are answers to questions about kinship itself, and our understanding of kinship phenomena generally will be enhanced by knowledge of why and under what circumstances some people adopt and others do not. The following chapters provide some answers to these questions by presenting an expanded body of ethnography on adoption and fosterage in several Oceanic societies.

NOTES

This chapter is a revised and expanded version of a paper presented at the 71st Annual Meeting of the American Anthropological Association, Toronto, 1972. I am grateful for the many suggestions and comments offered on a previous draft by Keith Morton, David M.H. Richmond, Michael Rynkiewich, Jerry Smith, and Carol Stack. For other vital input, I wish to thank Harold Scheffler, David Schneider, Bernd Lambert, Henry Lundsgaarde, Mac Marshall, and John Kirkpatrick. Their divergent but especially probing comments have changed the tenor and the substance of this chapter considerably.

1. A strictly a priori approach to identifying adoption cross-culturally is unsatisfactory because it risks introducing any number of unspecified assumptions concerning the actual sociocultural content of 'adoption' transactions in particular societies (Carroll 1970b: 11). The introduction of such assumptions can be especially disruptive when the analytic goal is not only to identify particular behaviors but also to predict their outcome (see Howard 1970; Keesing 1967, 1970, 1971).

2. See also Scheffler's review of Rivers' notion of "social kinship" and adoption on Mota, where, under certain circumstances, ". . . men other than presumed genitors pay midwives and thereby establish claims [for themselves and their wives] over children they did not engender" (Scheffler 1970:376).

3. Secondary jural parenthood can also be treated in terms of role-specific entitlements, such as those held by "aunts," "uncles," "mother's brothers," "grandparents," and so on (see Goodenough 1970b:399). But, insofar as these are entitlements to children as immature human beings, or to relatives who are classified as 'children' in any way by the persons who hold these entitlements, then it would seem that the label "parenthood" is appropriate and that a formal distinction between primary and secondary jural parenthood is analytically justified.

4. More evidence on 'sibling' adoptions is needed to make this point conclusively. Many of these cases may be buried in the literature under the heading of "formal friendship" (see, for example, Koch 1963; Finney 1964; Lambert 1970).

5. Schneider (1968, 1970) suggests that the biogenetic "facts" recognized in American kinship are best viewed as symbols for kinds of social relationships, and his interpretation of the meaning of kinship generally and how it ought to be studied is fundamentally at odds with the material quoted here from Scheffler and Lounsbury (1972).

6. The usefulness of universalistic genealogical models hinges directly on the empirical validity of such generalizations (cf. Schneider 1972:37). The persistence of incest taboo parameters relative to the adoptee's previous

kinship identity, even where the transaction is otherwise jurally exclusive of his previous identity, is probably a good indicator of the indissolubility of 'congenital' relatedness in local theory.

7. My use of the phrase "kinship identity" here incorporates shared 'blood' as a substantive and a symbolic identity feature, and binding behavior, or the "code for conduct" domain, as a normative and social kinship identity feature. This usage differs in part from that of Silverman (1971), who contrasts "identity" features with "code" features on at least one level of opposition in his analysis of Banaban kinship.

8. Adoptive kinsmen, however, " . . . are relatives by virtue of their *relationship*, not their biogenetic attributes" (Schneider 1970:377). In a similar light, Carroll (1970c) suggests that a "relative" is a person who acts like a kinsman should act according to the rules of his society, including persons who do and those who do not share consanguinity.

9. Carroll notes with reference to the Nukuoro that " . . . the initiating act itself is of such importance that events following are of little immediate import" (1970c:145).

10. Adults, of course, also may be 'fostered' (see Marshall, chapter 2).

11. On the premise that bilateral affinities may be disruptive of unilateral allegiances, it may be advantageous in jurally exclusive transactions to conceal the adoption event from the adoptee (see Scheffler 1970:378). Jurally inclusive transactions may require the opposite: the adoptee's knowledge of the bilaterality of the arrangement may be pertinent to maintaining the relationship among the principals in the long run. Knowledge of being adopted, however, does not necessarily mandate unequal treatment of the adoptee relative to other children in the adopter's household (but cf. Carroll 1970c:143). In fact, considerable effort may be expended by the adoptive parents to avoid such invidious comparisons (see Marshall, chapter 2; Brady, chapter 7). This may be viewed as an attempt to consolidate the arrangement in fact by bringing the emotional solidarity of psychic parenthood into line with the jural parenthood assignment made in the adoption transaction.

12. Variation in the scope of relationships involved also amounts to variation in the importance of adoption as an alliance feature. The event may involve the recruitment of 'adoptees' within a domestic context such that kinsmen other than the principals who negotiate the transaction may ignore the adoptive bond, or the event may be engineered explicitly to serve wider group functions, in which case the context of recruitment and scope of involvement of other persons is necessarily greater than that of the principal negotiators themselves (see Silverman 1970; Shore, chapter 8; Tonkinson, chapter 10). Either way, alliance functions are at stake and should be specified. (see also Brady, chapter 12).

13. Fosterage generally does not entail a formal renegotiation of incest taboo parameters. But the domestic context into which a foster child is recruited may be sufficient to imply restricted sexual access to the sponsors and the members of their immediate family. The ground rules governing fosterage

in the Ellice Islands are explicit in stating that, given no previous 'blood' ties, a 'foster child' can marry (and therefore should not be punished for having covert sexual relations with) his benefactors' natural children; formal 'adoptees', including foster children who subsequently become 'adoptees', do not have these rights.

14. The whole complex of *compadrazgo* and of 'god-parenthood' generally needs to be reexamined in this light.

15. The custom of exchanging children as adoptees between families, as Shore (chapter 8) points out, may serve both descent and alliance functions. Fosterage is also susceptible to similar kinds of bilateral arrangements. In the Gilberts, for example, and perhaps formerly in the Celtic-speaking parts of the British Isles, one child of a family line would be given as a ward to another specific family in each generation, ultimate jural authority being retained by the natural parents. The two descent lines were linked by repeated transfers of wards from one to the other (Lambert, personal communication).

2

SOLIDARITY OR STERILITY? ADOPTION AND FOSTERAGE ON NAMOLUK ATOLL

Mac Marshall

INTRODUCTION

Earlier anthropological work in greater Trukese society has viewed adoption as a consequence of demographic imbalance—especially as a result of high infertility rates caused by disease.[1] I intend to demonstrate that this argument does not adequately account for adoption and fosterage in Truk District and to offer a more comprehensive explanation.

Within the last few years, a great deal of excellent work has been published on the subject of adoption and fosterage in Oceania (Carroll 1970a; Keesing 1970; Monberg 1970). In this chapter, I draw upon two of many suggestions for the study of kinship and adoption found in a recent symposium (Carroll 1970a). The first of these suggestions argues that adoption and fosterage should be looked at from the point of view of the groups rather than simply the individuals concerned (Ottino 1970:115). The second suggestion holds that adoption should be seen as part of a larger pattern of sharing among relatives (Carroll 1970c).

When examined from a group point of view, the circulation of children by adoption and fosterage on Namoluk is discovered to occur largely within, rather than among, kinship groups. Close kin on Namoluk share physical substance, land, food, residence, labor, material goods, political support, and sometimes money. Paramount in importance among the resources shared by close relatives are land and people. Adoption and fosterage serve as mechanisms by which human resources (especially children) are distributed among relatives, and adoption plays a small part in land redistribution on the atoll. Namoluk adoption and fosterage can be explained as part of a greater pattern of resource sharing that is the essence of kinship solidarity.

ETYMOLOGY AND DEFINITION

The Namoluk word for adoption *muuti* 'adopt; take or break away from', derives from the root *muu* 'separate; divide'. *Muuti* belongs to a class of words that includes *muumu* 'an adopted person' and *muufeseng* 'divorce; break into two parts'. When one adopts a child, he is also said to *nauni* 'take as one's own' the child.[2] *Nauni* comes from *nau* 'child' and *-ni* 'suffix denoting possessive entitlement', and also is used to describe stepparent and stepchild relationships.

As regularly used on Namoluk, the word *tumwunuu* 'foster; take care of; watch out for', is not restricted in application only to persons. One may 'take care of' an animal, a plant, a material object, or a person, including oneself. For example, when discussing an ideal relationship of a chief or magistrate to his people, the word *tumwunuu* is used. A leader is said to bear responsibility for 'taking care of' his constituency. In the view of Namoluk people there is no difference between 'fostering' and 'taking care of' a person—they are one and the same thing.

While the word *tumwunuu* can be applied to the care that natural, adoptive or stepparents give their children, it is not normally used in this way. If a couple divorces and the parent retaining custody of the children remarries, the stepparent is said to *naulap* 'take as a stepchild' his new charge.[3] Should a child be orphaned, he would be fostered or adopted by a close relative of one of his parents, in which case the word *tumwunuu* or the word *muuti* would apply. Since foster parents may not claim to 'take as one's own' their foster children, stepparenthood on Namoluk has more in common with adoptive parenthood than with foster parenthood. Both step and adoptive parenthood may require the parties involved to observe new incest restrictions, whereas foster parenthood never alters incest restrictions (see Marshall 1971). Furthermore, there is no succession to jural parenthood by foster parents. Adoption and stepparenthood both involve a transfer of or succession to primary jural parenthood (see Brady, chapter 1), and this carries with it an obligation to provide the child with an inheritance. The linguistic connotations of the word *nauni* for adoption, stepparenthood, and fosterage permit us to define Namoluk adoption as "any customary and optional procedure for taking as one's own a child of other parents" (Carroll 1970b:3). The crucial distinction between adoption and fosterage in this definition is the phrase "taking as one's own." The crucial distinction between adoptive parenthood and stepparenthood is that stepparenthood is not optional.[4] Bearing these distinctions in mind, fosterage is defined as "any customary and optional procedure for taking care of (but not taking as one's own) a child of other parents."[5]

JURAL PARENTHOOD

Jural authority over children is vested primarily in natural parents. Persons having the next greatest claim over a couple's children are natural grandparents, followed by parents' natural siblings, adoptive siblings, stepsiblings and lineage siblings. To a lesser extent, parents' siblings in the same subclan have some claim over a couple's children. All of these people are considered to be close kin on Namoluk and all (except mother's brother) stand in a classificatory 'parent' relationship to a couple's children. All share in what might be called latent (or secondary) jural parental rights in a couple's offspring, and all bear a responsibility to 'take care of' a couple's children should a need arise. As a general rule the jural rights of matrilineal kin override those of patrilateral kin.[6] It is important to note in a consideration of jural parenthood that a party who wishes to adopt a child often approaches not only the child's natural parents but also his natural grandparents and parents' siblings. In any case, the child's natural parents usually consult their parents and siblings before agreeing to give a child in adoption.[7] Should any of these close kin object to a proposed adoption, it is extremely unlikely that the adoption would take place. Parental responsibilities, like everything else involving close kinship, are shared among close relatives.

NAMOLUK ADOPTION AND FOSTERAGE EVENTS

Adoption and fosterage are common events on Namoluk. Sixty-eight percent (23/34) of the households on the atoll in 1971 contained at least one foster child, and 41 percent (14/34) of the households contained at least one adopted child.[8] All adoptive relationships on the atoll are justified in terms of a prior relationship among the parties concerned—especially ties of consanguinity. Ninety-seven percent of Namoluk adoptions are by persons having some prior consanguineal relationship to their adoptive child (see table 1). In cases where genealogical connection is distant, justification for an adoption may be based on situational determinants of kinship, a past adoption among relatives of the involved parties, or on exceptional kindness shown one party by the other.

It is possible to foster another person in a variety of ways. To regularly make gifts of clothing or other material goods to someone is to foster him in that respect. To feed another person regularly is to foster him also. To sleep regularly in someone else's house is to be fostered by that person in the eyes of the Namoluk community. Generally speaking, these ways of caring for someone go together, but they need not do so for a fosterage relationship to exist.

TABLE 1.   Relationship between Adoptive or Foster Parents and Adopted or Fostered Children on Namoluk

Relationship	Adoptions		Fosterage	
	n	%	n	%
Parent is child's classificatory 'mother'	81	75	165	75
Parent is child's classificatory 'father'	16	15	21	9.5
Parent is child's classificatory 'sibling'	6	6	21	9.5
Parent is child's classificatory 'child'	2	1	7	3
No kinship relationship between parent and child	3	3	6★	3
TOTAL	108	100	220	100

SOURCE: Author's field notes, 1971.
★All of these involved the families of immigrant native pastors.

People usually foster relatives just as they usually adopt relatives. As with adoption, 97 percent of the fostering parties on Namoluk have a prior kinship relationship to their foster child (see table 1). Unlike adoption, adults as well as children are fostered. Fosterage may be initiated by the person being fostered, by the person who takes care of him, or by an interested third party not directly involved in the relationship. For adoption, on the other hand, only the persons wishing to adopt will initiate the transaction. Parents do not advertise their children for adoption, and children never initiate their own adoption. In these respects, adoption and fosterage relations on Namoluk are fundamentally different.

Informants give a host of reasons for adopting children, but the underlying condition always mentioned is a kinship tie that exists between them and their adopted child. Childlessness is often cited as a reason for adoption. Similarly, an informant may point out that he has only a son or daughter and wishes to adopt a child of the opposite sex. Also mentioned is a desire to adopt a girl when a possibility exists that one's lineage may die out for lack of fertile women. Adoption sometimes occurs to replace a child that has died. Yet another reason is to repay great kindness by an adoptive child's natural parents. Finally, adoption is often phrased as an act of generosity to help support a relative with a large family.

Childlessness is both a reason for adopting a child on Namoluk and a rationale for giving a child in adoption. People often remarked that they gave up their child out of sympathy for the adoptive parents who had no children of their own.[9] An important motive affecting natural parents' decisions to give up a child in adoption is the personal satisfaction that derives from an act of generosity. Such acts—particularly among close kin—are intimately bound up with the Namoluk conception of what it is to be a 'good' person.[10] Another reason for giving a child in adoption is basically economic: a child has been born out of wedlock and has no father to provide for him or to leave him an inheritance.[11] One of the motives in giving a child for adoption is a calculation that the child will benefit by inheriting land from his adoptive parents. This consideration is important in cases where a couple have many children among whom they will have to divide their resources.

Still another factor that enters a decision to give a child in adoption is the age of the adopting couple. If the adopting couple is in their fifties or sixties, the natural parents stand to benefit from giving up the child in several ways. First, as has been discussed above, the child probably will receive a larger inheritance than if he had not been adopted since his natural parents also are likely to make some provision for him. Second, the natural parents are relieved of the economic burden of supporting the child. Finally, the adopting couple is likely to die before the child reaches adulthood, at which time the child will return to his natural parents just as he is becoming an economic asset.

The ideal Namolùk family includes children of both sexes. It has already been mentioned that one stated reason for adoption is to obtain an opposite-sex sibling for one's natural child. Parents want children of both sexes to assist with labor in a society where there is a marked sexual division of labor. Young girls are worked much harder than young boys, and they are conditioned from an early age to cook, carry firewood and water, tend smaller children, wash clothes, and run numerous errands. Except for minor tasks, boys lead a carefree existence until they approach puberty. At this time, they begin to fish in earnest, assist in making copra, help work in the taro patch, and clear land.

Short-term fosterage arrangements frequently develop when a person prepares to travel off-island and decides to leave his children behind.[12] Under these circumstances, the individual who will be making the trip asks a relative or close friend to care for his children while he is gone. Sometimes when the traveler returns he resumes care of all the dependents he cared for before he left. On other occasions, fosterage relationships begun for this reason continue after the traveler has returned. When someone plans to be off the island for a time, it also happens that a relative or close friend may request to foster one or more of the traveler's dependents.

Sometimes, a person is fostered explicitly to help with work around one's house. This sort of fosterage relationship is overtly one of reciprocity: room and board are provided in exchange for services rendered. Fosterage relationships of this kind are instigated on Namoluk only by recent immigrants to the atoll (the family of the native pastor, for example) who have no relatives on whom they can call for assistance.[13]

Children of a deceased kinsman often will be fostered as a way of assuaging grief over loss of a loved one. Informants are explicit in stating that replacement of the deceased by his child is a major motivation for such a relationship. Grandparents sometimes foster the children of a son or daughter who has left the island permanently as a way of replacing their departed child (see Goodenough 1970b:401).

Occasionally, a person may just show up on one's doorstep unasked and unannounced. In such an instance, if the person has no other place to turn, he will be fostered, and no one will think it strange or unusual. To take in someone under such circumstances is considered a most praiseworthy act.

Most adoption on Namoluk is by couples, although single men and women may also adopt. Adopted persons on Namoluk are nearly always children. It is considered best to adopt a child when he is as young as possible so that he will not grow up knowing he is adopted and will not attempt to return to his natural parents. Namoluk people prefer to adopt young children because it is believed that they can be changed and molded to fit new situations. No special feast or ceremony marks adoption and fosterage events.

Namoluk adoption is always customary. There has never been a legally registered adoption on the atoll, in spite of provision for this in Trust Territory jurisprudence.[14] This is not surprising since Namoluk people have no need for legal adoption. Adoption is an act of generosity—a form of sharing among relatives—and, as such, legal trappings are superfluous. Indeed, such trappings would imply a lack of trust and solidarity and run counter to the very essence of adoption transactions.

Older people on Namoluk feel cut off if they have no young children around them. If they are not living in a household where youngsters are present, they will try to adopt or foster a child. An extremely common form of foster parenthood on Namoluk is that in which a child's maternal or paternal grandparents take him right after he is weaned and foster him until they die or he grows up and marries.[15] During these years a child may seldom go to eat or sleep with his natural parents, although they will usually contribute to his care. No formal transfer of jural authority takes place in such cases—the grandparents simply exercise their influence (jural rights) over their *own* children. In such circumstances, children find it very difficult to refuse their parents' fosterage requests. Since this kind of fosterage frequently occurs with a couple's first child (on grounds that a new mother does not properly 'know how to care for an infant'), it provides a strong motivation for a couple to reside with whichever grandparents foster their child. Such residence simultaneously permits a couple to satisfy their parents' fosterage request and still enjoy the pleasure of having their child in the same household.[16]

Ideally, a couple wishing to adopt a child will approach a woman who is pregnant (along with her husband if she is married) and make their wish known. Nearly always they will seek out a relative, since kin are less likely to refuse a request than non-kin. They will be sure to pick a relative who has several children, since they can then couch their request in terms of wanting to 'help' their relative by easing his burden of caring for a large family. Such a request is a delicate matter. The prospective adopting couple must be careful how they choose their words, lest their relative feel aspersions are being cast on his role as provider. The person approached about the adoption will discuss the proposal with his natural parents and siblings. If there is no objection to the adoption, the adoptive mother will move in with the natural mother and live with her from the time she gives birth. Babies are said to 'know' that their mother is the person who cares for them from birth so that by coming to stay with the baby from his birth an adoptive mother assures that her baby will be unable to differentiate between his two mothers.

When the adoptive mother comes to stay with the natural mother, she will provide the natural mother with as much good food and as many drinking coconuts as she can. This food is given because the child will be strong only so long as the woman who is nursing him is strong, and because the sooner the child grows big and healthy, the sooner he will be weaned, and his adoptive parents will be able to take him home.[17] Adoptive parents may also bring cloth for diapers, soap, and other small gifts. These gifts emphatically are *not* a payment to the child's natural parents. They are gifts to the child and demonstrate that his adoptive parents are already looking after his welfare.

Once an adoptive child is weaned (anywhere from six months to one year of age), he is taken home by his adoptive parents and does not return to his natural parents. A conspiracy of silence surrounds the adoption, and it is considered to be in very bad taste to tell a child he is adopted. While close kin of the parties concerned usually know an adoption has taken place, most other people in the community are uncertain whether the arrangement is adoption or fosterage. In more than a few cases, the conspiracy of silence endures until the child reaches adolescence. An adoptive child who knows he is adopted has a powerful lever at his disposal for shaping his relationship with his adoptive parents: he can threaten them with desertion. Should a child actually carry out such a threat, his natural parents have the responsibility of sending him back. Protection of the link between child and adoptive parents, rather than shielding a child from possible psychological trauma over knowledge of his adoption, appears to account for the secrecy surrounding Namoluk adoption.[18]

Sometimes an arrangement begins as fosterage, lasts, deepens, and subsequently develops into adoption. When this happens, a formal agreement by all parties may never be reached. Instead, the nature of the relationship shifts slowly and imperceptibly, with agreement that it has changed from fosterage to adoption obtained only implicitly. Needless to say, many of these changed or changing relationships may be contested.

A child may be fostered by a number of different people simultaneously or at various times in his life. Many people who have been fostered have a long history of being cared for first by one person and then by another. This is especially true for unwed mothers and children born out of wedlock.

To adopt or foster someone on Namoluk conveys messages of kinship, friendship, and assistance. Adoption and fosterage relationships are used to strengthen preexisting relationships among persons. Fosterage relations are particularly effective in this regard because they are informal, flexible, and breed no ill will if they are terminated. The value of this relationship is demonstrated by the fact that nearly all Namoluk people have been adopted or fostered at some point in their lives.

The differences between adoption and fosterage on Namoluk should now be apparent. Adoption involves a transfer of primary jural rights in a child, ideally on a permanent basis. Fosterage entails no permanent transfer of jural rights and is temporary, lasting only a few weeks or months in most cases. Unlike an adopted child, a foster child is free to return to his natural parents at any time of his own volition, and he will not be forced to return to his foster parents. Foster parents may terminate a fosterage relationship at any time, but no case is known where adoptive parents halted an adoption of their own will. Fosterage entails no obligation to provide an inheritance for one's foster child, whereas provision of an inheritance is one form of validation of adoption on the atoll. Kinship terms are not used between foster parents and children (except in a few cases concerning orphans) unless a preexisting relationship warrants it; parent-child terms are always used by adoptive parents and children in reference to each other. Finally, no effort at secrecy surrounds fosterage relationships, while this effort is always made in adoption.

KINSHIP AND SHARING

At its most basic level, kinship on Namoluk is shared physical substance. This derives from the Namoluk notion of descent. Namoluk people belonging to the same matriclan subscribe to a myth that they are *popusengi emen choput* 'descended from one woman'. This myth includes all people anywhere who are members of the same clan. As a result, people on Namoluk feel a distant but distinct bond of kinship with clansmen elsewhere in Truk District. This bond is expressed by saying all members of one clan are *eu aramas* 'one people'. The feeling of 'one people' is given as justification for rules of clan exogamy and as accounting for clan hospitality among relatives on different islands. Closer kinship connections among people on one or more island are expressed by the phrase *eu fütük* 'one flesh and blood'. This category is a subset of the category 'one people', and it corresponds in all particulars to a subclan. It is a group of people, arrayed in two or more lineages, who maintain a belief of being 'descended from one woman' in the comparatively recent past, although the exact genealogical relationship has been forgotten. Members of 'one flesh and blood' are considered to be 'close relatives'.

People on Namoluk recognize the role of both a man and a woman in begetting children. The male role in physiological paternity receives recognition in the Namoluk kinship system in a category called *afakur* 'descended from men'. One's patrilateral kin ties flow from being *afakuran eu ainang* 'descended from men

of one matriclan'. One's matrilineal kinship relationships follow
from one's membership in *eu ainang* 'one matriclan'. Actual and
mythologically shared physical substance with both matrilineal
and patrilateral kin is the basis for everyone's kinship universe.

Close relatives are expected to *tumwunuu fengen* 'take care of
each other' and to *alilis fengen* 'cooperate'. From the time they are
small, children are admonished to share with their relatives. Gifts
given one child are passed around for 'siblings' to use or play with.
Close relatives share all manner of material possessions. Such
sharing occurs via loan, outright appropriation, and joint ownership. If a close relative asks to borrow an item, it is very difficult
to refuse him. To refuse without good reason puts a strain on the
relationship. To refuse repeatedly, regardless of the reason, is to
repudiate or deny the kinship tie involved. Often a child, sibling,
or wife's brother will just *angai* 'take' or *tüngor* 'ask for' one's
possession with no intention of returning it. Such requests are
difficult to turn down or turn about for the same reason that it is
difficult to refrain from loaning something to close kin. Few
possessions are truly private property on Namoluk. The code of
kinship is mutual help and cooperation, with group interest placed
above individual desires.

Close matrilineal kin usually *möngö chu* 'share land' at the lineage
or subclan level.[19] In a large subclan, one or two pieces of land may
be designated 'shared land', with all other land held by members of
the subclan individually or by groups of siblings. A process of
fragmentation of 'shared land' during the past century has reduced
the total amount of land held in joint estate, and today 'shared land'
is largely symbolic. To share land with someone is, by definition,
to share close kinship.

Close relatives normally live together in extended families on
one *pei* 'homesite' or on adjacent homesites. Until the village
pattern on Namoluk was reorganized radically during the re-
building that followed a disastrous typhoon in 1958, close kin
generally lived together in a single large dwelling.[20] Today no
more than three nuclear families live in any one dwelling, although
it is common for several sisters and their husbands to live in
adjacent single family dwellings and to cook together in one
cookhouse.[21] A strong pattern of living uxorilocally with the wife's
parents or sisters (or on the wife's land) continues on Namoluk.
Virilocal residence is a less common alternative. Neolocal residence,

with no close kin on the same or adjoining homesite, is very rare. Living together implies kinship in the Namoluk view, and this feeling carries over to adoptive, step, and foster siblings when the relationship has endured for a long time. Genealogical considerations notwithstanding, marriage or sexual intercourse among people raised together as children on one homesite is viewed as being "like" incest.

Shared food on Namoluk symbolizes kinship and friendship. Close kin continuously take each other gifts of food, especially prepared taro, breadfruit, and fresh fish. Gifts of food (such as preserved breadfruit and salt fish) are sent to close relatives living temporarily or permanently off the island on every ship that calls at the atoll. Close kin working in the district center of Moen, Truk, send gifts of rice and canned food to their relatives on Namoluk at every opportunity. To eat together conveys feelings of close relationship because the produce has come from shared land or from labor that is the outgrowth of past assistance among kin.[22] To eat together regularly on Namoluk is to participate in a recurring kinship communion.

Near relatives often pool labor, talent, and money to make or purchase something to which they all have joint and equal rights. Things as varied as a canoe, a pig, or money for the education of a kinsman are handled in this way. To regularly share material possessions or money means to be 'kin' on Namoluk.[23] Closely related women cook, tend each other's children, make copra and handicrafts together, and so on. Closely related men assist each other in fishing, gathering breadfruit, husking copra nuts, and other heavy tasks. While joint labor is especially notable among relatives living together in one household, it frequently extends beyond the limits of a single household into wider kinship domains.

With so many shared interests, it should come as no surprise that political factions on Namoluk are largely composed of close lineal and affinal kin. Despite the slow disintegration of traditional, kinship-based political roles (which have been replaced by introduced, elective positions), kinship continues to play a decisive part in local level politics. Considerations of a candidate's relatives, more than his merit, determine the outcome in most local elections. Shared political interests are usually (though not always) shared kinship interests expressed in the political arena.

When very close ties develop between persons who trace no

genealogical relationship, a *pwiipwii* 'formal friend' relationship may be established. *Pwiipwii* is a reduplicated form of the kinship term *pwii* 'my same-sex sibling', however one may establish a 'formal friend' relationship with a member of either sex. In such cases, a "friendship" relationship is turned into a "kinship" relationship, and one behaves toward his 'formal friend' as he would behave toward a 'sibling'.[24]

'Formal friendship' is likened explicitly to 'adoption' by Namoluk informants, except that the person 'adopted' is a 'sibling' rather than a 'child' or 'grandchild'. Close relatives of two 'formal friends' are expected to 'take care of' each other *as if* the friends were natural siblings. Sometimes 'formal friend' relationships provide a basis for transmission of *rong* 'esoteric knowledge or skills' or for sales of land resources. This is significant because such knowledge and resources normally are transmitted only among close consanguineal or affinal kin. As with people raised together on one homesite, 'formal friendship' requires the friends to observe incest and exogamy restrictions with each other, and these restrictions extend to their children as if the 'formal friends' were 'siblings'.

From the above it must now be obvious that genealogical connection, in and of itself, is not sufficient to determine whether or not two people are 'close kin'. Shared land, shared residence, shared material possessions, 'formal friendship', and common political cause are among the situational determinants of 'close kinship' (see Swartz 1960).

ADOPTION AND FOSTERAGE AS RESOURCE SHARING

Inevitably, the answer to my question, "Why did you adopt or foster that person?" on Namoluk was, "Because he is my relative." In many cases, pressing for other reasons proved fruitless. Adoption and fosterage are viewed as an integral part of the pervasive pattern of sharing among close relatives on the atoll. Children (and sometimes adults) are shared for companionship, love, pleasure, a sense of personal worth and fulfillment, and a variety of economic reasons. To give one's kinsman a child in adoption or fosterage is simply one more way of expressing kinship solidarity by sharing valued resources.

A request to adopt a child is a request to *give* a "possession" to a kinsman. A request to foster a child is a request to *loan* a "possession" to a kinsman. Both adoption and fosterage requests accord with the rules that govern sharing of resources among close kin: to refuse such a request without good reason is to jeopardize the kinship relationship involved. Symbolically, the taking back of an adopted child by his natural parents severs the kinship relationship between the two sets of parents.

The majority of adoptions on Namoluk are by close kin. As table 1 illustrates, 90 percent of adoptive parents already stand in a classificatory parental role to their adoptive child before they adopt him. As grandparents or close 'siblings' of the parents, 49 percent of adoptive parents share parental rights in the child they adopt prior to adopting him. Adoption makes manifest these latent rights and provides the adopted child with an additional set of parents. Table 1 further shows that fosterage events also transpire primarily among close kin and that about 84 percent of the fostering parties stand in a 'parental' role to the children they foster prior to fostering them.

It is instructive to think of Namoluk adoption in the same way that Goodenough (1951:38–39) discusses divided ownership of property.[25] Like divided ownership, Namoluk adoption always involves two parties, the natural and the adoptive parents of the child. To give a child in adoption is to *liffang* him 'give as a gift' to the adopter. As with divided ownership of property, the parties to an adoption may be individuals or "corporations" (if we view a married couple as a "corporation" for purposes of this comparison). Giving a child in adoption divides title to the child between his natural and his adoptive parents. The natural parents retain the residual title. As provisional titleholders of a child, persons who adopt gain physical possession and take on full responsibility for support of the child. As residual titleholders, natural parents are free of the immediate concerns of child support, but they continue to enjoy certain rights in the child. For example, if a child is a minor, he will always return to his natural parents on the death of his adoptive parents. Should adoptive parents neglect or mistreat their adoptive child, natural parents have the power to reclaim the child, just as with physical property. Should this occur, the adopting party forfeits its rights in the child. Neither the adopting party nor the natural parents may give the adoptive child to someone else in adoption without the consent of the other title-holder.[26] These data suggest that a single cultural pattern underlies the rules governing adoption and divided ownership of property in greater Trukese society.

The most significant economic benefit resulting from Namoluk adoption and fosterage is that they provide a social welfare system organized around kinship. Since close kin have shared parental responsibilities for each other's children, no orphan goes uncared for on Namoluk. When a child is orphaned, he is immediately adopted or fostered by a classificatory parent or sibling. Unwed mothers also are provided for by Namoluk's social welfare system. Ordinarily, a single man or woman cannot fully exploit the food resources at hand. Ideally, an adult of each sex is needed. An unmarried woman with children must be assisted by a man if she is to support herself and her children properly. In such cases, it is common for a woman's father, brother, or sister's husband to 'foster' her, and usually she will go to live in a household containing a male relative. It can be seen in table 2 that children born out of wedlock are adopted more than twice as frequently as those borne by married women. Not only does this relieve the economic burden for a single woman of trying to provide adequately for her child, it also works to the economic advantage of a fatherless child who may count on an inheritance of land from his adoptive parents. Finally, adoption and fosterage promote the social welfare of the aged on Namoluk. Namoluk people fear the thought of reaching old age with no children to care for and assist them. Should a couple have no natural offspring, an adopted child substitutes

TABLE 2.   Adoption of Namoluk Children Born In and Out of Wedlock in the Last Two Generations

Status	Number of Named Children	Number Adopted	Percent Adopted
In Wedlock	380	40	10.5
Out of Wedlock	43	10	23.3
TOTAL	423	50	11.8

SOURCE: Author's field notes, 1971.

nicely. It has been noted above that grandparents frequently foster grandchildren, and this is at least partially accounted for by a fear of being left alone. As mentioned above, to foster grandchildren helps to keep one's own children in the same household.

Adoption and fosterage also lead to the maximum utilization and optimum distribution of available human resources. Couples without children may adopt children. Whenever an extra person is needed (for whatever purpose), a foster child may be taken. Large families with insufficient resources may relieve some of their economic burden by giving one or more children in adoption or fosterage. In these ways, many needs for companionship, labor, heirs, and the care of children are satisfied.

Fosterage—in the form of clan hospitality to relatives from other islands—has obvious economic benefits for the traveler. He can visit many other islands confident that he will not lack for food and shelter. Such hospitality assumes added significance today when so many people travel to the port town of Moen, Truk, in search of employment, education, excitement, and medical attention.[27] Even very distant adoptive relationships may be called upon when Namoluk people travel to Moen, need a place to stay, and have no close clansman to take them in. For example, one woman accompanied by her mother's adopted sister went to Moen to stay with the adoptive parents of the latter's daughter.

The transmission of land from adoptive parents to adoptive children serves both as an inducement to natural parents to give up children in adoption and as a means by which an adopting party may demonstrate their sense of obligation for the gift of a child. By providing an inheritance for their adoptive child, an adopting party at once shows their love for the child and partially repays their "debt" to the child's natural parents for sharing a child with them. In cases where a couple is childless, adoption of a close matrilineal relative of the wife works to the long-term economic advantage of the wife's lineage. The adoptive father will leave his adopted child an inheritance of land, and the complex system of marriage alliance and land transfer that exists among descent groups on the atoll will operate as if the marriage had resulted in natural offspring (see Marshall 1972). Adoption thereby plays a role in the recurrent redistribution of land resources from fathers to children on Namoluk.[28]

OTHER EXPLANATIONS FOR ADOPTION AND FOSTERAGE IN TRUK

Writing about adoption and fosterage in Trukese society, other anthropologists have explained the high rate of adoption as a consequence of a high incidence of sterility among women. Ann Fischer (1963) has argued that the relative infertility of Romónum women under age forty may be attributed to a particular method of intercourse practiced in Truk and to a greater occurrence of venereal diseases among younger women.[29] The former argument would not seem to account for differences in fertility when one reflects that the method of intercourse in question was practiced just as passionately by women over forty when they were in their prime. While venereal infections are a likely explanation for the infertility of Romónum women at the time Fischer gathered her data, such diseases do not begin to explain the Namoluk data.[30] Table 3 shows that while only one-half of the Romónum women age 30–39 were mothers, nearly all of the Namoluk women in this age group had given birth. While less than one-half of Romónum

TABLE 3.   Age, Motherhood, and Marital Status of Romónum and Namoluk Women

Age group	Number in Group		Mothers in each age group				Married women in each age group			
	Romónum	Namoluk	Romónum		Namoluk		Romónum		Namoluk	
			n	%	n	%	n	%	n	%
0– 9	29	40	0	0	0	0	0	0	0	0
10–19	17	38	1	6	4	10.5	6	35	4	10.5
20–29	23	31	11	48	18	58	21	91	18	58
30–39	18	23	9	50	22	96	17	94	15	65
40–49	19	13 }	25	83	36	90	17 } 63		9 } 63	
50 & over	11	27 }					2 }		16 }	
TOTAL	117	172	46	39	80	46	63	54	62	36

SOURCE: The Romónum data are from Ann Fischer (1963:528) and pertain to 1949. The Namoluk data derive from the author's field notes, 1971.

women age 20–29 had borne children, 58 percent of their Namoluk counterparts had offspring. Table 3 obscures the fact that although only about 10 percent of the Namoluk women age 10–19 had married in 1971, 100 percent of these had given birth. Even more striking is the fact that 17 out of 18 of the married Namoluk women age 20–29 had offspring by 1971. It is clear that women on Namoluk have been much more fertile than women on Romónum. When Fischer (1963:530) claims that ". . . the low rate of fertility naturally results in a high adoption rate," her statement does not explain the situation on Namoluk where adoption is even more frequent than on Romónum, but where infertility is not an issue.

More recently, Ruth Goodenough (1970) has tried to show that adoption and infertility on Romónum are positively correlated. She argues that

> . . . one might predict that the rate of adoption will fall off appreciably in the immediate future, back to a level that reflects a more balanced fertility picture.
>
> This last point rests on the observation that there are apparently no strongly operating factors to sustain such a high rate of adoption other than childlessness or the occasional orphaning of children (1970:316).

A comparison of her data with similar data from Namoluk (tables 4 and 5) clearly shows that infertility and childlessness alone do not explain the high rate of adoption on Namoluk. Nearly two-thirds of the Namoluk women married in the past three generations have had two or more children, as compared with less than one-half of the Romónum women. Furthermore, of the twelve adult Namoluk women who have not married as of 1971, or who have borne all of their children out of wedlock, six have had children and five have had two or more offspring.[31] Only 15 percent of Namoluk women were childless, as against 32 percent of Romónum women. It should also be realized that many Namoluk women with only one or two children have only been married for a few years and may be expected to bear other children. As table 5 illustrates, it cannot be said for Namoluk that ". . . the overwhelming number of adopting couples . . . were childless" (Ruth Goodenough 1970:316). Eight out of ten adopting families on Namoluk had at least one natural child.[32] Three-fourths of the adopting families on Romónum were

TABLE 4. Comparative Fertility of Women on Romónum and Namoluk

| | Women Bearing These Children | | | |
| Number of Named Children Borne | Romónum | | Namoluk | |
	n	%	n	%
0	56	32	19	15
1	40	23	27	21
2	33	19	18	15
3 or more	46	26	62	49
TOTAL	175	100	126	100

SOURCE: The Romónum data pertain to 1965 and are taken from Ruth Goodenough (1970:315). The Namoluk data are taken from the author's field notes, 1971.

TABLE 5. Comparison of Childlessness as a Factor in Adoption on Romónum and Namoluk

| | Number of Families | | | |
| Number of Natural Children in Adopting Family | Romónum | | Namoluk | |
	n	%	n	%
0	43	75	20	18.5
1	9	16	27	25
2 or more	5	9	61	56.5
TOTAL	57	100	108	100

SOURCE: The Romónum data pertain to 1965 and are taken from Ruth Goodenough (1970:316). The Namoluk data are taken from the author's field notes, 1971.

childless. Were Goodenough's prediction to have general validity for greater Trukese society, the rate of adoption on Namoluk should be much less than that on Romónum. In fact, the crude adoption rate for Namoluk *exceeds* the crude adoption rate for Romónum.[33] Clearly, while sterility is one factor in adoption and fosterage in greater Trukese society, childlessness alone does not explain the presence or persistence of such transactions. Some other "strongly operating factors" must exist to sustain the high rate of adoption and fosterage found in these islands.

CONCLUSIONS

I have argued that the simplest and most inclusive explanation for the high rate of adoption and fosterage practiced in greater Trukese society is that adoption and fosterage represent part of a larger pattern of sharing among relatives. This explanation has the additional advantage of accounting for fosterage as well as adoption —something the earlier work does not do. Children of close relatives on Namoluk are shared via adoption and fosterage in the same way that land, food, residence, labor, physical possessions, political support, and money are shared. As such, adoption and fosterage are not unique responses to atypical events. Rather, they flow logically from the system of kinship and represent just two of many ways for demonstrating what it means to be 'close kin'.

NOTES

Research on Namoluk Atoll, Eastern Caroline Islands, was conducted for a period of eighteen months during 1969–1971. The project was generously supported by Research Grant MH11871 from the National Institutes of Health, by related Fellowship MH42666, and by an Institutional Grant from the Department of Anthropology, University of Washington. Special thanks are due my research assistant, Sarel R. Agrippa, for the hours he devoted in helping gather the data on which this chapter is based. Ivan Brady, Vern Carroll, Ward Goodenough, and Leslie B. Marshall provided helpful comments on earlier drafts of this chapter.
Namoluk is a small atoll standing alone thirty-five miles northwest of the Lower Mortlock Islands and sixty-five miles southeast of Losap Atoll. Truk is 125 miles to the northwest. The resident population of Namoluk during 1969–1971 was approximately 275, with another 125 ethnic Namoluk people residing temporarily or permanently off-island. Namoluk is included in Truk District, one of six administrative units comprising the U.S. Trust Territory of the Pacific Islands. All residents of the atoll are Christian, and the island has a school reaching the eighth grade. While Namoluk has had some exposure to a cash economy, a majority of the inhabitants continue to live on a traditional subsistence basis.

1. Greater Trukese society refers to all of the islands and people of Truk District in the U.S. Trust Territory of the Pacific Islands (Micronesia).
2. *Nauni* also means 'to take something from someone else with an agreement to keep it'. In this sense it is contrasted with *naunau* 'borrow with an agreement to return'. Foster parents may be said to *naunau* their foster children.
3. *Naulap* literally means 'big child' and is composed of the root *nau* 'child', the infix *-lap-* 'big; old', to which is added a personal possessive suffix, for

example, *naulapei* 'my stepchild'. One informant speculated that the word refers to the fact that most stepchildren are taken when they are 'older' than adoptive children, who ideally are taken at weaning.

4. Marriage to someone with children from a previous marriage, or who were born out of wedlock, is optional, of course, but stepparenthood is involuntary and automatic once such a marriage is entered.

5. Ruth Goodenough (1970) chose to limit consideration of fosterage on Romónum, Truk, to cases of orphanage. This unnecessarily restricts the meaning of *tumwunuu* as it applies on Namoluk.

6. That matrilineal kinship ties are "stronger" is reflected in the comparative frequency of adoption and fosterage by matrilineal and patrilateral kin. Two-thirds of the adoptions and two-thirds of the fosterage events on Namoluk are by matrilineal relatives of the child. Less than one-third of the cases of adoption and fosterage are by patrilateral kin. The greater "strength" of matrilineal kinship ties on Namoluk is also seen when the subject of incest and exogamy is considered (see Marshall 1971).

7. Nason reports that on the closely related atoll of Etal, clan chiefs also have to be consulted before an adoption can take place (personal communication). No such situation exists on Namoluk.

8. For purposes of this analysis, a "household" is an enduring commensal unit, usually consisting of an extended family who eat together daily.

9. One criterion for adulthood on Namoluk, as on Romónum, Truk, is parenthood (see Ruth Goodenough 1970:330–333). To be an adult with no dependent children is, in some senses, not to be an adult and is a pitiable situation in the eyes of Namoluk people.

10. Nason has suggested that prestige and status accrue to the adopter on Etal and that adoption of children may be one means for demonstrating prowess as a 'big-man' (personal communication). The Namoluk data support this suggestion.

11. Land from one's father is especially important on Namoluk because, if one shares such land at all, he shares it only with his siblings. Land from one's mother is subject to jural rights of other members of one's lineage. Children born out of wedlock are at an economic disadvantage from birth because they have no father to provide them an inheritance (see Marshall 1972).

12. Although the infrequency of ships to and from the atoll means that such short-term fosterage may last several months, this kind of fosterage resembles Tongan *tokanga'i* arrangements in all other respects. Morton (chapter 4) describes these as being identical to the Western practice of babysitting.

13. Compare Shore (chapter 8) who records a similar situation for Samoa.

14. "In adoption cases, the child proposed for adoption must appear personally before the court. If the person seeking the adoption is married, both husband and wife must join in the petition unless the husband or wife is the true father or mother of the child. An adoption may not be granted without either the written consent of, or reasonable notice to, each of the child's known living legal parents who is not insane or has not abandoned the child for a period of at least six months. If the child is over 12 years of age, adoption

also may not be granted without the consent of the child" (U.S. Trust Territory of the Pacific Islands 1960:29).

15. Natural grandparents account for 25 percent of all fosterage relationships on Namoluk. When classificatory grandparents are included, the figure increases to 44 percent.

16. Instances where natural and foster parents reside in the same household have been counted as 'fosterage' only when both parties agree that the foster parents have primary responsibility for 'taking care of' the child. Fosterage does *not* automatically result from living in an extended family household.

17. Note here the symbolism of food: an adoptive mother indirectly nurses her child by providing its natural mother with foods said to insure a good supply of milk.

18. Secrecy about adoption events seems to hold throughout greater Trukese society (Ruth Goodenough 1970:325–326).

19. *Möngö chu* literally means 'eat together'. *Möngö* 'food; eat' is regularly used on Namoluk as a generic term for the following resources: *fanu* 'dry land'; *pwöl* 'taro plots'; *set* 'sections of reef'; *mae* 'stone fish weirs'; *mei* 'breadfruit trees'; and *nu* 'coconut palms'. All of these resources may be inherited, bought, sold, or exchanged.

20. Before Typhoon Phyllis destroyed all of the houses on Namoluk in 1958, dwellings were scattered widely about the islet in separate clusters. When typhoon relief provided materials to replace houses destroyed in the storm, a decision was made to lay out the villages in lines of adjacent dwellings fronting on "streets." This plan was copied from an illustration of a typical American main street found in a fourth-grade civics textbook.

21. Until missionary teaching finally put a stop to it more than twenty-five years ago, lineage siblings enjoyed rights of sexual access to one another's spouses under certain prescribed circumstances.

22. Close kinsmen feel they have rights to some of the fruit of their close relative's labor if they contributed materially to supporting him as a child.

23. Money is not shared as freely or as willingly as *pisek* 'material goods', and the incursion of a semi-cash economy is beginning to make small inroads into the cherished notion that kinsmen should share everything.

24. I am indebted to Reggie Kennedy for pointing out to me that the 'formal friend' relationship in greater Trukese society is very similar to 'going for siblings' in Black American culture.

25. See also Ann Fischer (1963:527) and Ward Goodenough (1970b:399), where it is suggested that adoption and fosterage involve access to people as if they were a form of property.

26. Although consent of both parties should be secured before an adopted child is given to someone else, two cases have occurred on Namoluk where mutual consent was not obtained. In both cases the natural parents took back their child without the consent of the original adoptive parents in order to give the child in adoption to someone else. The natural parents were widely criticized for their actions, and the relationships between the natural parents and the original adopters continue to be strained.

27. This form of fosterage works to the disadvantage of salaried workers employed and living in the district center. A steady stream of relatives from the hinterland passes in and out of their homes, resulting in a steady drain on their monetary resources. It may be expected that with time the cash economy on Moen will prove incompatible with the dictates of widespread clan hospitality and will perhaps diminish the range of traditional obligations for kinship reciprocity there.

28. If a child's adoptive mother is of a different clan than his natural mother, the land he receives from his adoptive mother also aids in land redistribution on the atoll.

29. This method of intercourse is also practiced on Namoluk and, according to Namoluk informants, has been practiced for a long time throughout greater Trukese society.

30. It is of interest that Namoluk women in 1971 are not marrying at as young an age as Romónum women in 1949. Expanded educational and employment opportunities for women probably account for this difference.

31. Adult women are those age twenty-one and over.

32. Table 5 does not consider whether the natural child was alive at the time of adoption. This, however, is more than offset by the fact that other adoptive siblings were not included in a determination of whether a Namoluk family had children at the time of adoption. Since a great many adopting couples adopt more than one child, this latter consideration is of some consequence.

33. The crude adoption rate on Namoluk in 1971 was 13 percent, based on 85 adoptions out of 654 named children born in the last three generations. Calculated in the same way, the crude adoption rate for Romónum in 1964–1965 was 10.9 percent (Ruth Goodenough 1970:314).

3

ADOPTION ON MANIHI ATOLL, TUAMOTU ARCHIPELAGO

Candace Carleton Brooks

INTRODUCTION

Despite at least a century of periodic attempts by missionaries, businessmen, and administrators to bring the behavior and institutions of the inhabitants of French Polynesia into agreement with European practices, the Polynesian way of life continues to resist fundamental change in many crucial areas.

The retention of traditional values and attitudes is particularly apparent in patterns of marriage, land tenure, and adoption. These patterns represent, in part, a complex adjustment to the problems faced by small populations in relatively isolated environments.

Most island populations are small, and, as such, they are particularly vulnerable to rapid demographic changes. On the one hand, unchecked population growth can quickly overburden the carrying capacity of the environment. On the other hand, some unpredictable disaster may lower population numbers below the minimum necessary to ensure continuation of some or all of the population's social groups. For example, an epidemic or loss of a fishing party in a storm may render a flourishing family virtually extinct within one generation's time.

Normally, marriage and land tenure patterns function periodically to redistribute needed resources and personnel throughout the population. Adoption provides additional means by which individuals and localized descent groups assure their access to the necessities of life.

This chapter describes current adoption practices in a French Polynesian community and suggests that the persistence of these practices, despite potential religious and legal penalties, derives from their continued function as a vital source of personal and group security.

MANIHI ATOLL

The atoll of Manihi lies at the northern end of the Tuamotu Archipelago, approximately 300 miles from Tahiti, the administrative and commercial center for French Polynesia. Except for a deep pass at its southwestern end, the roughly oval lagoon is completely encircled by reef and reef islets. Although the population was formerly spread around the atoll rim in localized landholding units, today everyone lives in a single village located on one side of the pass.

Manihi's village had a more or less permanent residential core of 171 persons in 1967. With the exception of the schoolteachers and their families, all residents were affiliated by birth or by marriage with one or more of the atoll's three localized descent groups, called *ngati* or *'ati*, through which claims to land on the atoll are validated.[1] By 1970 the composition of the village's residential core had changed somewhat, but its overall characteristics and general size had remained about the same.[2] Data used in this chapter were obtained from a population of 221 persons, which included members of the residential cores in 1967 and 1970, plus 6 adopted individuals who were off-island during both study periods.

ADOPTION AND RELATED PRACTICES

There are three basically different arrangements involving care of children by persons other than their natural parents on Manihi. These arrangements are referred to locally as *ha'apa'o*, *ti'ai*, and *fa'a'amu*.

The term *ha'apa'o* 'to heed; to obey; to watch' is used to refer to situations closely resembling babysitting in America. One may be asked or told to 'watch' a child for five minutes or for five days. For example, a child of four might be told to 'watch' its two-year-old sibling. If the younger child gets into trouble, the older child is held responsible. At the same time, the older child is not supposed to physically punish the younger one. Or, a mother may ask her neighbor to 'watch' her child while the mother collects drinking nuts outside the village. The neighbor assumes responsibility for the child's immediate welfare, but all punishment except verbal scolding is normally delayed until the return of the mother. In a 'watching' situation, the natural parents specifically retain jural control of the child.

The term *ti'ai* 'to keep; to foster' is used in situations where the parent is physically absent and at a sufficient distance to make immediate return difficult. In a 'fosterage' arrangement, the person left in charge assumes greater temporary control of and responsibility for the child than in a 'watching' arrangement, and longer periods of time are usually involved. The 'foster parent' has the right to punish the child for misdeeds, but the 'fosterage' relationship is explicitly regarded as temporary. For example, Ounu, a young widow with no land of her own, wanted to move to Pape'ete to find work. Ounu's mother reluctantly agreed to keep her young granddaughter on Manihi only after being assured that this was to be just a 'fosterage' arrangement. Ounu promised to send money and clothing regularly for the child as evidence that she planned to reclaim the child eventually, that is, she promised to demonstrate that she retained ultimate responsibility for and primary jural control of the child.

The term *fa'a'amu* 'to feed; to cause to eat; to care for a child as one's own' refers to true cases of adoption. In this instance, the adoptive parents and the natural parents agree that primary jural parenthood has been transferred from the latter to the former (see Brady, chapter 1). While the natural parents are expected to show continued affection and interest in their child, the child's first obligation is to its adoptive parents.

These expectations and obligations are explicit in the following incidents relating to one adoption: A young girl named Teio was adopted by Mahia and her husband. When Teio's sixth birthday arrived, her natural parents were on another part of the atoll making copra. Teio cried at the absence of her natural parents, and other villagers were mildly critical that the couple had not returned to show their affection on her birthday. Later on, Teio's natural mother, Tiare, pressed her into babysitting her three younger siblings without first consulting Mahia. Within a short time, Mahia came and took Teio home, and she reprimanded Tiare on the grounds that the little girl was now her adoptive child. Although Tiare is normally an aggressive person, she took the rebuke quietly and apologized.

In the eyes of the community, absence of regular support from the natural parents plays an integral part in establishing that a child has been 'adopted' rather than merely taken over in a 'watching' or a 'fosterage' arrangement. The most important difference between 'watching', 'fosterage', and 'adoption' appears to be an agreement between the natural and substitute parents as to who has ultimate jural control and responsibility for the child. For example, in fosterage transactions the natural parents are expected to periodically provide some tangible, token support for the 'foster child'. If such support is lacking, the 'foster parent' may declare that effective jural control of the child has been transferred to him by default and that the child is now an 'adoptee'. In such cases, community opinion usually favors the self-named adoptive parent.

A recent controversy illustrates such a status change: Hina, a young woman from another island, conceived a child by a visitor while residing on Manihi. Prior to the child's birth, Hina formed an alliance with a second visitor. This man was forced to leave the island just after the baby's birth, and Hina went with him. Because the child was too young to make the trip, Hina left her in the care of her kinswoman, Puahi, with the understanding that Puahi would 'foster' her until Hina's father, Po, could come for her. Over six months elapsed before Po finally arrived. By that time, Puahi had grown too fond of the child to part with her. Po left her in Puahi's care until Hina's return.

Four years later, Hina and her husband returned to claim the baby. Puahi and her fellow villagers said that the baby had been *fa'aruehia* 'forsaken', that only once had Hina sent a small amount of money (and that within the first year) for the child's care, and that the child was therefore 'adopted'. Hina claimed that she had sent money and clothes several times. She maintained that Puahi stole the child by refusing to give it to Po.

Was primary jural parenthood transferred by default to Puahi or not? Paramount among the factors upon which both parties to the dispute based their arguments were questions of the existence and frequency of support from the natural mother for the child.[3]

France controls French Polynesia as one of her overseas territories, and the Polynesians are French citizens. They may participate in national as well as local elections and are subject to the French civil code. Under the civil code, it is possible to adopt a child legally through the offices of the French courts. However, this method is not generally used by Polynesians, in part because the criteria for legal acceptability of the parties involved (such as the age of adoptive parents) differ from local norms. More importantly, perhaps, the entire court system is viewed by the islanders as French and therefore foreign and capricious. The legal system is viewed as a game in which the average Polynesian does not know the rules and perceives little chance of being able to consciously manipulate events to his advantage. None of the adoptions in this sample were formalized through the courts. The adoption of Hina's child by Puahi, described above, took place under unusual circumstances, and custody of the child was later contested in the courts.[4] The major reason for this unusual action seems to be the deep involvement of Hina's European husband in the quarrel.

Theoretically, the penalty for following local adoption practices rather than going through the courts is severe. Under French law, the right of an adopted child to inherit from his adoptive parents hinges on court recognition of his adoption. If he has not been legally adopted, he might be disinherited in a court case.

There are at least two ways to circumvent this problem, one used by the islanders and another by the court itself. First, in at least two cases from Manihi, a child taken at birth by its adoptive parents was registered officially in the civil records as their natural child.[5] It is uncertain what a judge would decide if a consanguine of the adoptive parents tried to contest such a child's inheritance at some later date. At the present time, however, adoptive parents feel that such registration strengthens the legal ties with their children. Second, some French judges have allowed Polynesian custom to affect their rulings. The court in Pape'ete has often honored the testamentary desires of adoptive parents, both in the rare cases where they leave written wills and in cases where the adopted child can show conclusively through witnesses that the deceased intended such gifts. For example, a woman's natural son recently tried to gain his adopted sister's inheritance through the ploy that she had not been legally adopted. The court upheld the adopted sister on the basis of verbal testimony by other relatives and fellow villagers as to her deceased parent's intent. However, the possibility of anyone's contesting an inheritance is often minimized because the adoptive parent is already a lineal or close collateral consanguine of the adopted child. The child's right to inherit is reinforced by his preexisting biological ties with the adoptive parent. In addition, adopted children today often receive land from both their natural and their adoptive parents.

Religious policy is another potential deterrent to local adoption practices. In isolated rural areas such as Manihi, community life centers around the church, and social status is gained or reinforced through religious participation. Normally, residents of such rural communities are sensitive to church attitudes.

The Sanito Church (Reorganized Church of Jesus Christ of Latter Day Saints), to which over 78 percent of Manihi's adult population belong, has expressed a strong negative position on adoption (see Ottino 1970:92–93). However, one of the more prominent local Sanito members, an adopted child himself, has let his adoptive parents adopt one of his own children. In conformity with Ottino's (1970) observations for Rangiroa Atoll, Manihi Sanito members tend to adopt grandchildren, but this is by no means a prescriptive rule. For example, recent adoptions of more distantly related consanguines in two prominent church households have aroused no local comment. Although the church is normally a powerful factor in controlling community behavior, on the subject of adoption, at least, its guidelines are largely ignored.

INCIDENCE OF ADOPTION

Adoption is common on the atoll. At least 25 percent of Manihi's recent residents have been or are presently adopted children. As the data are by no means exhaustive for islanders over twenty years of age, it is probable that the actual percentage of adoptions is much higher.

Examination of the fifty-five adoptions for which relatively complete data are available shows general agreement with trends noted in other rural areas of French Polynesia (see, for example, Finney 1965; Hooper 1970; Ottino 1970). As table 6 indicates,

TABLE 6. Relationship of Adoptees to Adopters on Manihi Atoll

Relationship	n	%
Consanguineal:		
Children		
sibling's child	14	25.4
Grandchildren		
child's child	13	23.6
sibling's grandchild	5	9.1
sibling's child's grandchild	3	5.5
parent's sibling's grandchild	3	5.5
parent's sibling's child's grandchild	4	7.3
more remote relationship	1	1.8
	(43)	(78.2)
Affinal:		
Wife's child	5	9.1
Parent's spouse's grandchild*	1	1.8
	(6)	(10.9)
Nonkinsmen	(3)	(5.5)
Exact relationship unknown	(3)	(5.5)
TOTAL	55	100.0

SOURCE: Author's field notes, 1970.
*The real and adoptive parents were reared together.

a majority of adoptions on the island have been among consanguines.[6] Most of these adoptions by consanguines (32 out of 43; 74.4 percent) are among the close lineal and collateral kinsmen of the *opu ho'e* 'womb'. This kin grouping comprises siblings and, by extension, their children and grandchildren. It formed the nucleus of the corporate landholding groups in the past, and it continues to be socially and economically important today.

Of the nine known nonconsanguineal adoptions, six were viewed locally as "close" in relative kinship distance because they involved affinally linked people living in the same household. One case involved exchange of a child by stepkin (a man and woman) who had been raised together, and, according to local norms, this made them functionally equivalent to 'natural' siblings. In five other cases, children of previous unions were adopted by their mothers' new husbands.

Another case of nonconsanguineal adoption involved the transfer of a child between two women who were very close and who had grown up 'almost as sisters' in adjoining households. Informants admitted that the women were not kinsmen in any accepted formal sense but insisted that their deep friendship and close association as children made them analogous to 'kinsmen'.

Of the thirty-three households on the atoll during the two study periods, seventeen included young adopted children. Sixteen households included no adopted children, but seven of these households had given children in adoption. Thus, nearly three-fourths of Manihi's households have been directly involved in recent adoptions.

Most of the nine households that have not participated in recent adoptions are established nuclear families with several children of their own. Kinsmen in the strongest position to request one of these children have already adopted children from other sources. Other prospective adoptive parents presently have closer kinsmen outside these households from whom they can more easily demand children. In time, it is likely that most of these households will either lose or gain a child in adoption. Most islanders participate either as donors, as adoptees, or as adopters in at least one adoption transaction during their lives.

MOTIVATIONS FOR ADOPTION

Reasons given by informants for adopting or for giving up a child correspond to those found elsewhere in French Polynesia. These include childlessness, easing a large household's economic burden, the need of older people to have someone younger near at hand who is strongly obligated to help them, and the desire to have a small child around the house. A close examination of actual cases suggests that the last of these reasons is the major stated motivation in adoption transactions.

On the whole, Manihi's present female population does not suffer from infertility. While three women have only one living child, the average number of children in residence in 1967 was 3.4 per mature woman. If children who have died or who are attending school off-island are considered, this figure increases to at least 5 children per woman.

Where infertility occurs, however, it provides a strong incentive for adoption. One of the island's two barren women has had no natural children from either of her two marriages, but she has adopted and raised ten children. Nine of these children were closely related to her, and the tenth was closely related to her second husband. The reasons given by her for each of these adoptions range from the poor health of the natural mother to the unstable relations between the natural parents. But the underlying motive readily attributed to her by neighbors is her possessive love for children.

The economic burden of a large household does not appear to be a common motive for giving children in adoption. Little cash outlay is needed to fulfill daily expectations of a 'good life' on the atoll. In addition, children enter the rural labor pool early and usually become an important part of the work force by the time they are ten years old. There was one family, however, that other villagers considered to be overburdened. The young couple had nine children, all under twelve years old. A kinswoman asked for their last child before its birth. This woman, the second of the island's two childless women, explained that she had only an adopted son from her husband's family, that the young couple had too many small children to care for comfortably, and that she wanted a baby she could care for. Informants suggested that the young couple were willing to give up the child in adoption because of the problem of guaranteeing adequate land for all their children.

Over one-half of the informants who were related as 'grandparents' to their adoptees stated specifically that they adopted a young child in order to have someone to care for them in their old age. These same persons usually added that their own children tended to be self-centered and to forget their obligations. It is possible that traditional support for the elderly is being increasingly threatened by adjustment of the local Polynesian social system to Western pressures such as a cash economy, individual ownership of land, and nuclear family households. However, personal observations suggest that the elderly parents of middle-aged residents are still being cared for directly by their children or, if they live apart, receive monetary support from the children.

Although old-age security may be hoped for or used as a rationalization for such adoptions, the prime motive on the part of grandparents is more likely to be the desire to raise a small child again. Usually an adoptee is taken as an infant and will not be in a position to support his already elderly adoptive parents for many years, by which time he will be in his teens, a traditionally irresponsible time of life for Polynesians. Formerly, teenagers remained economically valuable because they continued to reside in their parents' households and assisted with domestic tasks. Today, however, they frequently depart for the excitement of metropolitan Pape'ete.

An examination of specific cases reveals another reason for the adoption of children who are already related to the adopter as 'natural' or classificatory grandchildren. In at least eleven of twenty-eight such cases, the natural parents either had not entered into a stable marital arrangement or were working in Pape'ete. Small children are considered to be a burden to young parents in the urban center because the parents usually do not live in the sort of extended household arrangement that would provide babysitting when parents are away for work or recreation. Traffic hazards and potential danger from strangers are also cited as reasons to avoid keeping very young children in the vicinity of Pape'ete. Thus, many children are left with their 'grandparents' when their natural parents emigrate to Pape'ete.

A series of complementary population shifts seems to be taking place between rural Manihi and urban Pape'ete in which the adoption institution provides an important security function. These shifts are summarized in figure 3. Teenagers and young adults move to Tahiti for work and entertainment. Illegitimate children or children of young parents will be sent back to Manihi, usually to be adopted rather than fostered by their grandparents or other close consanguines. The adoptive relationship ensures that a child will be fully cared for, whether or not the natural parent sends financial aid regularly. In addition, both established couples and unattached individuals may return to the atoll for varying periods to relax from city life, to reassert residential and property rights, and sometimes to remain permanently.

At the same time, a few elderly and ailing islanders move to Pape'ete to be near the hospital where they are supported by close relatives already established on Tahiti or by money sent by

FIGURE 3. Population Movement Between Manihi and Tahiti.

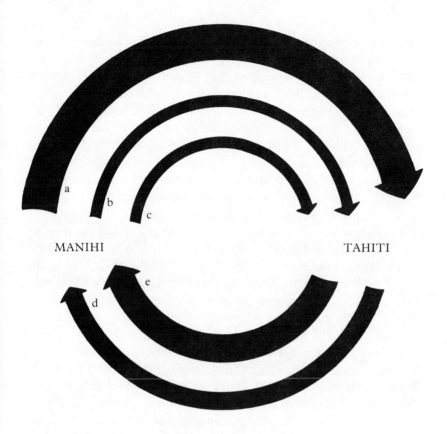

MANIHI

TAHITI

Width of arrow indicates relative flow

a   teenagers and young adults
b   older children for advanced schooling
c   elderly with support from children
d   young or mature adults for visit or residence change
e   small children

kinsmen from Manihi. Some children are sent by their parents to
Pape'ete for special or advanced schooling. They are usually
adopted by an elderly consanguine, whom the child's natural
parents may already be supporting. Again, close care and responsibility for the child by a close kinsman are assured.

CONCLUSIONS

The people of any small island face a relatively precarious existence. On atolls, even the land itself is an impermanent feature.
Manihi's aboriginal population had to cope with uncontrollable,
generally unpredictable, and unavoidable disasters such as epide-
mics, tsunamis, typhoons, and differential reproduction and survival rates. Adoption was one strategy utilized to maximize the
survival potential of the human population on the atoll by ensuring
maintenance and continuation of local descent groups.

The position of the islanders with respect to natural disasters
and differential fertility rates has not been changed substantially
by Western technology. Even now, for example, the exact path
of a typhoon cannot be predicted, and islands in actual need of
evacuation cannot be identified prior to the storm's arrival. Aid
to survivors is prompt, but the basic problem of surviving the
storm itself remains unaltered on a low island. Many of the conditions alleviated in the past by adoption continue to exist and to
provide a *raison d'être* for retention of adoption practices.

In addition, the increased physical movement of young adults
from family-oriented, rural communities to individual-oriented
urbanized areas, with the attendant increased potential for instability of parent-child bonds in the urban setting (see Kay 1963;
Finney 1965), provides a new need, or perhaps merely an inten-
sification of an old need, for guaranteeing emotional and physical
security to children. Adoptive relationships are utilized presently
as means to fulfill this need.

Levy (1970) has argued that French Polynesian adoption practices intersect with marital practices to convey a psychological
message to members of the society about the tenuousness of
emotional bonds between individuals. Parents can be lost through
death or other misfortune, as can spouses and children. It does
not pay to become too emotionally dependent upon any one
individual. The hazards of the local environment make this
message sound advice.

But there is a second, positive side to the message: All individuals
are replaceable. If parents, spouses, or children are lost, other
persons are always available to replace them. Security cannot be

assured through any one individual, but chances for security may be maximized through the maintenance of a group of potential substitutes. Common kinship as a recurrent theme among potential "givers" and "takers" in adoption provides a consistency and predictability needed by people living in a system in which roles form the constants, and most actors are interchangeable.

NOTES

My husband and I carried out our initial fieldwork in French Polynesia during eleven months in 1966–1967 as part of the requirements for my doctoral degree. The work was funded by a fellowship and a dissertation research grant from the National Science Foundation. An additional four and one-half months of post-doctoral work was done in 1970.

1. Membership in these localized descent groups was formerly exclusive. Today a person may utilize cognatic ties to claim membership in a number of descent groups. Normally, however, the most relevant groups are those of one's place of residence because land rights are traced through membership in them (see Ottino 1970:89).
2. Forty-eight people present on the atoll during the 1967 census were absent during the 1970 census. Of these, four had died and twenty-five had probably moved away permanently. The rest were considered to be only temporarily absent for health, education, or business reasons. Forty-four new people were recorded in the 1970 census, one-half of whom were children born to residents since the 1967 census, and another ten of whom were residents returning after lengthy absences.
3. Some visible token support of a child is probably most important when the 'foster parent' is not a natural grandparent.
4. The outcome of the court case is not known at this writing.
5. Ottino mentions similar behavior for Rangiroa residents (1970:109).
6. I have included as an adoption the care of Ounu's daughter by Ounu's mother, described earlier in the chapter. Although the initial arrangement was to be 'fosterage', in just two months community opinion and circumstances had visibly begun to alter the grandmother's attitude toward her charge. The grandmother had displayed unusual behavior in the first place when she did not immediately offer to adopt the child. It was obvious that soon she would be treating the little girl as her adopted daughter. It was also probable that Ounu would not challenge this change in status.

4

TONGAN ADOPTION

Keith L. Morton

INTRODUCTION

Tongan kinship is a dynamic system of social relationships that individuals can and do manipulate to attain goals in the form of psychological well-being, social status, and economic security. Generally, the kinship system is manipulable simply by a person's emphasizing those relationships advantageous to him and deemphasizing the less advantageous relationships. While this process may alter the intensity of kin relationships, it does not necessarily create new relationships or alter the membership structure of an individual's kinship network. However, adoption is a specific, formal process within the kinship system that both creates new kin relationships and redefines kinship networks. It is these special characteristics of adoption that invite individuals to utilize it for goal attainment, and it is with these characteristics in mind that I will describe and explain Tongan adoption as goal-directed kinship behavior.

The statistical data for this study were obtained from 240 households in a village of 260 households on the main Tongan island of Tongatapu.[1] At each household, information was gathered regarding the adoptive status of the household head and his real siblings, the household head's wife and her siblings, and the adoptive status of each of the household head's children. This means, then, that the adoptive statuses of all children in 720 families of orientation were recorded. From this information, plus census data from two other villages, it was determined that 12 percent of the Tongan households surveyed have either adopted a child or have given up a child in adoption. Specific information on eighty-one adoption transactions was recorded.

In my sample village, as in all other Tongan villages, the dominant household form is the nuclear family. Nuclear families are usually joined into a *matakali* 'residence group', whose members are linked by ambilineal ties to the group's headman. Membership in this residence group is loosely defined, but anyone thought to be related to a headman and living in the same village as the headman is eligible for membership. For most Tongan commoners the 'residence group' is the most inclusive corporate group in which they claim membership.[2]

Economy at the village level is based on horticulture and fishing. Primary emphasis in production and consumption is placed on subsistence needs, although most peasant farmers do some cash-cropping. Goods and services are distributed through a system of nonmarket exchanges that pivot on kinship and friendship obligations. Children are distributed through the system as adoptees but are considered to be especially valuable resources because of their central role in the maintenance and perpetuation of local kin groups.

ADOPTION AND RELATED PRACTICES

Nearly all adult Tongans have had some experience with adoption, either directly as adopters or adoptees, or indirectly through relationships with kinsmen who have been directly involved in adoption transactions. The Tongan government sanctions only a few of these adoptions. Few applications for legal adoption are made to the courts because the circumstances of Tongan adoption are often incongruent with the European model of adoption applied in the courts. In 1970, eighteen applications for adoption were made in the courts; sixteen were granted and two were refused (Roberts 1970:3). Only one case of legal adoption was recorded in the sample village discussed in this chapter.

In contrast to Western practices of child rearing, the rights

and duties of jural parenthood extend to a large number of kinsmen, neighbors, and friends. This has a determinant effect on
socialization responsibilities. For instance, a child is seldom called
home at mealtime if he is working or playing elsewhere; parents
assume he will be fed wherever he happens to be within the village.
It is also expected that neighbors will generally look after a child
whenever he is near their home. Parents frequently leave children
who are five years of age or older at home while they go to their
gardens or perform some other task, presuming that their children
will be looked after without any explicit arrangements having been
made. In return for such services, persons who temporarily
assume the duties of parenthood establish claim or reinforce
existing claims to rights as secondary jural parents with respect to
children cared for in this manner. For instance, adults can expect
neighbors' children to run errands and execute minor tasks for
them, and they may use corporal punishment to insure that orders
are obeyed.

When explicit arrangements are made for an adult to care for
another's child, the arrangement is described by the term *tokanga'i*
'to care for'. This type of transfer of parental role is only for short
periods of time, from a few hours to a few days, and is similar to
the Western practice of babysitting.

A partial, but permanent, transfer of certain aspects of the
parental role is the practice of *fakahingoa* 'to name' (see Aoyagi
1966:165–167). The namer is usually a high-ranking kinsman of
either the father or mother. Quite often the namer is the *meheki-
tanga* 'FZ', who is the highest-ranking kinsman in the first
ascending generation of the person to be named. Occasionally,
unrelated persons of high community status may be asked to
give a name; frequently these are high-ranking churchmen. The
namer assumes partial responsibility for the moral welfare and
training of the subject and may be called upon to assist the child
either through counseling or by material assistance.

A Tongan term that may be glossed as fosterage is *tauhi* 'to
protect' or in the nominal sense 'guardians'. Fosterage arrangements do not alter a child's formal kinship status or inheritance
rights. Following the definition of adoption offered by Brady in
chapter 1, Tongans practice two types of adoption. The first is
ohi, which refers to the 'adoption of non-kinsmen'; the second

type involves the 'adoption of consanguines' and is known as *pusiaki*, which literally translates as 'to rear a child away from its mother' (Churchward 1959:424).[3] The presence or absence of shared *toto* 'blood' is, according to Tongans, the primary distinction between these two types of adoption, and it is an important difference. The adoption of 'blood' kinsmen occurs with a much higher frequency than the adoption of other persons. Of the eighty-one adoption cases recorded, only two can be legitimately classified as 'adoption of non-kinsmen'.

Both of these adoption types result in a new parent-child relationship. All adoptees are adopted as 'children'. There are other situations similar to adoption, but these are not marked by formal transaction or jural recognition. For instance, a kinship term may be extended to include non-kinsmen classified as 'close friends'. Depending on the relative age and sex of ego and his or her friend, the term for sibling, child, or grandchild may be used. Such kin term usage demonstrates strong affection but not jurally binding kinship.

The remainder of this chapter will deal with 'adoption of consanguines', and henceforth the term 'adoption' will be restricted to 'adoption of consanguines' unless otherwise stated.

ADOPTION TRANSACTIONS

No numerical data were collected on the frequency of adoption requests, but it seems that requests are denied far more frequently than they are honored. Most requests are made just prior to parturition, or in the first few weeks following a child's birth. It is felt that it is best to make the request before the mother and child have become emotionally attached to each other. Although it is considered generous both to adopt a child and to give a child up for adoption, the denial of adoption requests does not usually upset relationships between parents and prospective adopters.

Adoptions are arranged through a procedure that minimizes conflict between prospective adopters and the natural parents of potential adoptees. Following this procedure, the prospective adopter makes the initial adoption request of a kinsman, who he feels will consent to the adoption of one of his or her children. Such a kinsman will usually consent to the adoption contingent upon agreement by the other natural parent—the one not related by blood to the prospective adopter. It is the latter that usually denies the request if a denial is forthcoming. Thus, the burden of disagreement in such an important matter rests between affines and not consanguines—an acceptable, if not ideal, situation.

Both husbands and wives must agree to the adoption of their children, but women seem to take more interest than men and so tend to dominate adoption negotiations. In those cases where only one adoptive parent was related by 'blood' to the adoptee, 68 percent of the adoptees were related to the adoptive mother.

If a prospective adopter finds parents who are willing to let him adopt their child, custody of the child is transferred without ceremony. Although there is no exchange of goods at the time of the transaction, adoptions are thought to bring the two sets of parents closer together, and mutual exchanges may increase in frequency. Adoptive parents have greater obligations to natural parents after an adoption event. However, any mention of money or goods owed is socially unacceptable and subject to censure. In one case, the natural parents of an adopted child approached the adopter and requested that he return the child. The adopter agreed to return the child if the parents would compensate him for having cared for the child. The parents, unable to pay the amount asked, made the incident known publicly, and the adopter was subject to local gossip for trying to 'sell a child'.

A typical example of the adoption process is provided by a man whom I shall call X. X did not marry until late in his twenties, and after three years of marriage his wife had not borne a child. He wanted a child from his own *kainga* 'kinsmen', so he went to his younger brother, Y, who had a two-year-old child and an infant of less than a month. X asked to adopt Y's younger child. Y was agreeable to the adoption, but the child's mother said she did not have enough children and denied the request. About a year later, Y's wife had another child and X renewed his request. It was again denied by Y's wife. X had no other close kinsmen with young children so he stopped trying to adopt one of his own kinsmen and allowed his wife to arrange the adoption of one of her sister's children.

Most adoption transactions are initiated by prospective adopters, but in some circumstances natural parents will actively seek adopters for their children. One such case involved a man whose wife had died, leaving him with several young children. The man found another woman willing to marry him, but she did not want his children; he then made arrangements for his brother to adopt the children. In general, it is far easier to find someone willing to adopt children than it is to find parents willing to give them up.

ADOPTION AS GOAL-DIRECTED BEHAVIOR

Unlike other kinship statuses and relationships, adoptive statuses and relationships are negotiated and defined more or less explicitly by the norms and principles of adoption transactions. Adoption is initiated only by the choice of individuals, and in that sense adoptive relationships are optional and manipulable. It is this feature of adoption that allows it to be utilized in pursuit of individual goals. As described above, adoptions are usually initiated by the adopters, and an understanding of adopters' goals is essential to a satisfactory explanation of Tongan adoption.

The goals of adopters vary with their age and their position in the household cycle. Tongan households generally pass through four phases of development and decline before termination. An initial phase, the dependent nuclear family, is characterized by a man and wife residing with the kinsmen of either spouse and being dependent upon those persons for housing and perhaps land and food. Dependent nuclear family members usually intend to establish a separate and independent household in the near future. The "lifespan" of a dependent nuclear family depends on several factors, including the husband's success in obtaining land or a wage-labor job, the maintenance of congenial relations with the host family, and the growth rate of the new family. This period of dependence often ends when the first child is born, at which time the couple establishes a separate household and begins to assume most of the duties and responsibilities of adults. The next period in the household cycle is the young household phase characterized by bearing and rearing of children and maintenance of an independent household.

Motivations for adoption in either of these first two phases are closely connected with achieving adult status. The Tongan community gradually extends adult status to its younger members;

there is no single criterion for adulthood, but rather a number of social and economic criteria must be met before an individual gains full recognition as an adult. For men, achievement of parenthood means the assumption of economic and moral responsibilities for rearing a child. For women, nurturance is a specific and highly valued role.

Single women were the adopters in about 5 percent of the adoption transactions surveyed, but there was no recorded case of a single man adopting. While men take a great deal of interest in infants and enjoy holding and playing with them, they do not like to assume responsibility for day-to-day care of a child.

The mother-child relationship is particularly intense in the first few months of infancy. During this period, a new mother devotes almost all her time to physically maintaining her infant and herself. Infants are held whenever they cry or show any sign of discontent. They are always held when going to sleep and only placed in bed after they are asleep. Infants are heavily bundled in wool and flannel clothing to protect them against the weather—even when the weather is pleasant. More importantly than protecting the infant, the extra clothing signifies the mother's competence in the eyes of others, and it gives her psychological comfort.

Tongan beliefs and values surrounding marriage reinforce parenthood as a goal for young adults. For instance, it is commonly believed that childlessness leads to discontent and unhappiness in marriage. A childless couple 'has no reason to remain together'. A correlate of this belief is that a childless couple experiencing discord can solve their problems by adopting a child.

Within the first two phases of the household cycle, parenthood itself is an important immediate goal. For couples who cannot bear children of their own, adoption provides a legitimate process for achieving parenthood. Adopters in these first two household cycle phases may also have more specific goals in mind. Parents who have children of only one sex often desire or need a child of the opposite sex and will adopt accordingly. The division of labor within the household is rigidly defined according to age and sex categories. By the age of ten or younger, boys are expected to contribute substantially to the material well-being of the family by gathering coconuts and firewood and caring for livestock. Girls assist by performing many household tasks and are often assigned the care of their younger siblings. Thus, a household without children of both sexes is considered to be as imbalanced as a household without any children. Again, adoption provides a means for establishing what is considered the proper composition of a household. In these cases, the goal of adoption is recruitment for specific roles. However, it should be noted in this regard that there was no overall preference in my sample for either male or female adoptees. Both sexes are adopted with about equal frequency.[4]

In a few cases, adopters stated that they adopted a son to provide heirs to their property. Legally, however, an adopted child cannot inherit land unless the adoption is recognized by the courts (cf. Brooks, chapter 3), and, as mentioned above, legal adoptions are infrequent. Another infrequent, but strong, motivation for adoption is grief for a recently deceased child. Parents experiencing such a loss sometimes turn to adoption to provide another child of the same sex and approximately the same age as the one they lost.

Adopters in the third and fourth phases of the household cycle have different problems and concerns than do adopters in the first two phases, and this difference is reflected in their adoption goals. The third phase, the mature family, is marked by cessation of child bearing, maturation of children, and, frequently, the presence of dependent families or individuals. The last phase is the declining household with few or no children present and an increasing reliance upon other households for subsistence needs. In these latter two phases, children are adopted by aged adults for companionship and for assistance in performing household chores and subsistence tasks. By adopting children in the third and fourth household cycle phases, adopters increase the number of primary kinsmen on whom they can rely for material assistance in their declining years. Ideally, grown children assist their parents economically whether they are 'natural' children or adopted. Table 7 shows the ages of adoptive mothers and natural mothers of adoptees; it also gives an approximation of the relationship between adoption and household development phases.

Adopters usually initiate adoption events, but the adoptees' natural parents sometimes encourage the adoption of their children for several reasons. Illegitimate children are preferably adopted by

TABLE 7.   Age Distribution of Natural Mothers and Adoptive
Mothers

Age	Household Phase	Natural Mothers		Adoptive Mothers	
		n	%	n	%
16–20	dependent	9	11	4	5
21–25	nuclear	18	23	5	7
26–30		21	26	6	8
31–35	young	14	18	11	14
36–40		9	12	13	16
41–45		4	5	9	11
46–50	mature	4	5	7	9
51–55		0	0	9	11
56–60		0	0	3	4
61–65		0	0	9	11
66–70	declining	0	0	2	3
71–75		0	0	1	1
TOTAL		79	100	79	100

SOURCE: Author's field notes, 1970–1971.

someone in the mother's family in order to give the child a socially
acceptable position and to 'free the mother to find a husband'.
Children thought to have been conceived in adulterous relationships are often not wanted by the mother's husband, and he might
insist that the child be adopted by someone else. Men who lose
their wives through death or divorce and are left with small children
usually allow them to be adopted, or they may actively seek an
adopter. Parents may also encourage the adoption of their child
if they believe an adopter could give the child educational or
economic advantages beyond what they could provide. Generally,
parents experiencing economic hardship, severe illness, or serious
marital instability are more willing to allow adoption of their
children than they would be in more normal circumstances.

Gratitude for services rendered sometimes results in adoption.
A woman who cures a sick child may be given the child as a gesture
of parental appreciation. Another example is provided by a man,

J, who was visiting an outer island. During his stay there, J had an argument with the kinsman he was visiting and was asked to leave. A non-kinsman, K, befriended him and looked after J until passage could be arranged back to Tongatapu. Out of gratitude, J asked K what he could do in return. K answered that he wanted J to adopt his son and take him back to the main island where the boy could receive a better education. This case is unusual in that it was not initiated by the adopter, and it resulted in the adoption of a non-kinsman, but it illustrates how adoption can result from obligation and how adoption can be utilized for attainment of the natural parents' goals.

The most common reason that natural parents consent to the adoption of their children is their general willingness to assist kinsmen who desire an adoptee. Willingness to give up a child comes from a genuine desire to help kinsmen in need and from the necessity of maintaining good relationships within the system of kinship reciprocity. It is believed that families with several children should be willing to give one to a childless kinsman, just as it is believed that one with an abundance of food should be willing to share with those less fortunate. Adoption, then, is part of a general system of kinship reciprocity, and children are resources whose custody can be negotiated and exchanged within that system (see Carroll 1970c; Marshall, chapter 2).

ADOPTION AND KINSHIP RECIPROCITY

The Tongan concept of kinship implies participation in reciprocity among kinsmen. Sharing is expectable kinship behavior. This concept is expressed as *fetokoni'aki* 'the spirit and reality of co-operation'. Nearly all goods and services enter into the reciprocity system and may be *kole* 'requested' or they may be *foaki* 'given freely'.

Generally speaking, adults give and receive goods with persons who vary from mere acquaintances to close kinsmen. The pattern is different for the flow of children in exchange (Morton 1972: 116–118). Children are highly valued resources. As such, the transfer of their custody is almost completely limited to transactions between 'blood' kinsmen. Tongans are less trusting of non-kin than they are of kinsmen as far as responsibilities for children are concerned. Women nearing parturition usually request that only their mothers or other close female relatives assist them in childbirth and in the infant's early care. Other persons are not to be trusted. This attitude grows more lenient as the child grows older so that more distantly related persons and even non-kinsmen may be entrusted with his care for short periods.

Table 8 illustrates that adoptees are usually close kinsmen of the adopter, generally the adopter's classificatory children or grandchildren. In 81 percent of the cases shown, adoption transactions were between principals who were related either as parent and progeny or as siblings and who at one time had resided in the same household.

Sibling and parent-child relationships are generally the most important ones for resource sharing. An examination of 310 exchange events in which goods were transferred revealed that 50 percent of the transactions involved these particular relationships (Morton 1972:115).

This pattern of resource sharing occurs within a system in which the basic unit of production and consumption is the *'api* 'house-

TABLE 8.   Relationships of Adoptive Mothers to Adoptees

Relationships	Adoptees	
	n	%
BC	17	22
ZC	14	18
SC	14	18
DC	13	16
HZC	7	9
HBC	5	6
BDC	3	4
BSC	1	1
MZDC	2	3
MZSC	1	1
HFBSC	1	1
HMMBSC	1	1
TOTAL	79	100

SOURCE: Author's field notes, 1970–1971.

hold'. As mentioned earlier, most households are composed of nuclear families, or small extended families. A few households may be linked by consanguineal ties to form a loosely organized residence group. This residence group is important in terms of resource sharing: a person is likely to share goods and services more extensively with members of his residence group than with nonmembers. Adoption also follows this pattern of sharing. About 56 percent of adoptees in the sample were obtained from members of the adoptive parents' residence group. Normally, the broadest parameter for sharing children is the 'bilateral kindred', which includes all persons to whom ego can trace consanguineal relationship.

The high frequency of adoption of ZC, BC, SC, and DC in table 8 can be accounted for as part of the general pattern of sharing among kinsmen (see Carroll 1970c). In a sibling relationship, a man is always obligated to assist his sister by giving her first fruits and other goods and services and by watching after her social welfare. Between siblings of the same sex, the elder takes precedence in rank and prestige and commands respect from the younger sibling. However, the behavior pattern followed between adult siblings of the same sex is one of greater balance in reciprocity and mutual dependency. This fact promotes a relatively high frequency of cases in which siblings are the principals in adoption transactions.

Excluding cases of grandchild adoption, 68 percent of adopters were from among the adoptive mother's kinsmen rather than from the adoptive father's kinsmen. This pattern is explained by two circumstances. First, women tend to dominate negotiations, and they choose to negotiate with their kinsmen rather than their husband's kinsmen. As explained above, adoption transactions are negotiated by consanguines, not by affines. Second, the kinship rank of a woman is higher than a man's with respect to siblings. Rank within the kindred determines social prestige, influences the allocation of authority, and has implications for resource sharing. Kin rank is relative to ego and is established by three criteria applied in the following order: agnates outrank uterines, females outrank males, and age outranks youth. Thus, a woman outranks all of her siblings except older sisters; a man is outranked by all of his siblings except younger brothers. A woman's higher rank with respect to her siblings means that her request for an adoptee is more likely to be honored by them than would a similar request made by her husband and directed to his siblings. As shown in table 8, adoptive mothers' siblings are sources of adoptees much more frequently than are adoptive fathers' siblings.

The large number of grandparent-grandchild adoptions results from the general obligation children have to assist their aged parents. Parental requests should be honored, including requests to adopt one's child. Grandparent-grandchild adoption is often ambiguous because of the age of the adopter and perhaps because of the adopter's general dependency on the household of the natural parents. A grandparent who adopts a grandchild may die before the adoptee reaches maturity, in which case the adoptee will probably return to his natural parents. A grandparent who adopts a grandchild also may be unable to care for the child's needs, so the natural parents may continue to look after the physical needs of the child under these circumstances. Although adoptions by grandparents are regarded as 'adoption of blood kin', they are understood to be special cases in which 'adoption' is not complete.

Goodenough (1970b:404–405) has suggested that in Polynesia the transfer of child custody should be viewed as an exercise of rights of jural parenthood beyond those of the natural parents. In reference to grandchild adoption, he says, "If grandparents have a right to have their grandchildren reside with them, then the taking of a grandchild into one's house does not represent a transfer of parental right from parent to grandparent but represents, rather, a simple exercise of grandparental right" (1970b:404). However, Goodenough's hypothesis that grandparents hold latent overriding rights of parenthood with respect to their grandchildren does not fit the Tongan data. Tongan grandparents can only take their grandchild as an adoptee after the natural parents have agreed to relinquish their rights in the child. Rather than grandparents holding overriding rights of parenthood, they only hold the right to make a request for their grandchild, and, of course, such a request can be denied. However, aged persons do expect support from their children, and providing one's child in adoption may be part of the obligation to assist one's parents.

In sum, children may be viewed as resources whose reallocation is manifest through the process of adoption. The direction and nature of such reallocation follows the usual pattern of resource sharing among kinsmen. The importance of children as resources and the strength of binding reciprocal obligations contribute directly to the high frequency of adoption transactions among close kin.

THE ADOPTEE

I have described adoption as a process that is used both by adopters and by natural parents to attain goals. Adoptees do not normally make any decisions with respect to the adoption transaction itself, but they do benefit from their adoptive statuses, and they manipulate their statuses to attain goals. Adoption has the overall effect of increasing an adoptee's options for group affiliation and access to resources. These options are greater for adopted than unadopted persons because adoption provides an individual with two overlapping kindreds instead of one.

The behavioral and conceptual content of an adoptee's natal kinship status reckoned through his natural parents is not altered by adoption, but the degree to which this status is stressed by the adoptee varies according to context. An adoptee may refer to kinsmen by adoption as though they were 'natural' kinsmen, or, if the occasion demands, an adoptee may stress that they are kinsmen by 'adoption'. When adopted by a kinsman, an adoptee finds himself in the position of being related to some persons in two different ways. For instance, if adopted by his MB, an adoptee's natural mother can also be considered his FZ. In referring to such persons, an adoptee's choice of terms will be determined either by the social context of the moment or by his personal preference. Since personal names, rather than kin terms per se, are used in address, the problem of selecting the proper term seldom arises.[5]

Adoption is particularly advantageous to the adoptee because it provides alternatives for the reckoning of rank within the kindred. For instance, if a female is adopted by her FZ, all of her natural siblings become subordinate to her by virtue of her new status as FZD, whereas before adoption her older sisters outranked her. Because adoptees have two sets of related parents, they also have two ranks with respect to those kinsmen they are related to through both sets of parents. Under these circumstances, adoptees may choose the more advantageous rank by stressing either their adoptive status or their status through their natural parents.

The adoptee's continuing relationship with his natural parents may range from infrequent to almost daily contact. The natural parents may bring gifts of food and other items to their child, and he may visit them on occasion. However, the more frequent and intense the contact between adoptee and natural parents, the more likely it is that friction will occur between the adoptive parents and the natural parents.

Adoptees frequently become the *pele* 'favorite' of their adoptive parents, and some Tongans think of adopted children as 'spoiled children'. An adoptee is in a position to get special treatment from his adoptive parents because he is more likely to be an only child, the only child of one sex, or the youngest or eldest child in the family. Forty-five percent of the adoptees surveyed were adopted into households where there were less than three other children present. Although the age of adoptees at the time of adoption varied from a few days to sixteen years, nearly 60 percent were less than one year old and 72 percent were less than two years old. These figures are consistent with the ideal of adopting very young children. Another possible reason for the special treatment of adoptees is that adopted parents fear that the child will return to his natural parents unless they treat him kindly.

Adoption also results in a redefinition of incest parameters. In Tongan society, the incest taboo, at least for commoners, applies to all persons with whom a consanguineal relationship exists, no matter how remote. Even unadopted persons have some difficulty in identifying eligible sexual partners. Three times in succession a young man began showing interest in a girl only to find out from an interested third party that he and the girl were related in some obscure manner and that their relationship could not continue. For adoptees this situation becomes even more difficult as the incest taboo applies to kinsmen related through adoptive parents as well as to kinsmen of natural parents. The extension of the incest taboo for adoptees underscores the fact that adoptees are accorded full kinship status through both their natural and adoptive parents.

An example will illustrate how adoption provides alternatives for an adoptee regarding access to resources and group affiliation. It will also show how an adoptee may manipulate his kinship status to achieve goals. L was adopted at the age of seven months by M and N; M was L's FMZ, but after the adoption L called M *fa'e* 'mother', and N *tamai* 'father'. M had a daughter of her own, but the girl married young and left home so M wanted another child. When L was nine years old, M became very ill, and L was sent back to live with his natural parents. M's illness continued for about a year and then she died; at that time L ran away and returned to live with N, his adoptive father. During the next few years, L's mother came several times to take him to her home, but each time he ran away and returned to his adoptive house only after she had left. During this period, there were a lot of hard feelings between N and L's natural parents. The last time L's mother came to take him back he was seventeen years old, and he told her that he was old enough to decide for himself that he wanted to stay with N.

When L's natural mother died he did not go to her funeral, but when his natural father died both he and his adoptive father attended the funeral. L inherited nothing from his natural parents; all of their possessions went to a younger son. When N died, L inherited all of his possessions. Both L's natural parents and adoptive parents resided in the same village, but the natural parents had few kinsmen within the village while the adoptive father had several. By stressing his relationship with his adoptive father, L closely aligned himself with six household heads within the village, two of whom held strong positions of leadership.

SUMMARY

I have tried to demonstrate that Tongan adoption is an integral process within the kinship system that provides for individual goal attainment and thus offers solutions to a broad range of social and economic problems. Young adults utilize adoption to attain the goal of parenthood and community recognition of their adult status. They also use adoption to recruit children to roles within their household in order to 'balance' the division of labor or to solve other specific social and psychological problems. Older persons adopt to secure companionship and material assistance from adopted children. People allow their children to be adopted because they are temporarily or permanently unable to care for their children, or because they believe the children will benefit from the adoption. The most important reason people allow their children to be adopted is because they feel obligated to assist kinsmen who request a child. Adoptees generally benefit from adoption because it enlarges their network of "close" kinsmen, endows them with the advantage of reckoning their kinship status through either their natural parents or their adoptive parents, and thereby expands and reinforces their access to strategic resources.

NOTES

This chapter is based on doctoral dissertation research completed in Tonga during 1970 and 1971, which was funded by a National Institutes of Health Traineeship administered by H. G. Barnett, University of Oregon. The primary field problem concerned the economics and social organization of Tongan villages.

1. Tonga is an independent nation consisting of three island groups in the Tongan archipelago. Tongatapu is the largest island and is the governmental, administrative, and economic center of the island kingdom. The total population is variously estimated at 85,000 to 90,000.
2. Tongan society contains four strata: *tu'i* 'kings', *'eiki* 'nobles' or 'chiefs', *matāpule* 'chiefs' assistants' and *tu'a* 'commoners'. This chapter deals only with adoption among commoners, who form the bulk of the population. For further information regarding social strata in Tonga, see Gifford (1929) and Kaeppler (1970).
3. *Ohi* also has a broader meaning: it is used to describe human nurturance of young animals.
4. In my sample of eighty-one adoptions, male adoptees represented 51 percent of the cases and females, 49 percent.
5. Tongan terms of reference for the parental generation are bifurcate-merging; cousin terminology is Hawaiian.

HOUSEHOLD, LAND, AND ADOPTION ON KUSAIE

Walter Scott Wilson

INTRODUCTION

This chapter describes the transfer or delegation of parental rights and duties from one party to another on Kusaie. A discussion of Kusaiean parenthood is presented, and the types of transactions and associated motivations recognized in transactions in parenthood are traced. Finally, the outcomes of such transactions are discussed in terms of household organization and land distribution.

DUTIES OF PARENTHOOD

In the Kusaiean view, the primary duty of parents is to *tufalla* 'nurture' their children. The same term is also used to describe the care of pigs and other domestic animals. Children are 'nurtured' until they are old enough to make a significant contribution to the household economy. The age at which a child is considered able to make such a contribution is about fifteen years, although younger children are assigned household duties according to their abilities.[1] While the primary duty for 'nurturing' falls on natural parents, other persons such as grandparents and parents' siblings share these duties. Older children are expected to help care for their younger siblings, and much of the care and feeding of children after they are weaned is performed by older sisters and, less often, by older brothers. As soon as they are old enough to perform any of the activities involved in child care, children learn to take care of their younger siblings.

A second concept relevant here is that of *karunanen* 'caring for'. The main difference between 'nurturing' and 'caring for' is that a person may be 'nurtured' only until he reaches maturity, but a person may be 'cared for' at any age. The concept of 'caring for' includes offering protection, being responsible for, and seeing that the other person's needs are met. Parents have a primary responsibility to 'care for' their children as long as they are able to do so, regardless of the age of the children. Grandparents have a duty to 'care for' their grandchildren as well as their own children.[2]

A person should 'care for' all those persons he or she refers to as *talik natik* 'my child'. Similarly, siblings should 'care for' one another, and adults should 'care for' small children, the elderly, and persons who are sick or require special attention, such as those who are away from home and in need of hospitality as generalized reciprocity (see Sahlins 1965; Brady 1972).

A primary duty of fatherhood is to provide children with land. During the period that a father is active economically, he may allow his children and members of his household to use land under his control. A man's own children do not have to reside in his household to use his land, but the rights of others to use such land are often predicated upon continued membership in the owner's household. A man's land is usually divided among all of his children who have families large enough to form independent households.[3] If a man dies before this division is made, it is his eldest son's responsibility to divide the land. If a man has left a will, his son is obliged to respect his father's wishes.

RIGHTS OF PARENTS

Parents have a right to have their children in their households although this right sometimes is conditioned by grandparental rights. A man's parents have a stronger traditional claim on grandchildren than a woman's parents, and, in the rare case of parental separation, the father rather than the mother has a customary right to take the children. A mother and her parents assume parental rights over children born out of wedlock. In such cases, the natural father has no right to his children solely by virtue of paternity.

As children approach puberty, they become valuable household workers. The word for 'the service which a child or other person performs within a household' is *kulansap*. This 'service' is expected by parents or by the head of a household from other members of the household; grandparents, parents' siblings, and older siblings may also request this 'service' when it is needed. Transfer of a child from one household to another for the purpose of 'service' either establishes or discharges an obligation between the adult parties involved.

Parents expect to be 'cared for' in old age by their children, and this is one of the most important rights of parenthood. To be surrounded by children and grandchildren in old age is one of the strongest motives to beget children.

The rights and duties of parents and children on Kusaie are not as exclusive as they are in Western culture. One result is a high rate of residential mobility within the community. At any time, there is a large number of children staying in households other than their own for periods of time ranging from one night to one year or more. These temporary shifts in residence are not necessarily associated with 'adoption'; many such shifts simply represent the exercise of secondary jural rights and duties rather than outright transfers of primary rights and duties.

ADOPTION

There are two types of adoption recognized by Kusaieans. The first involves the exercise of rights to *srukye* 'hold' their grandchildren. Out of 1,206 persons identified as Kusaieans, 40 had been 'held' by grandparents.[4] However, all children living with grandparents did not fall into the 'held' category.

Table 9 shows a breakdown of the forty cases by sex and relationship of the grandparents to the individual 'held'. A child living with a grandparent is different from one 'held' by a grandparent, and this difference is expressed on the part of the grandparents who 'hold' a child by stating that they have permanently assumed the rights and duties of parenthood. This transfer of primary jural responsibilities requires acquiescence on the part of the natural parents. Children born out of wedlock are

TABLE 9.   Children 'Held' by Grandparents

Relationship to Child	Number of Children		
	Male	Female	Total
Married Mother's Parents	8	12	20
Unmarried Mother's Parents	6	8	14
Father's Parents	1	5	6
TOTAL	15	25	40

SOURCE: Author's field notes, 1964.

usually 'held' by grandparents even if their mother later marries. This is done because Kusaieans believe that the stepfather and his family will not treat the other man's child well. In spite of this general belief, some accept their wives' children from previous unions and assume the rights and duties of parents.

Grandparental motivations for 'holding' a child are many. One motivation is to provide a fatherless child with a place in a household and an opportunity to inherit land. Another motivation is the strong bond of affection that exists between children and grandparents. In many cases when a man and wife establish an independent household, a child may remain with the grandparents. Another reason frequently mentioned by grandparents for 'holding' a child is to insure that there will be someone to 'care for' them in their declining years. Sometimes it is said that a child left behind is a substitute for loss of his parents' services. The household of the grandparents may require the 'service' of the child as a worker, and the child may be 'held'. In many cases, however, the child is too young to be of much help.

When a child is 'held' by grandparents, the natural parents do not cease to have rights and duties with regard to him, even though the child resides with the grandparents and is expected to contribute economically to the grandparental household.

A second type of adoption transaction is known as *nuti talik* 'to adopt a child as one's own'.[5] These transactions normally involve an explicit agreement between a child's natural parents and a set of adopting parents to share parental rights and duties. The way in which rights and duties are actually shared varies from little or no recognition of the adoptive relationship on the part of either set of parents or the child to the other extreme in which the 'adoptive' parents take over all the obligations of parenthood. In the latter event, the child performs all duties for his adoptive parents that he would normally owe to his natural parents.

On Kusaie the jural status of an 'adoption' depends not so much upon the contract involved as upon the performance of the parties to the relationship.[6] Even the claims of natural children depend upon their performance of duties because their parents have 'nurtured' or 'cared for' them and may be expected to provide them with an inheritance of land. In cases of adoption where existing 'parental' ties do not form the background for the adoptive parent-child relationship, performance becomes of even greater importance, although an emphasis upon reciprocity in the performance of obligations and in the claiming of rights is a general feature of Kusaiean culture.

Out of 1,206 individuals on Kusaie, 62 cases of explicit 'adoption' were identified. Forty out of ninety-eight households contained members who had experienced adoption. Of these forty households, twenty-five contained one adoptee, eight contained two such persons, five households had three, and one had six members who had been adopted. Of the sixty-two cases of adoption, sixteen of these individuals were living with their own parents, and twenty-six were living with their adoptive parents. Twenty were either heads of households or married. Table 10 shows the nearest kinship relationship between the adoptive parents and the adoptees in this survey. Children were adopted by parents' siblings in just over one-half of these cases. Parents' sisters were preferred over parents' brothers by twenty-four cases to nine.

The procedures involved in 'adoption' are informal. Ideally, adoptive parents request a child from the natural parents. It is considered impolite to refuse such a request. This is especially true when the person making the request is very close and trusted. Adoption by such persons usually means that the 'adopted' child will not be located far from his natural parents. This makes it easier for the natural parents to take the child back (by force if necessary) if he is mistreated.[7] If a child is taken back by his natural parents because of mistreatment, community sentiment normally is on their side. In any case, adopters have an obligation to take

TABLE 10.   Relationship Between 'Adopting' Parent and 'Adopted' Child

Adopting Parent's Relationship to Child	Number of Children		
	Male	Female	Total
Mother's Siblings			
MZ	6	6	12
MB	4	1	5
Father's Siblings			
FZ	9	3	12
FB	4	0	4
Other Relatives			
MMZ	1	2	3
FFZ	1	1	2
MMBS	0	1	1
MFBS	1	0	1
distant	7	6	13
Not Related			
'best friends'	4	1	5
other	2	2	4
TOTAL	39	23	62

SOURCE: Author's field notes, 1964.

good care of the child and to provide him with an inheritance. For this latter reason, most parents feel that it is to their child's advantage to be adopted.

Another characteristic affecting Kusaiean 'adoption' is the freedom that children have to wander from one household to another. This freedom of movement becomes somewhat curtailed for girls who are past puberty because parents feel an obligation to watch that they do not become sexually involved with boys. On the other hand, boys continue to be unsupervised, and the only effective limit on their mobility is their obligation to gather food and participate in other economic activities. Upon reaching the age where he is free to wander, an adopted child may prefer to stay with his natural parents, and in such cases the natural parents may request that the child return to his adoptive parents. Parents, however, cannot refuse hospitality to their own children, and a child's desires are generally respected.

A person of any age may be adopted on Kusaie. Yet, according to local theory, the best time to adopt a child is as soon after birth as he may safely be taken away from his mother.[8] At this time, a child is still young enough to form a strong emotional attachment to the adoptive mother. The natural parents' relationship with their child continues, however. The main right surrendered by natural parents in adoption is the right to be the child's boss. Even so, in many adoptions, the adoptive parents play the role of parents only for a short period in the child's life.

In Kusaiean customary law, the rights of natural children normally take precedence over the rights of adopted children. The rights of an adopted child, however, are strengthened considerably if he conscientiously performs the duties of a child toward a parent. The adopted child's rights are also strengthened if the adopting parents perform the normal duties of parents.

Motives for adoption vary considerably. One very important motive is to provide children for childless couples. A childless couple desires children both for reasons of affection and economic necessity. It is not unusual for a childless couple to adopt a child and later to have children of their own. It is also possible for a couple with children of their own to adopt additional children in order to insure that they will be cared for in their old age.

Another motive may be to symbolize and enhance the closeness of a tie between the two sets of parents. This is especially true where there is a 'friendship' relationship between one of the natural parents and one of the adoptive parents. Although I have classified *kawuk* 'best friends' as "non-relatives" in table 10, a 'best friend' is treated in all respects as a relative. The model of the 'best friend' relationship is the relationship between siblings of the same sex, and the exchange of children among such persons both symbolizes and further concretizes the closeness of the relationship.

The value placed on children as objects of affection leads to many adoptions that are motivated primarily by emotional reasons. Even unmarried women sometimes adopt children, enabling them to assume the role of mother. Sometimes such women also provide an inheritance for the child. One unusual case of adoption involved an unmarried mother, her child, and an unrelated infant. The child formed an emotional attachment to the infant and asked her mother to adopt the baby. The mother did so as soon as the infant was weaned.

Another unusual case of adoption illustrates how affection and 'nurturing' may lead to adoptive parental bonds. On a visit to a hospital, an unmarried young woman found one of her distant relatives there nursing one of her sick children. This relative also had another child sick at home, in this case an infant who was covered with sores. Since the mother could not tend each child equally, the unmarried woman offered to help by looking after the sick infant. The mother agreed, and the young woman took the infant home with her. She bathed the infant's sores and fed it milk and breadfruit. For several days, the young woman took care of the infant during the day while the mother looked after her other child in the hospital. Finally, the mother left the child in the care of the young woman at night. The infant recovered from the skin infection, gained weight, and generally looked healthier than before. At this point, the mother offered her child to the young woman in adoption. (This is unusual in that adoptions are normally initiated at the request of the adopting parent.)

The young woman intended to raise the child as her own. Sometime later, the young woman left the island to get married, leaving her parents to care for the child. The mother of the child came to the house and took the child back home where he has remained since. Whenever the adopting mother returns to the island for a visit, the child's mother dresses the boy up to visit his 'mother'. The boy usually hides because he is afraid that his adoptive mother will take him away. The desire for the welfare of a child may be the motive for both the adopting and the real parent in this instance.

One of the traditional functions of chiefs on Kusaie is to care for all members of the community. In order to be taken care of, an individual must be part of a household. A person brought into a household necessarily has a status similar to others in that household. This does not of itself, however, constitute adoption to the Kusaieans, although it is possible to adopt a stranger or for a stranger to adopt members of the community, both of which have occurred in the past.

REASSIGNING 'SERVICE'

In addition to transactions in parenthood that come under the category 'adoption', there is another relationship that is conceived to be temporary and yet constitutes a distinct change in status. This transaction involves reassignment of the 'service' of a young person from one household to another. A person is most likely to enter into a 'service' relationship after the age of fifteen and before marriage. The person in 'service' has the right to be fed and cared for and has the obligation to work for the household. The person in such a relationship does not necessarily acquire any permanent rights in the household in which he works. Service in this relationship does, however, create and discharge kinship obligations between households and families. These obligations may be intergenerational. For example, individual A took care of B's mother in her old age. Therefore, B's grandchild may be made to feel obligated to take care of A in A's old age. The motives in the 'service' relationship are predominantly economic.

FUNCTIONS OF TRANSACTIONS IN PARENTHOOD

The functions of the various types of transactions in parenthood on Kusaie fall into three main areas. The first is the symbolic value or the "message" that these transactions carry (Carroll 1970c). The ability of grandparents to 'hold' their grandchildren symbolizes the overriding authority of parents over children which does not end when the children marry. It also carries with it the message that parenthood, like other social relationships on Kusaie, is not exclusive. Kusaiean 'adoption' also stresses the overriding value put on generosity, cooperation, and sharing, even to the extreme of giving away one's most valued possessions. 'Adoption' further emphasizes the message that performance of one's duties and exercise of one's rights is necessary to validate them. It may also carry the message that one gains most in the Kusaiean system of reciprocity by investing one's energies in the service of others, thereby creating obligations. The message of the 'service' relationship is that one's duties are transferable: One's obligation to a parent can be discharged in service of a "substitute" parent.

The second function of the various transactions in parenthood is the distribution of land. Two types of problems are eased by discharging the duty to provide land to one who has performed the obligations of childhood. One problem is to provide land to poor families and to individuals who do not inherit land. The other is to provide a vehicle for the land rich to insure that they are fed and cared for in their old age. Land allocations through adoptions provide such insurance. The adoption of close relatives also helps to keep land within the kin group.

The third function of transactions in parenthood on Kusaie is to provide flexibility in the formation of viable households, that is, households that can cope with problems of subsistence. Out of ninety-eight households in Lelu, only fifteen had less than six members. This represented a total of only fifty-four people. The smaller households represented older individuals and married couples who had completed their families and who were dependent to some extent on other households. All viable households require a balance of membership that does not always prevail through birth recruitment processes. The actual membership requirements also vary according to the life cycle of the members of the households. For instance, a woman who is bearing children needs help in performing her normal household work. Kusaiean transactions in parenthood provide alternative means for increasing or decreasing the number and type of household members in accordance with fluctuating requirements.

SUMMARY AND CONCLUSIONS

The rights and duties of natural parenthood on Kusaie are shared by parents with their own parents and with siblings and even with older children. It is the natural parents, however, who have the primary responsibility to 'nurture', 'care for' and provide land for their children.

Three ways in which parental rights and duties may be transferred with varying degrees of completeness and permanence have been discussed above: 'holding' grandchildren, 'adoption', and 'service'. The 'service' relationship is perceived as temporary, regardless of the length of time it endures. This relationship emphasizes service in a household, and the relationship ends when the 'service' terminates. 'Holding' and 'adoption' are viewed as permanent transfers of primary parental rights and duties, with residual rights and duties remaining with the natural parents. Thus, both types of transactions may qualify as "adoption" in a generic sense (see Brady, chapter 1; Smith, chapter 11).

'Adoption' and 'holding' relationships vary considerably in the degree to which a change in residence is required for the child, whether or not the change of residence is permanent or temporary, and whether or not the child eventually receives an inheritance of land. The status of an adoption on Kusaie also depends upon the performance of the parties to the transaction. The natural parents may nullify an adoption by requesting the child to return home for an extended period and by reassuming the primary parental role. A child may affect the status of the adoption by returning home or by fulfilling all the normal behavioral expectations toward his adoptive parents.

Another transaction in kinship involves the *kawuk* or 'best friend' relationship. Like adoption, the status of such a relationship depends upon the performance of the parties to it. At one extreme, 'best friends' share most of the rights and obligations of siblings. Recognition of this relationship by other members of the families of the parties involved varies according to the extent to which the 'best friend' discharges kinship obligations to other members of the family as well as to the primary party to the friendship.

In short, these various transactions in parenthood and kinship on Kusaie are carried out for a wide variety of motives, and they have a number of important social functions. They appear to satisfy psychological needs to nurture and to be nurtured; they also function to redistribute land. These transactions sometimes provide a place in the community for children who are otherwise socially handicapped. Finally, the formation of viable household units is facilitated by 'holding' grandchildren, 'adoption', and the 'service' relationship. The wide scope of possible arrangements under these three main types of transactions adds an important measure of adaptive flexibility to Kusaiean social organization.

NOTES

Kusaie is the easternmost of the Caroline Islands with a land area of 42.3 square miles (Bryan 1946) supporting a population of 3,989 in 1973. The fieldwork on which this chapter is based was made possible by a fellowship (MF–12, 312) and grant (M–4323) awarded by the National Institute of Mental Health. Additional financial assistance was furnished by the Department of Anthropology, University of Pennsylvania.

1. Age categories on Kusaie are those of *talik fus* 'infant', which ranges from birth to one year; *talik* 'child', which ranges from one to fifteen years; *met fus* 'young person', which ranges from fifteen to thirty years; and *met mata* 'adult', which includes persons thirty and older. Transition from one category to another is not formally marked.

2. The Kusaiean system of kinship terminology has sibling terms that are extended to both cross and parallel cousins and parent terms that are extended to parents' natural and classificatory siblings. There are separate terms for grandparents, but the term for child includes grandchildren.

3. Both males and females may inherit land; but in many cases only males inherit, and females are cared for by their husbands or brothers. Formerly, daughters were sometimes given a piece of land called *tuka* when they married.

4. For complete censuses of native Kusaieans taken in 1960–1961 and in 1964 see Wilson (1968). It is unlikely that all cases of transactions in parenthood were identified in this sample since some transactions would have been forgotten by informants.

5. The term *nut* 'adopt' is also used as an adjective in *talik nut* 'adopted child' and in expressions like *pik nut* 'domestic pig' (as opposed to a *pik in ime* 'pig in the bush'). The kinship term *talik natik* may be translated literally as 'my child (object)'.

6. The system of jural relations and customary relations referred to here is the system recognized by Kusaieans and not necessarily that of the Trust Territory Code.

7. When a parent desires to take back an 'adopted' child, he may take the child home for a 'visit'. The child may then be shuttled back and forth until he eventually spends most of his time with his natural parents.

8. It is customary on Kusaie for a relative to wean a child by taking it away from the mother. Weaning usually takes place when the child is between one and two years of age; the last child, however, may continue to be breast fed until it reaches four years of age.

6

ADOPTION AND LAND TENURE AMONG ARNO MARSHALLESE

Michael A. Rynkiewich

INTRODUCTION

The day after my arrival to survey Arno Atoll, I found a plot of land on which to build a house. The local Peace Corps volunteer pointed out that there was an old cistern on the property and that the rock-bordered path leading through the brush to the lagoon also indicated former habitation. That night we went to see the owners. I could not speak Marshallese, and the volunteer was not sure which of the adults in the household was the manager of the plot. However, he went ahead and explained that I wanted to build a house and use the site for eighteen months. In exchange, I would clear the land, repair the cistern, and turn the improved site and house over to them when I left.

Through the translation it became clear that they had some questions before they would make the decision. They wanted to know if I were a kind man. Would I be happy to have them come visit me, would I help them in times of need, would I share my food, my goods, and myself with them? My culture-bound re-action was that I was in danger of being exploited. What I wanted was a clear-cut economic relationship: lessor and lessee and no more. I offered them rent as well. They did not want money; the important thing was the kind of relationship that would be established.

Though confused and embarrassed at my own culture shock, I said the terms were agreeable. Then one man, as if making introductions, turned to me and said, 'This is your Mama, and this is your Papa'. I repeated the words, looking first at the old woman who was the land manager and then at the wiry old man who was her husband. The look of concern on her face was somewhat lightened by the indication that our relationship would be Marshallese rather than American style. My wife and I became their adopted children because we were living on their land. On Arno, one either lives on land because he is related to the owners, or he is related to the owners because he is living on the land. Kinship and rights over land are interrelated; one is often the source of the other (see Lieber 1970:163; Silverman 1970; Brady, chapter 7). I was not being prepared for exploitation; I was being translated into the Marshallese social system through a transaction in kinship.

This chapter is a description of the forms, meanings, and functions of adoption events on Arno Atoll. Adoption on Arno is a process of creating or redefining kinship relations between individuals and between categories of individuals. Adoption does not occur for any single reason, nor is there a single outcome to the process. Adoption is, at minimum, a transaction in kinship. The specific content and the implications of each transaction for other social processes and relationships always remain a matter for negotiation. It is important to realize that the process of adoption on Arno does not automatically include changes in residence or inheritance, though these may occur. Other processes, namely matrilineality and patrifiliation, are more important and more closely tied to the recruitment of persons identified as coresident and heir. Adoption, as a process of kinship affiliation, serves as a contingency strategy in the realm of social action. Once an adoption has occurred, for any of a variety of reasons, the adoptive relationship can be extended to include coresidence or inheritance. Whether or not this will happen depends not so much on the context of the adoption event itself as it does on the subsequent social situations that develop relative to the wants and needs of the adopter, the adoptee, and the adoptee's biological parents. An adoption negotiated for one reason may be transformed to serve other needs at a later date. Adoption on Arno can only be understood as an institution with many sources, many functions, and a flexibility that allows for transformation of relationships over time.

In the sections below, a discussion of the meaning of Arno kinship will be followed by a description of the forms of adoption, and, finally, by an examination of the place of adoptive relationships in the recruitment of household members and the inheritance of land rights.

CULTURAL CONTEXT OF KINSHIP

Adoption is clearly one part of a cultural domain that might be called kinship sharing or reciprocity (see Carroll 1970:152–153; Marshall, chapter 2). In this domain there is an emphasis on sharing food, housing, and labor among kinsmen. The Marshallese phrase *kilai nuki* 'look after kinsmen' means that food, shelter, and labor are to be shared among kinsmen without compensation. Conversely, there is the clear implication that the people with whom one shares these things are 'kinsmen' in some sense. Thus, either the notion of existing kinship promotes sharing, or the appropriate behavior gives rise to the use of the kinship idiom. It is the expression of kinship, the message that one is behaving as a proper kinsman, that is important. For example, when a person is preparing for a party, he summons his kinsmen to attend and contribute. They all promise to help and to bring food, but they often show up only to stand around and talk. The actual assistance is not as important as the expression of a willingness and intention to participate. The existence of a kinship obligation is operationalized by consent, an act which presents a message of recognized solidarity.

The applicability of ground rules for appropriate behavior among Arno kinsmen is coordinate with the kinship terms used in the relationship. Since adoption often involves a change in the use of terminology and behavior, or a shift in emphasis, it is instructive to outline these basic relationships.

It can be seen in table 11 that nearly all kinsmen in alternating generations use reciprocal kin terms for each other. Behavior in these dyads is characterized by ease, familiarity, and relaxed joking. Alternate generation relationships pivot on mutually patterned disrespect and toleration rather than on respect and authority.

Relations between persons in adjacent generations, on the other

TABLE 11. Arno Kinship Terminology

+2 and above	*jimau* (all males including affines of females of these generations).	*jibu, bubu* (all females including affines of males of these generations).	*uleba* (all males in the relationship of mother's brother).
+1	*jema* (all males including affines of females of this generation, usually excepting mother's brothers).	*jinu* (all females including affines of males of this generation).	
Generation ±0	*jeu* (all elder siblings and cousins, occasionally including their affines).	*jetu* (all younger siblings and cousins, occasionally including their affines).	*reliku* (alternate term of reference for cross-cousins of opposite sex).
−1	*neju* (all males and females and their affines, occasionally including sister's sons if male speaking).		*mangeru* (all sister's sons if male speaking. Optional for female speakers and females spoken to).
−2 and below	*jibu* (all males and females and their affines).		

SOURCE: Author's field notes, 1969–1970.

hand, are characterized by strong avoidance of both sexual joking and references to bodily functions. Persons in the ascending generation are all authority figures. Persons in the descending generation are expected to show respect and deference in the presence of the older generation. There is, however, variability in the strictness of the relationship between parents and their own children. The children are ranked from eldest to youngest. Parents and eldest son and daughter should avoid each other to the extent of not knowing (or at least pretending not to know) when or where the other is eliminating or bathing. This restriction is somewhat relaxed with the middle children, and the youngest child is free from nearly all such restrictions except those pertaining directly to sex. The folk explanation of these differences is that the youngest child is still around the household when the parents become old and infirm. Where the eldest child would never think of accompanying his parents in eliminating and bathing, the youngest child often has no choice but to help.

The rights, duties, and obligations of jural parenthood are shared to various degrees by all of a parent's siblings, real and classificatory. But it is clear that presumed biological parents have prior claim to their children as household members. Those with the next strongest rights are real siblings of the parents, particularly the father's sisters. Sisters are in a privileged position of respect; their requests are difficult to refuse, including requests to adopt a child. In one case involving this principle, an Arno man evidently was genuinely grieved when he returned home one day to find that his sister had taken his only son to her home elsewhere on the atoll. He knew she had already asked to adopt the child but did not expect a change in residence so soon. Though the matter had not been fully negotiated, he had little recourse against an elder sister.

Another strong 'parental' right is held by the mother's brother; his authority increases as his sisters' sons come of age. He controls their legal destiny in an important way because he allocates specific use rights to the lineage estate. With this property relationship in mind, mother's brothers often adopt their sisters' sons to solidify the lineage and bring their heirs into their own household.

The parents' own parents also share jural parenthood. Children who marry and move away from home are always under pressure to provide a grandchild as a replacement. Grandparents feel that they have a right to take at least some of their grandchildren as coresidents. The younger the couple, the more likely that they cannot resist the demands of their parents to provide their first-born children for adoption. As the couple matures and the union stabilizes, it is more difficult for their siblings or parents to press them in the matter of adoption or to further negotiate an adoption that includes a change in residence.

Relations in the same generation include the full range of variations described above, and more. The strongest kinship tie is that between siblings, those who call each other *jeu* 'my elder sibling' and *jetu* 'my younger sibling'. In genealogical terms, these are siblings and parallel cousins. In the Arno kinship system, they are persons from one's own generation whom one treats with respect and a sense of obligation for mutual aid and support. Younger siblings defer·to elder siblings, male siblings defer to female siblings. Siblings of the opposite sex must avoid being alone together, and other people must avoid reference to bodily functions in their presence.

The most uninhibited relationship is also between persons of the same generation, that is, between cross-cousins of the opposite sex. They may call each other by sibling terms, but they also refer to each other as *reliku*. This term applies to anyone who is or could be a 'spouse' and anyone with whom sexual joking and intercourse are permitted.

The use of kinship terminology to describe one's kinship domain thus includes a code for appropriate behavior. The code may be seen as a continuum with authority and respect on one end (as in parent-child and sibling-sibling bonds) and freedom and joking on the other (as between grandparents and grandchildren or in reciprocal cross-cousin relations). Mother's brother–sister's son relations fall in between by combining authority with permitted disrespect through joking.

The Arno system of reckoning kinsmen includes the possibility of manipulating through extension and denial both the substantive and behavioral attributes of 'kinship'. Actual genealogical connection is not a necessary condition for classifying and treating another person as a 'kinsman'. Similarly, existing genealogical status may be undermined by denying that a kinsman is any longer a kinsman and adjusting the code for conduct accordingly. In collecting genealogies and kin terms, the following incidents occurred that illustrate some commonplace manipulations of Arno kinship.

One informant discounted kinship ties with kinsmen of her mother's father. She said he was a bad man and that the blood had been dissipated—that is, the relationship was no longer significant in terms of the code for conduct that normally binds consanguines together. Another informant claimed a kinship tie to a person on the basis that their great-grandparents had lived on the same piece of land. This informant regarded the other as a 'sibling' because of this great-grandparental union. A third informant gave the following account:

> I could say that I am not related to L, but the truth is that she is my kinswoman. The reason I say she's not is that she has thrown us off the land. And the reason she threw us off is that she says we are not her kinsmen. But, we are all related, in that place J lives and in K (referring to two pieces of land). K is the real home of J, he has the worker rights there.

These cases illustrate that the effective domain of 'kinship' on Arno is not necessarily restricted to relations among consanguines, and that, where consanguinity is recognized, the code for conduct that normally binds consanguines together may be manipulated to the point of insignificance in actual behavior. Kinsmen may be added or eliminated through transactions in behavior, residence, and land rights. Adoption is one of the processes involved in these transactions. It is a primary means of defining or redefining kinship in its applicability as a cultural domain to specific persons.

THE CULTURAL CONTEXT OF ADOPTION

Several types of adoption transactions occur in Arno social life, and each includes a variety of possible outcomes. All involve the creation, redefinition, or reaffirmation of kinship relations. The meaning of the relations depends on the form and intended function of the adoption.

The most common and effective form of adoption is *kokajriri*, the 'adoption of children'. The etymology of this word shows that the process is patterned after consanguinity. The word for child is *ajri*. The prefix *ko* or *ka* is an activator which, when used with 'child', means either 'to make' or 'to gather'. *Kajri* (*ka* plus *ajri*), in fact, means 'to gather children'. The reduplicated ending, -*riri*, is often used to indicate patterned behavior. Thus, *kowainini* (*ko* 'to make' and *waini* 'coconut meat') means 'the act of making copra'. Therefore, *kokajriri* (*ko* 'to make', *ka* 'to gather', and *ajri* 'children') means 'the act of making children by gathering them' or 'a way of gathering a child'.

The 'adoption of children' usually occurs while the adoptee is still a baby. The adopter takes the adoptee as his own 'child' and uses the kinship term for 'my child'. The child reciprocates with the terms for 'my mother' and 'my father'. The adopters and adoptee follow the behavior appropriate to the parent-child relationship. Since most adoptions occur between kinsmen, this often entails the overshadowing of a former kinship relationship. In the cases of grandparent-grandchild and mother's brother–sister's son, the new relationship is stricter than the old one, and changes in behavior must reflect the new status relations. As one informant stated, "Now that I have adopted her, I will treat my grandchild after the customs appropriate to one's own children." If the adopter and adoptee already stand in the parent-child relationship, then there is a shift in intensity, not a change in kind.

The 'adoption of a child' also establishes or redefines a number of other relationships besides those between adopter and adoptee. First, the adopter and the adoptee's natural parents consider themselves to be 'siblings' after the adoption takes place, with the exception that persons who adopt their own grandchildren do not become 'siblings' to their own children. Adopters and adoptee's parents who do become or reemphasize their siblingship call each other by sibling terms. They may also call each other *jeman ju* 'father of my child' or *jinin ju* 'mother of my child'. People in this relationship are expected to assist each other without recompense in activities and responsibilities related to their 'children', such as in preparing birthday parties. Second, the adoptee becomes a 'sibling' to all classificatory children of the adopter. A man and his sister told me that each has adopted a child of the other in order to establish a sibling tie between the children. This tie overshadows the original cross-cousin relationship and prevents intermarriage. Nearly 16 percent of the adoptions surveyed effectively prevent cross-cousin marriages, but whether this was an actual motivation for adoption in every case is not clear.

At minimum the 'adoption of children' involves agreement between the adopter and the child's natural parents that an adoption has occurred. Some adoptions are never validated beyond the informal announcement that primary jural parenthood will be shared between the adopter and the adoptee's biological parents. Whether or not an adoption involves a shift in the major responsibility for the child from the natural parents to the adopter, a change in residence for the adoptee or an inheritance of land rights for the adoptee is always a matter for further negotiation between the adopter, the adoptee's biological parents, and, in some cases, the adoptee.

In Arno adoptions, the adoptee retains his ties with his biological parents, as well as his other natal kinship affiliations. This jural inclusiveness recognizes that adoption is revocable: biological parents retain the right to invalidate an adoption, especially if they think that the adopter is not nourishing the child properly or is bringing him up wrong. Revocation of an adoption is frequently an ambiguous act. One couple implied that their adopted child had been reclaimed, but they were vague about the ultimate outcome. In another case, a mother explained her unruly child's behavior by saying that he had been adopted by her husband's relatives and that they did not know how to bring him up. Nonetheless, the child had not been reclaimed.

A second form of adoption is *kokajriri in raeleb* 'adoption in the afternoon'. This means that the adoptee is adopted later in life—when he is already an adult. Such adoptions often serve to formalize an existing teacher-apprentice or proprietor-tenant relationship. For example, a man in his thirties was learning traditional medical practices from several people, including his elder brother. One of his teachers was an older woman who had not borne children but who had adopted children. She adopted the man because of the teacher-student relationship that existed between them. He used the kin term 'my mother' in addressing and referring to her, and each acted toward the other appropriately as 'parent' and 'child'. He provided food and generally looked after her and her husband's welfare.

A third form of adoption involves shifting the initiative for the transaction. In a sense, this form applies adoption procedures in reverse: A person may take another person as his parent and become the child in the relationship. For example, a woman who had some painful problems with her teeth was cured by an old man with Marshallese medicine. She had no other way to repay him so she *boke bwe in jeman* 'took him as her father', and his wife as her 'mother'. She took care of the old couple by bringing them food and nursing them in their sickness. As a consequence of this care, before the old woman died she persuaded her brother to give a piece of land to her adopted daughter. In this instance, a cure led first to a symbolic kinship relationship, then to an active economic relationship, and finally to a legal relationship with the adopted daughter as recipient of a gift of land.

A fourth form of adoptive kinship is to *boke bwe in jein* (or *jetin*) 'take someone as an elder sibling (or younger sibling)'. In this case, the new relationship is not one of parent and child but one between siblings. For example, a woman had no brothers, her sons had grown up and moved away, and her husband was handicapped by partial blindness. She 'took as her elder brother' a man whose son had fathered her daughter's son. The elder man had adopted their common grandson, and, since he was a good worker, she invited him to come and live on her land. The two families lived in one household (two sleeping houses and one common cookhouse) and shared all food and labor. Thus, the elder man had gained a sister, a house, and land to work, and she had gained an elder brother, a worker, and a food provider. Their relationship was characterized by 'appropriate' sibling behavior.

A fifth kind of adoptive transaction is to *jeraik* 'befriend' another person. An Arno person usually 'befriends' only one other person in his lifetime, unless that person dies. This kind of friendship is symbolically equivalent to siblingship. The friends call each other *jera* 'my friend'; their respective kinsmen treat them as 'siblings' and act out their own relationships accordingly. Friends depend on each other for mutual aid, support, and hospitality.

A sixth kind of transaction is to *ninnin ibben* 'nurse with' another person. A mother may have insufficient or poor quality milk and her child must then nurse with another woman. Sometimes one mother can nurse the two children soon after the births but not later. At that time, the other mother may be able to nurse although she could not do so before. The two children involved consider themselves to be 'siblings', and their mothers consider themselves to be 'siblings' because of the sharing of nursing obligations. These relationships are not as strong as those between friends. Nevertheless, they are not forgotten, and persons who have nursed together call on each other for help in such matters as preparing for parties. Sometimes one may even transfer land to the other. One such case occurred before 1885 when a chief gave some land to a commoner with whom he had nursed as a child. The chief's rationale was that he was compensating the commoner for his loss of milk as a child.

All of these adoptive transactions provide room for manipulation since they include, as a minimum, only the establishment of the code for appropriate behavior between those who are involved. Either party to the arrangement may then negotiate further transactions along the path already established. An adopter may request that the adopted child be added to his household if he has need of a child to help with work. Or, an adopter may promise land to an adopted child who stays with him and cares for him. Another possibility is for an adoptee to care for his adopted parent in old age and eventually receive a gift of land. Whether or not these additional transactions occur depends on the particular social context of the adoptive relationship through time.

CASE DISTRIBUTION, MOTIVATIONS, AND SOCIAL CONTEXT

Adoptions function to realign or reemphasize kinship relations, to reciprocate for a former adoption, to replace children lost through death or migration, and to provide children for childless adults. Adoptions may serve any one or any combination of these purposes. Lacking specific data for each of these different functions, this section will only outline the primary motivations for Arno adoptions, specifying social context where possible.

Among the 1,229 residents of Arno in 1969, 456 cases of 'adoption of children' in which at least one of the parties involved was still living on the atoll were recorded. In most cases, a couple had done the adopting. However, for clarity, the cases have been sorted according to the relationship between the adoptee and the partner who was his kinsman prior to the adoption (table 13).

There are some exceptional cases that cannot be sorted in this manner, especially those involving the adoption of grandchildren by grandparents, since both grandparents are equally related to the adoptee.

I have data for only a few kinds of transactions other than the 'adoption of children' for two reasons: the existence of some transactions was not apparent to me until after I had conducted the census, and I neglected to ask some adults whether or not they had been adopted. Therefore, I shall describe in detail the social context of adoptive 'children' transactions, and only incidental reference will be made to the other kinds of transactions discussed above.

Table 12 illustrates that most adopters were female and that

TABLE 12.   Adopters and Adoptees by Sex

Adopter	Adoptee			
	Male	Female	Total	%
Male	86	88	174	38
Female	139	106	245	54
Couple	23	14	37	8
TOTAL n	248	208	456	
%	54	46		100

SOURCE: Author's field notes, 1969–1970.

TABLE 13.   Adopters and Adoptees by Kinship Tie

Adopter	Type of Kinship Bond				
	neju 'child'	mangeru 'sister's child'	jibu 'grandchild'	Other	Total
Male	55	19	62	38	174
Female	70	36	87	52	245
Couple	0	0	17	20	37
TOTAL n	125	55	166	110	456
%	28	12	36	24	100

SOURCE: Author's field notes, 1969–1970.

more adoptees were male than female. Table 13 shows that 36 percent of the adoptees previously stood in the relationship of 'grandchild' to their adopters. These adoptions entail a significant change in the use of terminology and a realignment of formal behavior between the adopter and adoptee. As one informant explained it:

> L is my grandfather, but because he adopted me, now I call him 'my father'. If I see him I use his name. I often refer to him as 'my grandfather' because we can joke with grandfathers. However, even though I sometimes refer to him as grandfather, I cannot joke with him because he adopted me.

As mentioned above, grandparents often adopt grandchildren to replace absent children. When grandparents adopt a grandchild and request their own children to allow the adopted grandchild to reside with them, their own children often claim that the adopted grandchild is too young to leave home. Alternately, children may allow a parent to take their child away for the summer on the promise that it will be brought back when school starts. However, some young couples find it difficult to resist strong-willed parents.

Twenty-eight percent of the adoptees enumerated in my census already stood in a 'child' relationship to their adopters. In these cases, no change in terminology and little formal change in behavior occurs. There is only a shift in emphasis in which the adopters become, at least, persons with the major alternative rights to jural parenthood or, at most, the primary jural parents (see Brady, chapter 1). In any case, the biological parents never completely lose their rights as 'jural parents'. The process of adoption merely emphasizes the rights of a particular parent over the child. Adoption of a person to whom one already stands in the relationship of 'parent' often has less to do with relations between the child and the adopter than it has to do with relations between the adopter and the adoptee's biological parents. The adopter and the child's biological parents indicate by their request and acceptance that they are indeed 'siblings' and will act accordingly. To show that this is the case, one will adopt the other's child, thus solidifying the relationship.

Twelve percent of the adoptees were already the adopter's classificatory sister's son. This is again a matter of solidifying relations between siblings. The shift from being a 'sister's child' to being a 'child' involves no drastic reallocation of authority, but it does place more restrictions on the child's behavior. The child can no longer be mischievous with his biological mother's siblings, especially a mother's brother who has adopted him. Adoption of a 'child', 'grandchild', and 'sister's child' may emphasize and redefine relations between people who are already 'blood' relatives.

The reciprocal exchange of adoptees among kinsmen is also common on Arno. All such transactions are bound by the traditional constraints and incentives of kinship reciprocity. Often the descriptions of these adoption events include the words 'give' and 'take'. One informant stated "L adopted me when I was young. Later when I grew up, they (L's kinsmen) gave me K to adopt." Another informant said, "They adopted me, so later I adopted K (one of them)."

Figure 4 illustrates five cases of reciprocal exchange in which the numbers indicate the order of adoption events. In example A, a man adopted a girl, and his sister's daughter adopted a boy. After the two children grew up, the girl adopted her adoptive father's ZDS, and the boy adopted his adoptive mother's MB adopted DD—that is, the first adopted girl's daughter. In example B, a man adopted a girl, and the girl later adopted the man's BSS— that is, her classificatory sibling's son. In example C, a man adopted a girl, and his sister later adopted the girl's daughter. In example D, a man adopted a boy; later the man's biological daughter adopted his adopted son's children. Finally, in example E, a man adopted his wife's daughter, and the daughter later adopted the man's BS as her child. Reciprocal exchange of adoptees reinforces relations among kinsmen and helps keep them "close."

The importance of 'sharing' as an aspect of kinship solidarity also pervades these transactions. When a man is in need, he counts on kinsmen to fill that need. One felt need is for children because children are loved and because they also can become useful household members. There were 181 adopters in the survey of adoptions on Arno in 1969. In 68 of the cases neither the adopter nor his spouse had children by any marriage. It is reasonable to assume, therefore, that 37 percent of Arno adoptions involved childlessness as a direct or supporting motivation. However, child-

FIGURE 4.   Five Examples of Reciprocity in Adoption.

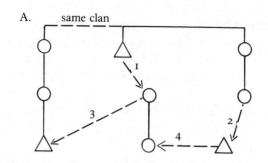
A.   same clan

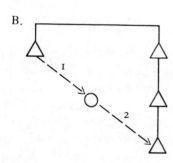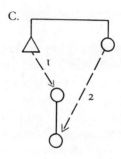

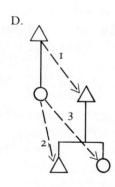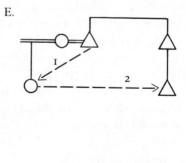

lessness is rarely stated explicitly as a factor in an informant's own adoptions. One reason for this is that it is embarrassing for some people to admit that they have no children; another is that all persons are likely to have a number of classificatory children that offset any absolute notion of childlessness. Nonetheless, childlessness does seem to be an implicit motivation for many adoptions.

In sum, adoption is a frequent event on Arno, usually involving persons who are already kinsmen. Kinsmen adopt to reemphasize their kinship obligations, to replace lost children, to reciprocate for former adoptions, and to share children with childless kinsmen. The variety of motivations is matched by the variety of functions the adoptive relationships serve, and this complexity and flexibility helps explain the high frequency of adoptions on Arno.

ADOPTION AND RESIDENCE

The household is not an important ideational group among Arno Marshallese, but it is an important action group. From an outsider's operational viewpoint, the household is that group of people who at any given point in time 'share a common cookhouse' (Kiste 1968:218; see also Tobin 1967:96–97; Spoehr 1949:104). A household always includes a sleeping house and a cookhouse on a cleared plot that is covered with coral gravel. The household area may also include a copra drier, cistern or well, and a pig pen. The group of people who live in the cleared area, sleep in the one or two dwellings, and eat together regularly constitute the household group. This group is neither named nor corporate. It owns no property and does not perpetuate itself as a distinct entity. In fact, the household as a total unit is quite ephemeral— group composition is fluid, and household sites periodically fall into disuse and are resurrected. Within a single year (1969–1970) over 100 of the 155 Arno households experienced a change in membership attributable to factors other than birth and death.

Arno households average about 7.9 members, somewhat below the average for other atolls in the Marshalls.[1] Although households are quite flexible in membership, there are some functional prerequisites for household development and maintenance. In general, households need a member who has some right to the land on which they are living. Second, they need one member who can make copra and at least one other member who can help, even if he is unable to do the work alone. Third, each household must have someone who can repair the buildings and tools as well as someone who can fish. Fourth, each household must have someone who can cook and make mats. Finally, each household usually has, but does not require, children.

At minimum, a household consists of one person. It is possible for one person to carry on most of the necessary tasks by himself, though single-person households are usually dependent on other people for some necessities. For example, a man who lives alone may depend on his sisters or daughters for mats. A woman who lives alone rarely makes copra for herself or repairs her own house. Thus, the sexual division of labor promotes at least two-person households. The optimum household, in the Arno view, includes an old man or woman, an adult couple who are their children or grandchildren, and four or five children under twenty years of age. Alternately, a household may be composed of a pair of adult siblings, one or both of their spouses, and four or five children.[2]

As stated, there is no functional necessity for children, but 93 percent of the households include children under twenty years of age. The mean number of children per household with children is just under five. The mean number of adopted children per household with children is just over one.

The adoptive tie is not the only or even the most important option or strategy for recruiting coresidents, but it is an important and common method. Adults also recruit their own children, younger siblings, sibling's children, grandchildren, and other relatives. However, except for the case of own children, the rights of jural parenthood are generally more clearly specified in the case of adoption than in the others.

Of the 1,229 residents of Arno in 1969, 173 were 'adopted children' living with their adoptive parents. These children represent 14 percent of the total population, and 26 percent of the total number of children under twenty years of age. Of the 155 households on Arno, about 7 percent include no children, and about 39 percent include children, but no adopted children, as residents. Adopted children were residents in 54 percent of the households.

The pattern of distribution of adopted children indicates that households that already have four or five children are unlikely to recruit new residents from among their adopted children, as illustrated by table 14. Table 14 shows the percentage of adopted children in each size household ranked according to the total number of children in the household. Households with four or fewer children have a larger percentage of adopted children than households with six or more children. Households with four or fewer children include as residents 57 percent of the adopted children but only 34 percent of all children. Only two households have more than four adopted children. The households with eleven and fourteen children are somewhat unique in having more than one resident married couple.

Table 14 also shows that more than one-half of the children in households with only one or two children are adopted. One reason for this is that young couples are likely to lose their first few children to parents and siblings through adoption. Thus, if they want to keep children in their own households at an early stage,

TABLE 14.   Natural and Adopted Children per Household

No. of Children	No. of Households	Total Children	Percent Adopted
0	11	0	0.0
1	13	13	53.0
2	18	36	55.5
3	22	66	43.9
4	28	112	37.5
5	18	90	20.0
6	16	96	16.6
7	8	56	16.0
8	7	56	8.9
9	7	63	12.6
10	0	0	0.0
11	4	44	20.4
12	1	12	8.3
13	0	0	0.0
14	2	28	32.1
TOTAL	155	672	$\overline{M}$ 25.7

SOURCE: Author's field notes, 1969–1970.

they must also adopt. Another reason is that mature couples who have lost all of their own children through residential changes are likely to bring in a few adopted children as replacements.

In sum, adoption provides one of several strategies for recruiting new household members. The usual pattern is for established adoptive ties to be renegotiated to include a change in residence for the adoptee. Adopted children are most likely to be made coresidents when four or fewer children already are resident in the household, when young couples do not have resident children, or when mature couples do not have resident children.

ADOPTION AND LAND TENURE

Various forms of Arno adoption have been described above as transactions in kinship that emphasize particular kin relations in symbol and substance. The adoptive tie, once created, is occasionally renegotiated to include a change in residence for the adoptee. Less frequently, adoptive ties are renegotiated to include the transmission of land rights from adopter to adoptee. In order to understand the role of adoption in land inheritance, it is first necessary to describe briefly the political and legal structure of Arno society.

The ideology of descent among Arno Marshallese is strongly matrilineal. Affiliation with the clan and lineage includes 'the children of women only'. The order of succession and inheritance puts 'the children of women first'. Themes in myths and parables stress that 'mothers' are the source of nurture, status, and land.

The largest unit recruited through descent is the *jou* 'clan', a named category of dispersed lineages. Kinship terms and appropriate behavior are extended to all clan members on the basis of generation and sex. The clan structure prohibits intraclan marriages and insures hospitality to travelers through the obligations of kinship.[3] Clans do not own property, nor do they have special religious or ritual functions.

The *bwij* 'navel' or 'those of the same umbilicus' is a matrilineage (Spoehr 1949:155; Tobin 1967:88). A matrilineage may be eight or more generations deep though the term is applicable to any branch or even to a mother and her child (Kiste 1968:163). Lineage branches are formed by sisters and ranked according to their birth order. Lineages are not localized; they do not reside or work together as a group. They are corporations holding rights over certain parcels of land as the lineage estate. No individual member may dispose of lineage rights; neither can he be prohibited from sharing in his lineage rights in land unless he has grossly mistreated his lineage mates.

The matrilineage provides a genealogical charter for succession. All lineage members possess shared rights to a lineage estate, but members of the lineage are ranked and differ in their control of lineage land rights. The *alab* 'lineage head' succeeds to his position on the basis of his sex, age, generation, and lineage branch. Ideally, the 'lineage head' is the eldest male in the senior surviving branch of the oldest generation.[4] The 'lineage head' has the power to allocate specific *rijerbal* 'worker' or use rights to his lineage mates, and beyond them to their nonlineal kinsmen. The sons of the lineage males in particular often obtain 'worker' rights though these are liable to be revoked after their fathers die. The 'workers' on each piece of land and the 'lineage head' share the proceeds from the copra made on the lineage estate (see Rynkiewich 1972).

Clans and lineages form the matrilineal descent units of Arno society. The major alternative process of affiliation is a category called *batoktok* 'blood', meaning in this instance the 'children of the males of the lineage'. This is not a descent construct but rather a filiation construct that emphasizes the single tie between sibling sets and their fathers' lineage (see Scheffler 1966; Schneider 1967). This process is here called 'patrifiliation' and the category a 'patrifiliage'. Thus, any given sibling set with the same father and mother is at the same time part of the patrifiliage category of their father's lineage and part of the membership of their mother's lineage. Either relationship may be emphasized, depending on the situation at hand.

Under certain conditions, one sibling set in the patrifiliage category may be recruited as primary heirs to their father's lineage estate. There are two major sets of circumstances under which this takes place. The first is when a strong lineage head of a declining lineage is able to alienate the rights to all or part of the lineage estate and grant them to his own children. The second, and more common, circumstance is when the lineage head is the last surviving member of his lineage—that is, when there are no children of lineage females to perpetuate the corporation. In this event, the eldest male of the patrifiliage (sibling set) becomes an *alab*. The word *alab* in fact has at least three possible interrelated glosses: 'lineage head', 'land manager', and 'mother's brother'. Ideally, as Arno Marshallese conceive it, the head of a lineage is also the manager of the lineage estate and is mother's brother to lineage males in the descending generation. In fact, the term *alab* is applied to persons holding any one of the three identities whether he holds the other two or not. Thus, the eldest male of the patrifiliage is a 'land manager'. The remaining siblings hold approximately equal rights to the estate and are often assigned worker rights to portions of the estate by the land manager. The sibling set as a group is said to *ninnin* 'nurse' the land from their father.

When all the siblings have died, the group that inherits their rights comprises only the children of the female siblings. That is, the original inheriting patrifiliage transforms itself after one generation into a landholding matrilineage.

These two processes, matrilineal and patrifilial, account for the majority of succession events on Arno. Succession to the position of lineage head and inheritance of land rights are both subsumed in the phrase *binij jenkwan* 'to step into his footprints'. In all, Arno Marshallese say that there are three *lukun lajaruk* 'real lines of succession': *bwij* 'matrilineal', *ninnin* 'patrifilial', and *kokajriri* 'adoptive'.

The conditions under which an adoptive relationship is renegotiated to include a transfer of land rights from adopter to adoptee are even more narrowly defined than for transfer to a patrifiliage. In the absence of matrilineal and patrifilial kinsmen, the adopter *may* grant his estate to his adopted children. There is less certainty that he will do so in adoption than under circumstances of matrilineal or patrifilial inheritance. If the adopted child of a land manager does not live with him and care for him, then the adopter is not likely to grant him land rights. The land manager has several other options for transmitting land available to him: lacking primary heirs, he may give the land rights to his spouse, to someone who has nursed him in sickness, to someone who has worked for him, or to his paramount chief. Thus, an adopted child is only in a slightly better position to inherit than other nonlineal and nonfilial kin and even non-kin, unless he 'proves his worth' as a child by 'caring' for his adopted parent.

Historically, adoption has become increasingly important as a mode of inheritance of land rights, and there appear to be two related reasons for this change. First, the power of paramount chiefs to confiscate land from commoner matrilineages has declined. Second, the number of matrilineages that have become extinct and have lost their estates to patrifilial, adoptive, and other heirs has increased. These two trends have contributed directly to the increased frequency of adoptive inheritance.

Arno social order is divided into aristocrats and commoners. Commoner rights in land have been discussed. They are the 'land manager' and 'worker' rights that are usually held within the matrilineage but occasionally are held in a patrifiliage or among adoptive and other heirs. Aristocratic rights in the same estates are identified as 'paramount chief' rights and 'lesser chief' rights. The former always are held by an aristocratic lineage; the latter usually are held by an aristocratic lineage or by a patrifiliage of an aristocratic lineage. Sometimes a paramount chief confiscates commoner land rights and either holds them for his own lineage or reallocates them to another commoner lineage or to a single commoner. This was the case more often in the past. In 1885, paramount chiefs on Arno held commoner rights to 4 percent of the land parcels and had recently redistributed another 14 percent to commoners. They were deeply involved in manipulating commoner land rights. However, under three successive colonial regimes, the chiefs lost their power to confiscate and reallocate land. Table 15 shows the decline in percentage of land parcels held or redistributed by chiefs from 1885 to 1970.

As the chiefs lost their power to interfere in commoner inheritance, the incidence of patrifilial and adoptive inheritance and other modes of gift giving increased. In 1885, 76 percent of the land parcels were held by matrilineages, and only 2 percent had been inherited or given as gifts by commoner land managers. In 1914 and 1944, the percentage of land parcels held by matrilineages remained about the same, while the percentage of land parcels inherited by 'patrifiliages' or adopted children or given as gifts to others increased. These increases indicate a shift from chiefly interference to land manager options for the allocation of rights. The percentage of land held by matrilineages remained about the same because as many lineages were becoming extinct as there were patrifiliages and other groups transforming themselves into line-

TABLE 15. Parcels of Land Held and Redistributed by Aristocratic and Commoner Lineages*

		1885		1914		1944		1970	
		n	%	n	%	n	%	n	%
Aristocratic	Held	29	4	5	1	12	2	9	1
	Redistributed	97	14	47	7	31	4	22	3
Commoner	Held	532	76	535	76	521	74	380	54
	Redistributed	14	2	95	13	122	17	280	40

SOURCE: Adapted from Rynkiewich (1972:201, 206).
*About 4 percent of the parcels is held under miscellaneous title in each period.

ages by handling the inheritance of land rights in a matrilineal pattern.

By 1970 a major change had occurred. About one-third of the matrilineages holding land in 1944 had become extinct by 1970. These matrilineages had their longevity undermined during the German and Japanese periods because the female members failed to bear children. However, the last members did not die until the American period. This mass extinction of lineages shifted many estates out of matrilineal hands and into patrifilial and adoptive hands. Thus, in 1970 only 54 percent of the land parcels were held by matrilineages and 40 percent were held by patrifiliages, adoptive children, and recipients of gifts. The place of adoption in land transfers can now be traced more specifically.

In 1885, none of the land parcels inherited from or given by land managers was held under adoptive title. By 1914, one estate of six land parcels had been inherited by an adopted child. These represent less than 1 percent of the total number of land parcels. By 1944, nineteen parcels of land had been inherited by adopted children, representing three times the number of parcels held under adoptive title in the previous period. By 1970, thirteen land managers held thirty-two land parcels under adoption title. The use of adoptive inheritance and gift giving thus has increased steadily since 1885.

The elimination of chiefly interference in commoner affairs and the increasing extinction of matrilineages has made adoption a more important factor in the manipulation of kinship ties for social and economic security. Adoption is sometimes used as a strategy both by those seeking land and by land managers seeking heirs, depending on the circumstances and the location of the estate.

The case of R is a good example of the problem some land managers are having. R's lineage became a landholding unit when it received a gift of patrifilial land. The rights passed for three generations in the lineage, but R is the only surviving member. He has no sons nor did his deceased parallel cousin, the only other member of R's generation in the lineage. R claims six adopted children, four of whom are living with him. He has other adopted children that he no longer talks about because they have left him. He states frankly that his adopted children should stay with him, and those who do not stay will not receive an inheritance when he dies. R's problem is that his four plots of land are not in a major population center of the atoll. The population, once spread fairly evenly throughout the atoll, now has concentrated on major islets where there are stores and churches and where large ships most often anchor. Land in these centers is consequently at a premium, and most people will exercise any right they can to get a place there to live and work. In contrast, in the more remote areas of the atoll, people like R who are without lineal or filial heirs often have trouble finding persons who will stay and care for them long enough to receive a gift of land.

Two other cases illustrate both the decline in the power of the chiefs and the growing importance of adoption as a mode of inheritance. One case involves a member of an aristocratic lineage; the other, a member of a noble lineage. Both have acquired estates when the line of inheritance was uncertain. In both cases the land is in population centers. In the past, both would have been able to make their claims valid because of chiefly rights to confiscate unused or disputed land. However, both chose to base their claim on an adoptive tie with former 'land managers' of the estates. People complained that these two should not take both the commoner and the chiefly share of the land, but no one opposed them openly because they back their adoptive claim with their remaining chiefly legitimacy.

In a situation where lineages are either dying out or their members are emigrating, and where people have individual preferences about places to live and work, there is a need for redistribution of land rights. Adoption on Arno often serves as a strategy for both adopter and adoptee to transfer land rights for mutual benefit.

If a person cannot gain rights as a land manager, he may settle for worker rights to a parcel of land. In 1970, there were fifty-three workers on sixty-six plots of land who had been recruited and received their worker rights through an adoptive tie. This constituted 9 percent of the total number of land parcels. Five more people were workers on five plots of land because one of their parents had been adopted by a former land manager of the estate. Two other people have worker rights to two plots of land because the biological parents of their adopted children gave them rights. Beyond this, an uncounted number of people work temporarily on plots of land because they are the adopted children of either the land manager or the worker on the plot. They do not acquire worker rights, but they work as long as their adopter maintains his rights.

Those who do acquire worker rights through an adoption do not seem to be in a strong position when their adopter dies. An adoptee's ties with his adopter's lineage mates are weaker than those with his adopter. Successive heirs do not necessarily feel the same concern for the adoptee's welfare. A dispute occurred during my study involving a man from another atoll who was adopted by an Arno land manager. The land manager gave his adopted son the worker rights to three plots of land. Later, the land manager's successor wanted to confiscate the worker rights and reallocate them to his own children and grandchildren. The adopted child of the former land manager made a counterclaim that he had been granted the land manager rights to one of the plots. The dispute escalated to the municipal court on Arno. The judgment was that one had the legal identity of land manager and the other the legal identity of worker, so they should each exercise their own rights and not infringe on each other. In many other cases, land managers have been successful in removing adoptive workers who had been given rights by previous managers on the pretext that the worker did not make proper use of the land. Arno Marshallese recognize that holding worker rights through an adoptive tie is tenuous, but, given the present uneven demographic pressure on the land and the uneven distribution of rights to land, they often have little choice in the matter.

SUMMARY AND CONCLUSIONS

Adoption is clearly a multifunctional institution on Arno. Its essence is a transaction in kinship: a negotiation and allocation of kinship identities and relationships where such ties are otherwise absent or of a different quality. As such, adoptive kinship is represented widely on Arno Atoll.

Arno people engage in adoption primarily for one or a combination of the following reasons: (1) to realign or reemphasize existing kinship relations; (2) to reciprocate for a former adoption; (3) to replace children lost through death or migration; and (4) to share children with childless adults. Adoptions structured on these bases may also be renegotiated or extended to serve other functions, such as coresidence and the transfer of commoner land rights. Land manager rights are inherited by adoptees under certain circumstances, such as the lack of matrilineal and patrifilial heirs. The uneven distribution of the population over the atoll forces some land managers to seek heirs, while in other places landless adoptees work hard to obtain land manager and worker rights. Adoption facilitates the needs of the principals in each case.

In sum, adoption on Arno involves the manipulation and creation of kinship ties and obligations to enhance social and economic security for the participants. It is desirable to adopt people to increase the number or quality of supportive kinsmen, and because the adoptive relationship, once established, can be put to many other uses advantageous to both adopter and adoptee.

NOTES

Fieldwork on Arno Atoll was carried out between June 1969 and December 1970 under a grant from the National Institutes of General Medical Sciences, GM01164, administered by E. Adamson Hoebel and the Department of Anthropology at the University of Minnesota. Preparation for and introduction to the field were accomplished under the guidance of Robert C. Kiste, to whom I am grateful. Earlier drafts of this chapter were read by Robert C. Kiste, Leonard Mason, Jack Tobin, Mike Rose, Ivan Brady, Mac Marshall, and others in this volume, to whom I am thankful for criticisms.

1. Other atolls average the following number of household members: Majuro 8.8 (Spoehr 1949:103), Bikini 14.6 (Kiste 1968:220), Kili 13.6 (Kiste 1968:271), and Namu 13.4 (Pollock 1970:132).

2. Spoehr's ethnography on Majuro (1949:113–133) contains some excellent examples of residential group structure that closely parallel the range of variation found on Arno.

3. There are some exceptions to clan exogamy. These and the question of incest prohibitions are discussed fully by Kiste and Rynkiewich in a forthcoming publication (Carroll n.d.) on incest prohibitions.

4. The rules for succession are contradictory under certain conditions. Sometimes a male of a senior branch but younger generation of a lineage is older in years than a male in a junior branch but elder generation. Disputes that arise on this account may result in conflict or fission in the lineage estate, or both.

7

SOCIOECONOMIC MOBILITY: ADOPTION AND LAND TENURE IN THE ELLICE ISLANDS

Ivan Brady

INTRODUCTION

The nine coral islands of the Ellice group lie south of the equator in western Polynesia, in the southern part of the Gilbert and Ellice Islands Colony. They have been under British administration since the establishment of a protectorate government in the area in 1892.[1] Life strategies for the inhabitants of these tiny islands ultimately concern kinship, land tenure, and land availabilities. Subsistence is heavily dependent on traditional use of the land, and the most direct means of access to land derives from kin-group membership. Adoption and fosterage, as kinship phenomena, are normatively and symbolically embedded in considerations of land tenure and land group constitution. This chapter analyzes these relationships, with special focus on the role of relative land hunger in adoption and fosterage transactions.

The analysis delineates some of the many ways in which adoption and fosterage serve as vehicles for socioeconomic mobility in Ellice communities. Adoption, in particular, is shown to be an important alternative to birth as a mode of recruitment to membership in property groups and households. It is also suggested that the movement of people and resources through adoption and fosterage mitigates relative land hunger to some extent by increasing individual access to land (see Goodenough 1955:81), by promoting continuity in land estates, by encouraging efficient household production, and by reinforcing kinship solidarity.

I shall begin with a brief discussion of the nature of land hunger in Ellice communities, go on to describe local kinship and property group structure, and then proceed to an analysis of adoption and fosterage in this context.

COMPLEX INSUFFICIENCY: LAND HUNGER

Coconut trees and taro gardens are basic subsistence resources that are controlled by a multiplicity of corporate landholding groups in each community.[2] Land rights held by these groups are reallocated from time to time to accommodate inclusion of new members and displacement of others. Normally, land tenure and inheritance rules provide for an orderly transmission of property, but the particular form of each reallocation depends on a number of variables. One such variable of increasing importance is relative land hunger, that is, an actual or perceived scarcity of land. Land reallocations in property groups that suffer from land hunger differ in scope and quantity from those that transpire in circumstances of greater resource abundance. A similar pattern applies to personnel movements between groups. Relative land hunger may be sufficiently intense to stimulate displacement of existing land group members or to deter incorporation of new members, or both, depending on the situation at hand. Because of the strategic place of land in Ellice culture, careful consideration is given to relative land hunger in all decisions and processes that pertain to aligning people and resources.

With a total de jure population of about 6,500 persons living on approximately ten square miles of territory, some two square miles of which is taken up by sandy beaches, coral flats, and plots otherwise unsuitable for production, the average population density in the Ellice Islands is about 800 persons per square mile of productive land. The optimum density is probably about 640 persons per square mile, all other things, such as cash income from employment and dependence on marine resources for subsistence, being equal (Brady 1974). But, because such factors as high plot

fragmentation and a maldistribution of resources also contribute
to overall land hunger, population densities alone are inadequate
indicators of land hunger magnitudes. Moreover, the perception
of relative land hunger does not require an absolute grounding
in fact to affect behavior (see Sahlins 1961:341).

Ellice land hunger has not yet reached a level of intensity
whereby most of the islanders are faced with imminent starvation
on account of insufficient or maldistributed resources (cf. Turnbull 1972). Some groups are decidedly disadvantaged; others are
not. But there is much talk of people being *fiafai manafa* 'land
hungry' or *maativa manafa* 'land poor', and the perception of these
conditions does not coincide with the range of demonstrable
poverty in particular groups. Land is generally viewed as scarce
and deprivation as relative, to the extent that most land groups
regularly attempt to maximize their associations with other groups
that are perceived to be better off. Some of these associations
provide for the movement of persons from land hungry groups
into circumstances of greater abundance, thereby leveling some
inequities in pressure on local resources. Such movements also
may create new or reinforce existing channels for supplementary
income through kinship reciprocity. Concomitantly, the groups
that feel the most pressure to displace some of their existing members are also likely to be the most emphatic in attempts to maintain
control over the property that they do have. Gifts of land to other
persons are kept to a minimum under these circumstances, and
voluntary increases in total group membership are likely to be
denied unless they can be turned to immediate production advantage.

Overall, despite some disparity between actual and perceived
land hunger, local land hunger problems have contributed to the
demise of several customary modes of land conveyance, intensified
conservatism in the giving of land in title to non-kinsmen, restricted
traditional mobility by undermining the range of optional affiliation
among related land groups, inflated estate fragmentation and
fission rates, and increased litigation over estate boundaries and
inheritance rights (Brady 1974). What remains to be specified
here is the relationship of adoption and fosterage to these patterns.
Prerequisite to this is a summary of Ellice kinship and property
group structure.

KINSHIP AND LAND

The concepts of *toto* 'blood', *manafa* 'land', and *fakatasi* 'sharing' or 'acting as one' represent central dimensions in Ellice kinship. Kinship identities and relationships are calculated largely by the manner in which blood, land, and proper conduct are shared with other persons. These elements are joined normatively and "in essence" by a traditional rule that provides access to land by birthright. In a purely symbolic sense, land and blood are isomorphic to the extent that shared access to either element implies common kinship (see Silverman 1971; Lieber 1974). Both elements symbolize nurturance, growth, communion with the ancestral past, and social solidarity as meaningful constructs underlying the kinds of relationships held to be appropriate among 'kinsmen' (see also Schneider 1968a, 1969, 1972).

With respect to the land tenure system itself, two types of tenure predominate. Some portions of land are held in *fakangamua* tenure as 'communal land' by all bona fide members of the local community, that is, by all persons in residence on the island who were born there, or who are descended directly from or formally adopted by someone who was born there. Most of the land, however, is held in *fakangamuli* tenure as 'private land'; it is shared unequally by the corporate land groups previously mentioned.[3] Kinship relations are implied (if not actualized) under both types of tenure, although shared land as a kinship construct on the community level is a diffuse rather than a specific category of relationship.

Land group structure and performance are operationalized most directly through joint participation and residence in *fale* 'households' or 'household clusters'. As a result, recruitment to fill vacant domestic work roles in households through birth or adoption necessarily carries important implications for changes in land group composition and tenure patterns. Simple fosterage represents an exception to this rule, as will be seen below. But household membership and production strategies generally cannot be divorced from land tenure considerations, whether they are functionally specific or diffuse, and domestic recruitment processes of all types take these patterns into account.

The community itself normally is consolidated as a single village on each island.[4] Villages range in size from about 300 to 1,000 persons, and each of these units contains representatives of several unrelated or distantly related descent categories. These descent categories, corresponding to the Ellice *ngafa*, can be identified as maximal ramages.[5] Each ramage is further subdivided conceptually by two types of descent lines. Alignments traced to a common ancestor through males only are known as *toto maalosi* 'strong blood'; those that include one or more intervening female links are called *toto vaivai* 'weak blood'. Cognatic reckoning thereby gives every person a network of 'strong' and 'weak blood' relatives who are combined in various ways as 'ramage' segments and corporate landholding units. The focal point of each land group is the senior *fanaunga* 'sibling set' that shares land and blood by birthright in a particular ramage segment. Brothers normally represent the dominant link within this configuration because the 'strong blood' bias in descent reckoning also favors men over women in matters of rank, inheritance, and authority.

At the heart of the system is a ground rule that automatically provides natural children with inheritance and residence rights in at least one landholding group at birth.[6] In principle, cognatic reckoning links every individual with at least two such groups, one for each parent. But parental residence and tenure options determine whether primary affiliation at birth is to be with an existing land group on either the mother's or the father's side, or with a new land group that has been formed by estate divisions in the parents' natal groups (see Brady 1974). This primary affiliative bond is activated through household participation and residence in sufficient proximity to make regular use of the land held by the group in joint tenure. Absentees from each group generally retain the right to reactivate their membership on return to the island.

Entitlements to active membership in land groups other than that of natal affiliation are rated on a scale of priorities that includes a consideration of residential, jural, affective, and genealogical proximity to the *pule* or *matai* 'manager of resources', who is normally the senior male in the group (see Brady 1972, 1974). The final decision to incorporate persons other than direct descendants and formal adoptees rests with the incumbents in the group being petitioned, however; and this level of jural integrity has been supported by colonial legislation. Current land legislation upholds and encourages the rights of individual land groups to deny distant or secondary claims on its property, even if the claims are such that they might have been honored more readily in the past (see Brady 1974:144). Furthermore, when a decision is made in favor of incorporating persons in other than their natal groups, adoption is the most common means for doing so.

Persons who marry into a land group can become primary members by pooling a portion of their natal estate with the new group as joint holdings. When land is pooled in this manner, the jural distance between the children on that estate and the members of the incoming spouse's natal group is increased. The land given to the incoming spouse by his or her natal group is supposed to represent the share transferred to subsequent heirs through inheritance. Concomitantly, the optional affiliation strategies and privileges of those heirs are weakened with respect to the incoming spouse's natal group. Not pooling land at marriage tends to perpetuate the affiliation and inheritance options established at birth, provided that the marriage bond itself is cultivated satisfactorily (see Brady 1974:145).

Jurally, a landholding group comprises all persons who *kaitasi* 'eat as one' from a common estate.[7] This refers to sharing rights in the disposition of land produce as well as to rights in the land itself. Obligations of kinship reciprocity promote a more or less regular diversion of some household produce beyond the level of individual land groups. But this flow is generally classified as *meaalofa* 'gift' exchange, and it does not necessarily compromise the jural or corporate integrity of the land groups involved. The development of a primary membership in one land group as opposed to all others in which a person might hold active or latent rights mitigates much of the conflict of interest that may result from these overlapping reciprocity networks (see Brady 1974:142ff).

The size of each landholding group depends on fecundity and the rate of property division in each generation. Dividing the land held in joint tenure dissolves the parent group into segments from which new land groups are formed.[8] Regular fission increases the number and decreases the average size of land groups in each ramage. Today, most land groups are made up of nuclear, lineal, or small extended families whose active cores contain eight or nine members on the average but whose total dispersed membership may range from two to about sixty persons. These groups were generally much larger in the past. Increased competition for land has stimulated fission rates in recent years (see Brady 1974).

The broadest concept of kinship in this system is the *kaainga* 'bilateral kindred'.[9] People who share a demonstrable or assumed 'blood' link of any kind, as well as those who 'eat as one' from a common estate are conceived to be 'kindred'. Specific reckoning of a shared blood tie in this context may go back as far as the founding (or remembered) ancestors in the maximal ramage category of each parent. Collateral calculations may include persons as distant as *tua faa* 'fourth cousins'. Blood links to more distant persons tend to be forgotten in time, and the 'kindred' category fades out into 'non-kin'. These calculations intersect with land tenure interests on the assumption that all persons who share blood can be connected ultimately to a common ancestral estate, whether or not they actually share land at present as members of the same corporate group. Variations in residential proximity, shared blood, and common land interests are thereby integrated by the concept of the 'kindred' on both a functionally diffuse and a functionally specific level (see also Lundsgaarde and Silverman 1972:106–107). Overall, the broad field of the kindred represents the basic social and symbolic context in which particular kinship identities surface and are played out by individuals as members of households, kin groups, and local communities.

With this brief outline of the intersection between land group constitution and certain principles of kinship and descent in mind, we may now summarize more formally the place of differential sharing of land, blood, and appropriate behavior as cultural constructs. These constructs combine in various ways to produce several broad categories of kinship identities and relationships that are pertinent to understanding the nature of adoption in Ellice society.

"MUD AND BLOOD" IDENTITY COMBINATIONS

Borrowing heavily from the works of Silverman (1970, 1971) and Schneider (1968a, 1969), and allowing for certain culturally specific permutations of the nature and meaning of shared land, the cultural constructs underlying my Ellice kinship data can be formalized in terms of "in nature" and "in law" distinctions. The culturally posited 'facts' of biogenetic relatedness constitute kin relationships "in nature." These relationships are symbolized in terms of shared 'blood', and they are generally viewed as immutable bonds in the substantive sense (see Brady, chapter 1). They are also assigned specific code for conduct features that govern appropriate behavior according to the degree and kind of 'blood' connection shared. Shared land emerges as one of several normative or "code" entailments of consanguinity on this level, and the result is a kinship identity that obtains "in nature" and "in law." Kin relationships that lack shared blood as a 'natural' or 'substantive' construct, but which include binding code for conduct features, may be said to exist "in law" or "in custom" only (see also Shore, chapter 8). However, the symbolic isomorphism that obtains between land and blood means that shared land is as close to shared blood in its 'natural' qualities as the system permits, and it is treated as both a 'substantive' and a 'code' construct in calculating kinship identities. Kinship identities that exclude shared blood but include shared land and appropriate behavior thus do not obtain "in law" only in the local perspective. Such identities depend in part on shared land as a 'substantive' construct. The following categories are generated by the juxtaposition of these constructs.

Persons with whom one shares consanguinity, land, and binding code for conduct theoretically represent the main body of one's 'kinsmen'. Such persons are relatives "in law" and "in nature" (blood + land + appropriate behavior). Persons with whom one shares appropriate behavior and only blood or land, but not both, are structurally more peripheral 'kin'. The first of these two subcategories (blood + appropriate behavior) is produced by estate divisions *i loto te kaainga tonu* 'inside the true (consanguineal) kindred'. Estate divisions do not alter 'blood' ties, of course; but the code for conduct features of the former relationship ideally change in accordance with the increase in social and jural distance produced by dividing the estate, and formally shared land becomes a diffuse rather than a specific kinship construct. The second subcategory (land + appropriate behavior) is produced by formal allocations of land to persons *i tua te kaainga tonu* 'outside the true (consanguineal) kindred'. Shared blood as a 'natural' construct does not apply. Instead, the relationship pivots on shared land as 'substantive' construct, and binding code features are applied accordingly. Both of these subcategories thus represent kinship identities that obtain "in law." They differ in terms of the 'substantive' bonds shared.

Affines and purely adoptive kinsmen are *fai kaainga* 'created kinsmen' or kinsmen "in law," as opposed to persons who are *kaainga tonu* 'true kinsmen' or kinsmen "in nature" and "in law." Shared land also mediates this opposition in 'substantive' terms. Formal adoption is intended to 'create' kin relationships as if they derived from birthright in a particular matrix of shared land and blood. Parallel to the rule that automatically entitles natural children to share in their natal group's estate, formal adoption obligates the adopters to provide land for their adoptees. Allocating land in this manner to nonconsanguines creates both a new code and a 'substantive' bond (land + appropriate behavior), as outlined above. However, as a result of a preexisting relationship, adoptees also may share 'blood' with their adopters ([blood] + land + appropriate behavior). In this case, the transaction redefines relations by supplementing rather than creating totally new bonds (see also Carroll 1970c), the supplement being the addition or realignment of formal rights to the adopter's estate.

The bilateral prohibition placed on marriage between persons more closely related than fourth cousins eliminates shared blood as a significant dimension for affines. The key 'substantive' variable in affinity is therefore shared land ([land] + appropriate behavior). As suggested previously, affines may pool land with their residential sponsors at marriage. The result is a kinship identity and relationship that pivots on both a substantive and an "in law" feature. If land is not pooled, then the affinal identity obtains "in law" only and can thereby be differentiated from both formal adoption and other affinal bonds that include shared land.

Kinship identities that are predicated on sharing both land and blood are believed to be *piliatu* 'closer' and *maalosiatu* 'stronger' than those based on sharing only one of these elements. However, adherence to the code for conduct governing appropriate behavior is crucial for the effective maintenance of kinship identities of all types. A relative who fails to behave appropriately is, at least de facto, not a kinsman at all (see also Schneider 1970; Carroll 1970c).

Furthermore, as a result of variations in estate divisions, personal characteristics, affective or sentimental ties and residential proximity, among other considerations, some purely adoptive relationships may actually become 'stronger' in perceived obligations and 'closer' in overall social distance than many relationships that are based on shared blood and land by birthright. The reverse is equally possible, that is, where circumstances combine to diminish the importance of adoptive kinship as a structural bond.

ADOPTION AND FOSTERAGE CATEGORIES

The Ellice term for 'adoption' is *pukenga*, from *puke* 'to take' with the nominalizing suffix *-nga*; 'fosterage' is *tausinga*, from *tausi* 'to guard' or 'to take care of (someone or something)'. Fosterage transactions produce *tamatausi* 'foster child' as an identity. Adoption transactions produce greater variation. The three most common adoptive identities found today are *tamapuke* 'adopted child', *tamapuke tonu* 'true adopted child', and *mokopuna puke* 'adopted grandchild'. The category known as *tama kumii* 'smothering child' disappeared as a result of missionary and colonial practices, but it once represented a child adopted in order to save it from infanticide (see Brady 1975). A *tamatii* 'child thrown in' in former times was normally a young boy from a woman's kin group who was taken in as an adoptee by the woman's husband on his deathbed to insure the woman's continued access to his estate. On death of the husband, the wife became the primary guardian of the adoptee and the estate willed to him by his adoptive father.

Another adoptive identity, *taina (tuangaane) puke* 'adoptive sibling of the same (opposite) sex', is rare nowadays as a transactional category in its own right. One purpose of adopting a person as a 'sibling' in former times was to establish a close and egalitarian relationship between rivalrous groups to insure against continuing hostilities or surprise attack by the donor group. Such adoptions were confined to chiefly ramages, and the candidates were seldom, if ever, persons other than the elder sons of high-ranking chiefs. Persons of high rank were also adopted as 'children' by rivalrous groups for similar reasons. The 'adoptive sibling' identity persists today primarily as a residual category between adoptees and the 'natural' children of their adoptive parents—that is, as a byproduct of a transaction in 'parenthood' rather than as an explicit transaction in 'siblingship' (see Silverman 1970:228–230; Brady, chapter 1).

The identity referred to as *taungasoa pele* 'best friends' is similar to 'adoptive siblingship'. Friendship bonds of this sort are formal rather than casual and are patterned closely on same-sex sibling relations. They normally begin between age-mates prior to adolescence. If the mutual interests and solidarity of the pair endure through childhood and on into the later phases of adolescence, the relationship may be concretized and formally validated by a reciprocal feast and gift-exchange ceremony between the two families involved. The ceremony is supposed to bind the participants to mutual aid and hospitality in perpetuity, even if one of the partners fails to live up to certain obligations (see Koch 1963). Formal friends are expected to adjust to each other's idiosyncrasies. They also use kin terms to refer to each other's parents and siblings of the same sex. The wider network of kinsmen on both sides reflects the change in code for conduct and relative social distance by assuming stronger obligations to share strategic goods and foodstuffs with each other.[10] The net effect is *fakasoko maalosi* 'to increase solidarity'. Friendships between age-mates of the opposite sex are considered to be *faamau* 'affairs' and do not qualify as 'formal friendship'.

Transactions in formal friendship constitute "adoption" in the general analytic sense insofar as they produce a change in kinship identity for the participants (see chapter 1). Extending kin term usage to cover a friend's immediate relatives of the same sex and activating the increased obligations for mutual sharing and hospitality exemplify such changes. But no land allocations or alterations in inheritance profiles are mandated by the transaction, and this is what differentiates 'formal friendship' from 'adoptive siblingship'. The lack of shared land and blood as substantive constructs makes 'friendship' bonds inhere in "custom" or "code for conduct" only. 'Best friends' who do exchange landholdings become 'adoptive siblings' by definition. This may be done directly as part of an 'adoptive sibling' transaction, or it may be done indirectly by the mutual exchange of children as adoptees at a later stage in the friendship. Either way, the transfer of land in title differentiates the relationship from 'formal friendship'. Formal friends otherwise approximate 'created kinsmen'.

Transferring land as part of the transaction is also a fundamental point of differentiation between 'adoption' and 'fosterage', although fosterage also differs from both adoption and friendship in terms of intended duration of the relationship. Fosterage explicitly does not obligate the foster parents to provide land rights other than temporary usufruct for their foster children (cf. Hanson 1970:148). Foster parents assume only a temporary responsibility to look after a foster child's subsistence and welfare needs. Actually giving or publicly promising permanent land rights to a foster child transforms the arrangement into formal adoption. Moreover, the negotiation of kinship as code for conduct in these transactions is such that a foster child recruited from beyond the fourth cousin range can marry his benefactor's daughter, while strict exogamy applies to all formal adoptees in their adoptive context and to all foster children who subsequently become formal adoptees.[11]

Formal adoption does not necessarily entail a change in residence for the adoptee, but fosterage is nearly always precipitated by some kind of residential shift in a child's natal group. Close relatives, preferably classificatory parents, may look after children whose primary parents are away from home for employment, or, in some cases, while the children themselves are relocated away from home for school. The primary parents temporarily allocate rights and duties concerning the children to the foster parents without actually surrendering those rights and duties (see Goodenough 1970b:409). Because inheritance rights to land are not transacted, fosterage is described more accurately as a form of temporary association rather than permanent affiliation with a particular land group; it represents recruitment primarily on the household level.

Children may be fostered by persons with whom they already share active land rights, but these rights do not derive from the fosterage transaction. As a result, a foster child's status is never equal to the jural position occupied by formally adopted or natural children on the same estate. Similarly, the status of 'adopted child' is jurally subordinate to that of the adopters and their natural children, if any, on the same estate. Adoption as a 'true child' is intended explicitly to override this difference. Persons recruited to this category of adoption are granted jural rights in their adopters' estate that are equivalent at least to those held by the adopters' own 'blood' children of the same sex. A person adopted only as a 'child' does not necessarily acquire more than one plot of coconut land and one garden pit from his adopters in the long run, and this may be much less than the inheritance allocated to the adopters' natural heirs of both sexes. In any case, neither adopted nor natural children are granted an active voice in household or land group affairs until they reach adult status, and even then their wishes remain subordinate to those of the 'manager' and all other adults senior in age or generation with a share in the estate.

Whether an adopted child of any type ever becomes sociologically equivalent to a *tama tonu* 'true child' in his adoptive group depends largely on the attitude of the adoptive parents toward the child and on the behavior of the child toward the adoptive parents through the course of their mutual association. A failure to live up to the adopter's expectations may preclude this kind of identification with natural children, even if the adoptee was taken in at the outset as a 'true adopted child'. Where these differences apply, however, they are seldom discussed by the parents in the presence of the children. Parents who are responsible for a mixture of adopted or fostered and natural children generally understate the differences by referring to all of the children equally as *tama* 'child'. Understating the overt distinction among children who have been recruited to a common group in various ways is said to enhance the cooperation and solidarity needed for effective household performance.

Of the three most common identities generated by contemporary adoption transactions, 'adopted grandchild' is the most consistently ambiguous in terms of reallocating kinship constructs. It is exceedingly rare for any person other than a real or classificatory grandchild to be adopted as a 'grandchild'. The candidates are therefore nearly always persons who share 'blood' and latent or active rights to land with their adopters. Moreover, because all second descending generation kinsmen are lumped together terminologically as 'grandchildren', the adoption of these persons as 'grandchildren' does not mandate a change in core kin-term usage.[12] These transactions do qualify as 'adoption', however, and they are conceptually distinguished from 'fosterage'. They normally, but do not necessarily, involve a change in residence for the adoptee. The primary element negotiated is kinship as domestic code for conduct. The transactions take advantage of the sociology of close kinship and household domestic roles in a way that reinforces property relations and revises the range of primary domestic authority between the adopters and the adoptees.

In households mature enough to have grandchildren, if the midlevel or 'parental' generation is disrupted, because of residential separation, illness, or for other reasons, the obligation to care for the aged falls most directly on productive individuals in the succeeding generation. Children are morally obligated to honor all requests designed to provide domestic security for their elders, including requests to give up one or more of their children in adoption, if necessary. Adopting a 'grandchild' as a 'grandchild' increases the level of primary domestic authority commanded by the adopters with respect to their adoptees, and it also increases the level of primary domestic allegiance owed by the adoptees to the adopters. This is an important means for insuring household service when it is needed most, that is, when the adopters' own children are unable to provide it for some reason and when the adopters are least capable of providing it themselves.

Adoptive grandchild transactions are important in that they are convenient means for formally expanding domestic loyalty and service without much disruption to political and property relations in the adoptive group. Adoptees may acquire additional or renewed access to land through these transactions, so long as they continue to fulfill their obligations. But, since natural and 'true' adopted children generally acquire higher priority rights for inheritance and jural disposition in the affairs of their natal and adoptive groups than either natural or adopted grandchildren, adopting a grandchild as a 'grandchild' is not likely to have much effect on the actual distribution of political power and property in the sponsoring group. The adoptee becomes a primary heir under these circumstances only if his or her parents have died and there are no other heirs senior in generation or relative kinship distance to the adopters. For these reasons, persons adopted to insure an immediate heir to an estate are nearly always adopted as 'children' rather than as 'grandchildren'.

Finally, it should be mentioned that most adoptions begin on an informal or ambiguous basis. A child is often taken in as a member of his or her adoptive group with the understanding that the land allocation needed to transform the arrangement into an explicit and formal 'adoption' might be forthcoming if the adoptee's behavior is satisfactory in the long run. These transactions are best regarded at the outset as transitional between simple fosterage and formal adoption. The arrangement may terminate with or without a gift of land, depending in part on the child's performance to the satisfaction of his benefactors, and in part on the nature of the agreement reached between the natural and the adoptive parents at the beginning of the transaction. It is also important to note that the failure to make firm property allocations at the outset gives these prolonged fosterage or informal adoption transactions a tenuous quality that is especially adaptive under conditions of land hunger in the sponsoring group. Maintaining an ambiguous adoptive relationship allows persons or groups to fill vacant domestic work roles in their households or to look after indigent children on a basis more permanent in intended duration than through simple fosterage, while at the same time minimizing the risk of unwarranted or unnecessary land allocations. Most such arrangements eventually are clarified, sometimes in the Island Court in litigation over the child's land rights. But the principals may not force the issue of clarification for several years, if at all.

SUCCESSION TO PRIMARY JURAL PARENTHOOD

Goodenough (1970b) notes that "the term 'adoption' has been applied indiscriminately to what appear to be instances of succession and of the exercise of overriding grandparental rights, as well as to instances of sharing and the outright transfer of jural parenthood" (1970b:409). The empirical range of 'adoption' in the Ellice Islands covers each of these contingencies in a variety of contexts, but the questions of what jural parenthood is, who may succeed to it, and under what circumstances, warrant special consideration.

Ellice children are born into a network of jural parent relations. Jural parenthood is not limited to coincidence with actual biological parenthood, although biological parenthood that is not disqualified by marital ground rules concerning 'legitimacy' establishes priority rights and a set of duties in relation to children for the biological parents (see Goodenough 1970b:394ff). The priority rights that accrue to the biological mother by virtue of her having borne a child under 'legitimate' circumstances, and to the (presumed) biological father by virtue of his role as genitor and his relationship to the child's mother, *may be* transferred in whole or in part to other persons through adoption and fosterage. But all of the biological parents' real and classificatory siblings also acquire at least secondary 'parental' rights in and jural obligations toward the child at the time of birth, and they do so independent of adoption and fosterage transactions. Jural parenthood is a matter of degree under these circumstances, and what is at stake in adoption and fosterage transactions is how, under what conditions, and to whom *primary* jural parenthood is to be transferred or otherwise reassigned (see chapter 1).

When adopters are blood kin who already stand in the relationship of 'parents' or 'grandparents' to the adoptees, adoption redefines the allocation of primary jural parenthood established at birth. It does not 'create' jural parenthood per se, as in instances of adopting nonconsanguines. The essential difference between these two domains, therefore, is one of transactions in parenthood that either: (1) involve succession to primary jural parenthood by persons with an existing but perhaps latent entitlement as 'parents' or 'grandparents' relative to the adoptee; or, (2) entail a transfer of primary jural parenthood to persons who would otherwise not be entitled to jural rights as 'parents' in the adoptee (cf. Goodenough 1970b:394–395). Cognatic kinsmen of a generation equivalent or senior to that of a child's natural parents theoretically qualify for transactions of the former type in the Ellice system. All other persons theoretically qualify for transactions of the latter type.

The secondary jural parenthood entitlements underlying succession transactions are rated in part on a priority basis of genealogical proximity to the primary jural parents in much the same fashion as jural rights in property are allocated among related landholding groups. Similarly, the actual strength of secondary obligations to succeed to primary jural parenthood includes a calculation of the residential, political, and affective or sentimental distance that obtains among the principals. Negotiations in terms of these criteria make some transactions more volitional than others, and the outcome of each event tends to be situationally rather than structurally determined to that extent.

Apparently, no one has overriding rights of succession to primary jural parenthood while the incumbent parents are still alive, married, and meet the customary requirements for the care and socialization of their children. The only contingency that seems to disqualify primary jural parents in the eyes of the community is open neglect or physical abuse of their children sufficient to alarm kinsmen nearby, and perhaps of a magnitude sufficient to be demonstrated nowadays in the Island Court. Coresident kindred in each village always share in the socialization, provisioning, and public defense of their 'children' to some extent; so 'parental' or 'family' neglect is at best diffusely defined in all instances except direct physical abuse, and such mistreatment is rare. Minimal property allocations that are not attempts to disinherit children completely do not disqualify persons as primary jural parents, although disagreements here may lead to estrangement between parents and their children.

Succession to primary jural parenthood is always in order when both of a dependent child's primary parents die. If only one parent dies, remarriage of the surviving parent normally is sufficient to offset the need for succession by classificatory parents. A stepparent may adopt his spouse's children from a former marriage if he chooses to, although he is under no obligation to do so simply on the basis of his marriage to the children's mother.[13] If the 'next-of-kin' feel that the stepparent will not care for the spouse's children properly, however, they may press for an adoption on the principle of succession to primary jural parenthood. When parents with mature children die, there is generally no need for such succession transactions. Adult survivors inherit their deceased parents' estate, succeed to positions of authority within it, and look after their own welfare.

If the claimants for succession to primary jural parenthood are members of a landholding group that is physically or socially distant, formal adoption is nearly always necessary for them to exercise their latent entitlements to a child. On the other hand, formal adoption is not always necessary to activate minimally shared jural parenthood among 'siblings' in related land groups if the distance involved is not so great as to preclude a child's continued assistance in his own household and land group complex. Ambiguous fosterage is a legitimate and commonplace alternative under these circumstances. This does not mean, of course, that formal adoption is precluded by such proximity. In fact, the temporary realignments in working, eating, and sleeping patterns for children who move around in the village to assist their kinsmen often build up strong affective ties that culminate in a formal adoption transaction.

Succession to primary jural parenthood is also possible on the strength of previous adoptive bonds. Adoptions normally are expected to endure for the lifetime of the principals. In cases where the original adopters die before their charges are mature, however, the adopters' natural children may succeed to primary jural parenthood over the adoptee if these potential successors are adults, and the adoptee's natal group does not object. In adoptive grandchild transactions, the adopters' natural heirs already stand in an adoptive 'parent' relationship to the adoptees. The right to succeed to primary jural parenthood under these circumstances is always implicit in the initial transaction, so the relationship may endure beyond the lifetime of the original adopters. If the original transaction concerned an adoptive 'child' rather than an adoptive 'grandchild', the adopters' natural heirs may continue to look after their adoptive 'siblings' informally. But the usual mode of continuance in such cases is for the natural heirs to renegotiate the initial transaction on behalf of dependent adoptees with the original parents, or, in the event they have passed away, with their next-of-kin. It is also common for adoptees to return to their natal groups with an award of land in title from their deceased adoptive parents or grandparents.

In general, if a need for adoption is precipitated by death of one or both of the primary jural parents, or by their divorce, remarriage, incapacity, or voluntary waiving of claims (see Goodenough 1970b: 408), the strongest claims for succession to primary jural parenthood ideally come from the primary parents' real siblings. Same-sex siblings normally take precedence over cross-sex siblings in this regard, but FZ and MB also occupy strategic positions concerning their cross-sex siblings' children.

A FZ represents the terminus of a 'strong blood' linkage insofar as she does not transmit 'strong blood' alignments but is a 'strong blood' relative to her BCh. Her role is terminologically equated with that of M and MZ, but her responsibility toward her BCh may be subordinate only to that of the children's mother. A FZ is encouraged to hold her BCh at birth and otherwise to establish and maintain sentimental and social ties that will insure her continued interest in the children's welfare. If her B fails to live up to his responsibilities as a parent, she is expected to chide him into appropriate behavior. If a M neglects or mistreats her children, or if she dies, FZ is expected to assume primary parental responsibilities for those children immediately, if only temporarily. FZ is also entitled to respect and obedience from her BCh as a matter of course.

MB occupies a complementary position on the matrilateral side. He is the key male in the 'weak blood' alignment that connects him to his ZCh. His role is not terminologically equated with that of F and FB, however, and he is expected to behave in a much less authoritative and hence more egalitarian way toward his ZCh than is either F or FB. Although a MB may hold more sway than a FZ in influencing the economic and political affairs of their cross-sex siblings' children, the identification of adoption as primarily a domestic function and the traditional bias that grants higher rank to 'strong' rather than to 'weak blood' alignments may nevertheless give FZ some priority over MB for enduring rights of succession to primary jural parenthood. FB is also likely to hold a similar priority over MZ insofar as the resolution of conflicting matrilateral versus patrilateral claims for succession tends to favor the latter in principle and because men generally hold more authority than women. The culmination of these dimensions in opposition helps to define the special position that FZ (strong blood + female sex) and MB (weak blood + male sex) occupy in Ellice kinship and parenthood networks.

Lineal grandparents are generally considered to be next to a child's parents' siblings of either sex in order of priority for succession to primary jural parenthood, although grandparents may derive a first priority claim for adopting their grandchildren through the rights they hold in their own children. A child's parents' classificatory siblings are theoretically last in this order of succession priorities. As in all other instances, however, the actual order may be altered by a number of situational factors such as

residential proximity, land group affiliation, and other considerations of relative social distance.

POLITICAL SUCCESSION RIGHTS OF ADOPTEES

Under certain circumstances, an adoptee may succeed to the
position of 'manager' in his adoptive land group. If the incumbent
manager dies without children of his own, and if his estate is held
in *vaevae* 'individual' tenure (thus eliminating the priority claims
to land his collateral kin may wish to pursue), then there usually are
no obstacles to prevent a formal adoptee from succeeding to the
position of manager'.[14] The chances are minimal, however, that an
adoptee will be designated manager over the adopters' natural
heirs, unless all of them are female and the adoptee is an adult male
in good standing with all concerned.

VALIDATION OF ADOPTION EVENTS

Today, Ellice adoptions involve one of two types of contracts:
(1) a legal contract, in which the adoption event is negotiated
through the island government and registered with the local
Lands Court (see Brady 1974:137–138); or, (2) a customary
contract, in which the adoption event is negotiated orally and
independent of the court (see also Lundsgaarde 1970; Monberg
1970:107). A customary contract is expected to endure for the
lifetime of the principals, as mentioned above. A legal contract is
discharged formally when land has been transferred to the adoptee,
regardless of the duration of the arrangement.

For an adoption to be legal, a person must give notice of his
intentions to adopt; the adopter must show that the allocation of
land required for the adoptee will not deprive the adopter's
natural heirs, the primary jural parents of the potential adoptee
must give their consent (if the candidate is a dependent child),
and the Lands Court must agree that all of these stipulations have
been met before the adoption is approved. The Lands Court may
disallow an adoption if the adopter has landholdings that appear to
be insufficient for the support of an additional dependent. Customary contracts are not recognized by the court unless they can
be registered and made retroactive to the time of the original

transactions.[15] To do this, the adoption event must be proved before the court to have existed in accordance with the customs of the island on which it takes place. The adopters may elect to register the event as adoptive 'child', 'true child', or 'grandchild', according to the demands of the moment.

In general, adoptions are validated through mutual consent, firm land allocations, and appropriate behavior. They are codified by registration in legal adoptions. They may be further validated by small feasts that signify the delegation, sharing, or outright surrender of primary parental rights in the adoptee. A lack of overt celebration in adoptions often indicates an activation of latent rights of succession to primary jural parenthood. On the other hand, greater validation than the agreement itself is said to be especially appropriate in formal transactions among non-kinsmen because of the relative social distance involved. Small gifts may flow back and forth between the adopters and the adoptees' natal groups for the duration of the arrangement. It is important to recognize, however, that while such gifts do help to maintain solidary relationships, they are not prerequisite to the successful maintenance or validation of adoption events themselves. Some fosterage transactions also rely more heavily than others on gift exchange as a maintenance or validating mechanism.

In many fosterage transactions, the primary and foster parents openly pledge themselves to mutual support of the children. When the reason for the transaction is parental migration for employment elsewhere, leaving some children behind to be looked after by other persons, the primary parents are expected to contribute some of their income from time to time to offset the increased costs in the foster household. In exchange for this, the foster parents agree to look after the social and economic welfare of the children until the primary parents return. Default by either one or both sets of parents may lead to accusations of parental neglect that are voiced widely among kinsmen and friends. If the primary parents fail to send money home to the foster parents, the latter may deliberately fail to give the primary parents a welcome feast on their return—a public indication of dissatisfaction. Perhaps of more consequence, however, is that default in explicitly arranged fosterage transactions may create an atmosphere of disapproval such that future requests for assistance may be denied by a substantial segment of the community. Persons subject to these negative sanctions for any length of time generally attempt a reconciliation with the injured parties through gift exchange. Other, less formal, fosterage transactions are easily contracted and easily broken without much consequence.

INHERITANCE RIGHTS THROUGH ADOPTION

Inheritance within the natal group is normally bilateral, but a larger share of land may be awarded to male rather than to female heirs when an estate is divided, the eldest son ideally being entitled to receive the largest share. Consequently, the average man's holdings on each island are larger than those controlled by women, and both sexes are likely to inherit most of their land from their fathers.[16] Usufruct rights, barring differences in the sexual division of labor, are approximately equal for both sexes.

Current land legislation is coordinate with Ellice rules for inheritance through adoption insofar as all demonstrably adopted persons must be provided for unless they are guilty of neglecting or abandoning their sponsors. A legal adoptee is entitled to at least one plot of coconut land and one garden pit under 'individual' tenure from the sponsor's estate. Lacking any single gift of land from the adopters, an adoptee may become a coparcener on the sponsors' estate and thereby acquire at least a minimal right to share in any subsequent divisions of it.

Adoption legislation is not fully understood by many of the islanders. Despite the fact that legal adoptions can be revoked on petition and proper hearing from the court, many adopters feel that registration of an adoption event is irrevocable and may prevent them from withdrawing from an adoption arrangement even with cause. For this reason, people who formally adopt children on a customary basis, and who have sufficient land to warrant a legal adoption, often prefer to avoid the court at the outset (see also Marshall, chapter 2; Brooks, chapter 3). Legal registration is also impractical, of course, when the unstated goal of the principals is to keep the arrangement informal and ambiguous. Adoption legislation does not take traditionally ambiguous adoptions into account. The possibility of letting an informal arrangement play out in time without entitling the adoptee to an award of land is surrendered overtly to the Lands Court through registration. Legal adoptions necessarily become formal and unambiguous adoptions.

On the other hand, when there is reason to suspect that an adopter who agrees to a formal but customary adoption may renege in the long run, the adoptee's natal group may press for legal registration immediately. Without a legal contract, the intestate death of the sponsors increases the possibility of the adoptee's being disinherited. In the event litigation develops in such cases, the burden of proof that some kind of adoption event actually transpired may rest entirely on the adoptee, his natal group, or his descendants. Legal contracts provide security against disinheritance, all other things (such as the adoptee's support of his sponsors) being equal. Several court cases on each island have involved attempts by "disinherited" adoptees to secure land from persons alleged to be their formal adopters. The defendants in these cases may maintain that no formal adoption ever transpired according to either colonial or Ellice rules, and the lack of legal registration is thereby a handicap. The defendants may argue that the claimant was not an 'adoptee' at all, but only a foster child who was fortunate enough to have a benefactor or two to look after his or her welfare.[17]

Land that has been legally awarded to an adoptee reverts to the donors' kin if the adoptee dies without children of his own. If the adoptee does have children, the donors subsequently lose their right of reversion.[18] Prior to the settlement of long-standing land disputes by the Lands Commission after World War II, this reversionary right was institutionalized on a community level at Nukulaelae. Periodically, the island leaders there ordered coconut plots and gardens given to adoptees to be returned to the donors.[19] These reversions applied more to persons adopted from outside the donors' kindreds than to persons who could demonstrate at least remote 'blood' ties to the donors. Land given to adoptees during this period was not supposed to represent a permanent transfer unless the donors expressly so stipulated. Land given under the same title on the other islands in the Ellice group was seldom registered, generally being viewed as an *aaongaa* 'loan' that reverted to the donors automatically on maturity or marriage of the adoptee. Land given to formal adoptees today is permanent throughout the Ellice district, barring the death of the adoptee without natural heirs of his own.

An adoptee's inheritance profile also is affected by another contingency. Access to land through formal adoption into another group does not require forfeiture of the adoptee's land inheritance rights in his natal group. Although this lack of jural exclusiveness (see chapter 1) potentially doubles the adoptee's access to strategic resources, the proportion of the resources given to an adoptee by the sponsor is nevertheless likely to take both relative land hunger and the existence of double inheritance privileges into account. The adopters may take on a greater or lesser burden than the adoptee's natal group in contributing to the adoptee's inheritance profile, depending on the availability of resources in each group. So formal adoption does not necessarily double the adoptee's access to land in a quantitative sense. Adopters also are more inclined to accept a larger share of the burden if the adoptee can be taken in as a coparcener on their estate, rather than agreeing to an individual award of land in title to the adoptee at the conclusion of the arrangement. Individual awards of land in title to persons from elsewhere contribute directly to estate fragmentation and thereby to relative land hunger.

Inheritance rights in adoption have not always been jurally inclusive, however. There is some precedent indicating that a child adopted in former times could be disinherited by his or her natal group once adopted securely into another ramage. Kennedy (1931: 309), for example, suggests that once a man was adopted on Vaitupu in aboriginal times, he might be denied reentry into the *tausoa* 'section meeting house' of his natal group. He was effectively disassociated from the former house and absorbed into that of his adoptive group instead. The elders surveyed on each island do not all agree that this was necessarily done, but many believe that this kind of disassociation was frequent and that it was sanctioned as 'customary' behavior. The net effect altered primary access to land to the exclusion of previous holdings, representing a jurally exclusive shift in kinship identity for the adoptee (see also Koch 1963). Some contemporary transactions involving orphans may result in a de facto exclusivity of the adoptee's previous situation. But these are rare circumstances, and an outright transfer of primary jural parenthood presently excludes the right of the adoptee's natal group to formally disinherit him on the grounds that the adopters will provide for him.[20] Moreover, the shift in kinship identity for the adoptee is always jurally inclusive with respect to the incest taboo parameters established in his natal group.

In general, inheritance and affiliation principles prescribe that even de facto disinheritance by one group must be at least in complementary distribution with the assumption of obligations by another group, thereby protecting the adoptee's customary birth-right to some land and garden holdings. Fulfillment of these obligations has prevented the emergence of a landless class. In aboriginal times, to be without land was to be without ancestors, adoptive kin, or affines on the island, and the custom of absorbing even *tino fakaalofa* 'strangers' into the community through formal adoption or simple fosterage persists today. Colonial legislation, however, now restricts the freedom of islanders who wish to award land outright or through formal adoption to persons who come from outside the colony (see Brady 1974).

ENCUMBRANCES ON THE NUMBER OF ADOPTEES

Parallel to the notions of resource scarcity and management that led to the acceptance of infanticide prior to the arrival of mission-aries and the colonial government, some restrictions on the number of adoptees allowed for each person or household have surfaced from time to time in the Ellice. A fairly recent example comes from the island of Nui. The people there reportedly passed an island regulation in 1948 that limited the number of formally adopted children to one consanguineal kinsman, and the common ancestor of the principals was not to be more remote than great-grandfather to the adoptive parent. The adopter had the option of replacing the first adoptee with a second if the first one died. Formal adoptees were also limited in the past to two children for each adopter at Nukulaelae and to only one child at Vaitupu.

These restrictions are inoperative today, not because relative land hunger and population management are any less a concern, but rather because the regulations were difficult to enforce—they were ignored by most of the local citizens. The only restrictions that remain in force are practical considerations: a person may adopt as many dependents as he can support without depriving his natural heirs of their subsistence requirements.

ADOPTION RATES, LABOR MIGRATION, AND LOCAL EMPLOYMENT

Adoption and fosterage are widespread in the Ellice group as means for initiating or perpetuating alliances within and, to a lesser extent, between islands. But the frequencies of adoption and fosterage vary widely from island to island according to a variety of circumstances.

The surveys I conducted in 1969 and 1971 revealed that about 83 percent of all households at Funafuti (95/114), 75 percent of those at Nanumanga (60/80), and about 55 percent of those at Nukufetau (50/90) contained one or more adopted persons. These persons either had been adopted previously by persons elsewhere or were attached to the households being interviewed as adoptees.[21] The latter category showed the most variation among these three islands. Nearly 55 percent of the households at Funafuti, 30 percent of those at Nanumanga, and about 17 percent of those at Nukufetau actually were sponsoring an 'adoption' at the time of the surveys.

Reliable quantitative data on fosterage were difficult to obtain because of the relatively informal and diffuse responsibilities involved. Nevertheless, about 30 percent of the households at Funafuti reported having one or more 'foster' children at the time. Comparable data from Nanumanga and Nukufetau suggest that from 50 to 70 percent of the households on each island may have sponsored foster children in recent years.[22]

The circumstances that generate these distributions are multiple and complex. Among the many contingencies that bear on contemporary adoption and fosterage strategies, differential labor migration and local employment opportunities have become important, and each of these variables pertains to land hunger. Labor migration by individuals in a land hungry group decreases the pressure on local resources and increases the income of the donor group through kinship reciprocity claims on money earned elsewhere. Local employment also adds to incomes and offsets some of the adverse effects of land hunger by providing cash that supplements subsistence and has the advantage of not disrupting the group by migration.

Most labor migrants from the Ellice district work for a few years for the phosphate-mining industries at Ocean Island or Nauru. In either case, labor contracts generally do not allow the laborers to bring more than one or two immediate dependents with them.[23] Housing is in short supply on both islands, and the wages paid are normally insufficient to support a large family away from home. This poses problems for the maintenance of dependent children who must be left behind, especially when the migrants are the primary subsistence source in their households.

Several strategies are used to offset these problems without foregoing the benefits of employment elsewhere. The most practical arrangement for households with a full complement of people to fill domestic work roles is to encourage labor migration by members of the appropriate age, sex, and marital status whose domestic duties can be covered with the least difficulty by those who remain behind. Young, unmarried, adult males are the usual nominees. A household that can send a few of its members off to employment elsewhere without creating new dependencies beyond its normal operating level can easily add the benefits of extra income.

On the other hand, when the migrants are the primary subsistence source in their households and some of their children must be left behind, the demand for fosterage, and to a lesser degree, for adoption, increases. Fosterage is the preferred arrangement under these circumstances because it involves only a temporary reallocation of primary parental rights and duties. More permanent transactions are seldom necessary because labor migrants usually do not stay away for more than a year or two at a time. It is also much easier to place dependent children in foster homes because of the existing secondary jural parenthood networks than it is to find someone willing to adopt a child simply on the basis that the primary jural parents must move away from the island for a while. Temporary separation by itself is viewed by many islanders as a "morally inappropriate" reason for giving children up for adoption.

The apparently higher rates of fosterage at Nanumanga and Nukufetau than at Funafuti correspond with a lower rate of labor migration from Funafuti than from the other two islands at the time of my study. Funafuti is the seat of the district government, and there are various opportunities for local employment there that do not occur on the other islands in the group.[24] Local employment gives households extra income without creating as much demand for fosterage as employment off the island.

Not all fosterage transactions are triggered simply by labor migration, of course, nor are all the choices between adoption and fosterage negotiated only, or even primarily, on the basis of parental absences. Funafuti's high proportion of households with adopted children is partly the result of local wealth: it has the highest per capita income in the Ellice.[25] Concomitantly, the capability for absorbing children from indigent groups, or for being able to support adoptees, is theoretically much greater on Funafuti than elsewhere in the group. Funafuti is held in high esteem by people from the outer islands for these reasons. The "port town" life styles on this island also make it a primary target for sponsoring adoption and fosterage.

However, the wealth in Funafuti's heterogeneous population is not evenly distributed, primarily because such economic levelers as obligatory reciprocity among close kinsmen are not so easily implemented when the kinship, residential, or affective distance between people is great (see Brady 1972). Moreover, excluding the income of immigrant employees who have no kinsmen or land-holdings on the island, land hunger at Funafuti is probably higher than on most other islands in the group (see Brady 1974). The result is that many local people are not as affluent or capable of absorbing additional dependents as the outer island attitudes suggest. In fact, the high probability of having at least one kinsman who is employed on the island and the priority given to local needs for adoption and fosterage have combined to keep the number of off-island adoptions to a minimum. Most adoption and fosterage transactions at Funafuti are strictly local arrangements.

Nukufetau also has a high degree of land hunger, and the islanders there consider it wise to avoid making a firm commitment of land to a potential adoptee in case his behavior proves to be unsatisfactory in the long run. This conservatism minimizes the number of formal adoptions and maximizes the number of ambiguous or "informal" adoptions in force at any given time. Similar concerns may contribute to the apparently higher rate of fosterage at Nukufetau than on the other two islands surveyed. Nanumanga is middle range in all respects in this distribution.

MOTIVATIONS SUMMARIZED

The household surveys at Funafuti, Nanumanga, and Nukufetau yielded detailed information on 134 separate adoption events. Preliminary comparisons showed no significant differences in adoption patterns on each island, other than those already noted, so the results have been combined here for ease of presentation. Most of the data are drawn from Funafuti.

Table 16 lists the reasons given by informants for their participation in adoption events in rank order of the frequencies reported. The most common reasons given for adoption pertain directly to filling a domestic work role, either because the sponsors had no children of their own or because all of their children were of one sex. Adoptions negotiated to assist the aged with their domestic needs, to provide a male heir to an estate, or to provide a sibling for the sponsors' natural children were also included in this category. Adoptions undertaken specifically because the adoptee's primary jural parents were indigent, relocated, dead, or divorced comprised the second most frequent category. More than half of these (21/37) were stated to have been undertaken to relieve over-crowded households or landholding groups of some of their members.

Overall, the data available from matched interviews and third party testimony suggest that about 41 percent of the total cases (55/134) involved negotiations specifically to relieve land hunger in the adoptee's natal group. But the range of this particular motivation is probably greater than was reported. Indigent families are often reluctant to admit to their insufficiencies because of the prestige associated with large landholdings. Similarly, persons who adopt indigent, abandoned, or otherwise neglected children often are reluctant to discuss the actual circumstances of the event for fear of casting aspersions on the child's natal group, thereby on the child itself, and ultimately on the adopters.

Adoptions negotiated primarily on the basis of strong affective ties among consanguines who were separated residentially, or on the basis of 'friendship' bonds, were third in order of frequency reported. Most of these cases were explicitly intended to balance,

TABLE 16.   Stated Motivations for Adoption

Reasons given	n	%
Fill vacant domestic work roles	52	38.8
Child's parents indigent, relocated, dead, divorced	37	27.6
Strong affective ties, friendship alliances	24	17.9
Incorporate illegitimate child	5	3.8
Provide school assistance for child	5	3.8
Nurse a sick child	4	2.9
Establish local identity for pastor's child	4	2.9
Succession to a previously established parental adoption	2	1.5
Wanted apprentice for carpentry	1	.8
TOTAL	134	100.0

SOURCE: Author's field notes, 1969–1971.

maintain, or reassert alliances between the adopters and the adoptees' natal groups. The strategy in adoptions negotiated primarily for alliance purposes is the same as that in marital alliances: sociability, solidarity, and economic security are intensified by increasing the number of positive links between persons or groups who would otherwise be distant. Ideally, the greater the number of links between such persons or groups, the less fragile is their relationship, and the greater is their mutual *alofa* 'solidarity' value.

As previously mentioned, 'best friends' may exchange their natural children through adoption as an expression of mutual solidarity, although this practice is less common today than it once was because of a growing conservatism toward giving land to distant kin or unrelated persons for any purpose. The strongest expression of enduring friendship and mutual support between 'best friends' is for each to relinquish an eldest son for adoption. Traditional inheritance and succession biases favoring the eldest male in each landholding group make relinquishing such children for adoption by others a particularly generous act, and one that is often politically advantageous. Nearly all of the adoptions among persons other than 'blood' kin in this sample were reported to have been negotiated between 'best friends' acting in their capacity as 'parents'. It is conceivable, but unlikely, that some of the 'friend-ships' developed out of the adoption transactions. Child adoption appears to function more as a maintenance rather than as a starting mechanism in friendship transactions.

The first three categories of stated motivations in table 16 comprise nearly 85 percent of the total. The remaining categories occur relatively infrequently, but they are still important. One of these categories, "succession to a previously established parental adoption," has already been discussed in detail. Another, that of adopting pastors' children, warrants further consideration because of what it reveals about adoption strategies in general.

The adoption of pastors' children is commonplace. These children usually come to the island from elsewhere in the colony or from Samoa. Adoption is an important means for absorbing them into the local community. The adoptees acquire positions in particular kinship matrices and firm land allocations concretize and validate the transactions. A local kinship identity for the immigrant pastors themselves is established by extension in principle of their children's adoptive identities. But this extension does not entitle pastors to share title rights in the adopter's estate. Community support and the pastor's role as "quasi-chief" preclude the need for pastors to have local land of their own for purposes other than prestige. Some small parcels of land may be given to a pastor by members of the community for prestige purposes.

As was the case for aboriginal chiefs, pastors are excluded from manual labor, unless they choose to act to the contrary. *Mataaniu* 'community producers' and *fatamaa* 'personal sponsors' ideally provide all that is needed to free a pastor for concentration on the duties of his office.[26] 'Community producers' are usually household heads who undertake a formal responsibility as members of the pastor's church and the island community to contribute money, produce, and people for domestic duties to the pastor's household. 'Personal sponsors' are charged with the responsibility of orienting the new family in the ways of the community. They are also the most likely candidates to adopt a pastor's child. But the normal relationship between a pastor and his 'personal sponsor' is not 'adoption'. It is classed instead as a form of adult fosterage that is extended to all community leaders who come to the island from elsewhere. This includes teachers and local government officials as well as pastors. Formal adoption transactions per se are above and beyond this level of community service.

ADOPTION CANDIDATES AND COMBINATIONS

Adoption arrangements may be negotiated jointly by the adoptive parents, although in most cases only one person actively participates in the negotiations as the principal adopter. Only about 11 percent of the three-island sample (16/134) involved both adoptive parents as the principal negotiators. Still, when one person undertakes a commitment for adoption, the spouse is likely to be consulted for an opinion before the transaction begins. Ideally, consent from all of the adults in the adopters' land groups is prerequisite for undertaking a formal adoption because of the land allocation implicit in the arrangement.[27] Adoptions negotiated without such permission may eventually lead to litigation in the Lands Court.

Adoptions that are not sponsored jointly by husband and wife also can lead to problems. For example, in cases where a woman adopts a child on her own initiative, the husband may become sentimentally attached to the child and bequeath it some land. If the adoption is not registered, the land given to the adoptee may later be successfully reclaimed by the adopter's natural heirs. If the gift is registered, the natural heirs may claim at a later date that the adoptee (or his natural heirs) has no right to the land because the child was never adopted by the husband in the original transaction, only by the wife. Where a husband and wife have pooled their landholdings as a joint estate, such litigation over single-sponsor adoptions becomes irrelevant.

The survey data show a marked tendency for boys to be adopted by male sponsors. Excluding joint sponsorship by a man and a woman as the principal adopters, male adoptees had primary sponsors of the same sex in nearly twice as many cases (48/73) as male adoptees with female sponsors (25/73). This parallel sex bias is not so apparent in the adoption of girls. The distribution of men as primary sponsors for the adoption of girls (23/45) is about equal to that of women as primary sponsors for the adoption of girls (22/45). The proportion of boys adopted overall by both individual and joint sponsors is also greater (84/134) than that for girls (50/134). Similarly, the island lands registers indicate that boys are given land in title as adopted 'children' (64/82—73.5 percent of all entries under this title) more often than girls (18/82—26.5 percent).

This distribution probably is substantially influenced by the traditional agnatic biases in residence, inheritance, and succession patterns, and by the fact that men are much more likely than women to vacate domestic work roles for labor migration, thereby inflating the demand for male adoptees at home. Women who adopt boys usually are widows with no sons. Adoption is a primary means for them to balance the division of labor in their households or to provide male heirs for their estates. Men who act as primary sponsors for the adoption of girls appear to do so in the majority of cases for similar domestic reasons.

Most informants agree that competition for land has made it more difficult nowadays for a landholder with a large family to acquire a son through formal adoption. Adopting a girl, or, for that matter, a boy, without registering the event generally represents less of a drain on the adopters' resources than would otherwise be the case. Female adoptees who mature and marry out are expected to rely on their husbands' resources more than on their natal or adoptive groups. Adoptive parents often find it easier under these circumstances to reduce the share of land given to female adoptees. Nonetheless, if the desire to adopt a child is strong enough, or if the need to do so is pressing enough (as in the case of an indigent child), the adopters may forego all of the above considerations and negotiate an informal adoption to meet the demands of the moment.

A person of any age is eligible for adoption, but only a little more than 5 percent (7/134) of the adoptees were recruited as 'adults', that is, as persons over sixteen years of age at the time they were adopted. Nearly 66 percent (88/134) of the sample involved the adoption of 'children', persons ranging from about two to about sixteen years; 30 percent (39/134) involved the adoption of 'infants', persons under two years of age.

Adoptions that involve adults as candidates have contingencies that differ from those involving the adoption of children, besides the obvious difference in the age of the candidates. For example, a crippled and unmarried man with a large estate at Nanumanga adopted a twenty-three-year-old woman from Vaitupu when she came to Nanumanga as part of an entertainment committee.[28] This man also adopted another woman from Tabiteuea in the Gilberts when she came to Nanumanga with her schoolteacher husband. Both women have been formally adopted and registered with the Lands Court as 'children'. The adopter stated that he adopted the women to assist him with household production and to provide heirs to his estate.

There are several aspects to this case that deviate from the normal range of adoptions involving children as candidates. First, the adopter was unmarried and generally incapacitated to the extent that he had to rely on neighbors and kinsmen for nearly all of his produce. Second, rather than balancing the adoption transactions with an adoptee of each sex who would take up residence with him, he adopted two women, neither of whom has become a regular part of his household. Third, he made the two women primary heirs to his estate, in spite of the traditional agnatic bias that normally prevails in such cases. These are unusual strategies for the adoption of 'children', although they do not contravene the rules for 'adoption' per se.

Most informants agree that there were no encumbrances in former times concerning the source of an adoption candidate. Even so, there is a stated preference to adopt a 'blood' kinsman in all types of adoption. Traditional rights of succession to primary jural parenthood and obligations to care for indigent relatives before undertaking responsibilities for non-kinsmen help determine this preference.

Many of the same informants also state categorically that there is "less alienation" of land entailed in providing for a consanguine than for other persons who are adopted. If land is transferred to a consanguine through adoption, it is argued, then there is a better chance that the land can be reclaimed in the long run, or that at least usufruct rights to its produce can be maintained, or more easily regained, through kinship prestations. Since adoptees may acquire title rights to their sponsors' estates and retain their natal holdings at the same time, adoptions among 'blood' kin also may permit a partial consolidation of previously divided ancestral landholdings, especially if the adoptee is given and retains a joint instead of an individual share in the estate.

The preference for adopting a 'blood' kinsman is also rationalized in terms of "knowing what kind" of person is being recruited in the adoption of someone of common ancestry, while the risk of getting the offspring of a *kaainga paie* 'lazy family' or a *kaainga masei* 'bad family' is believed to be greater in the adoption of other persons. It is also argued that favorable knowledge of this kind tends to reduce the uncertainty toward formally registering an adoption with the Lands Court at the outset of a transaction. The survey data provide modest support for this preference. There were about 20 percent more adoptions of consanguines (80/134) than other persons (54/134) in the three-island sample.

It is also obvious from the survey data that the importance of adoption as a process of alliance between nonconsanguines should not be underestimated (see Shore, chapter 8; Tonkinson, chapter 10). From the standpoint of the principal negotiators, nearly 19 percent (25/134) of the total adoptions surveyed were conducted through affinal ties; nearly 22 percent (29/134) were negotiated strictly on the basis of 'friendship' bonds. The notion of adoption as an aggregating process is also modestly supported by the distribution of adoptions among 'blood' kinsmen. A greater number of these adoptions transpired between persons linked through 'weak blood' (44/80) than through 'strong blood' (36/80), although the margin is slight. A somewhat larger proportion involved classificatory kin (52/80) as opposed to 'real' siblings and lineal kin (28/80). The balance of recruitment through adoption lies with what are ideally the weakest ties in all instances.

The survey data also suggest that adoptees tend to be taken in as 'children' more often than in the other formal adoption categories. Nearly 70 percent of the cases involved the recruitment of adoptees as 'children' (93/134), as opposed to the more solidary extreme 'adoption as a true child' (17/134) or adoption as 'grandchildren' (24/134).

Finally, it should be noted that there is no way to determine the differences between an unregistered formal adoption and an informal or ambiguous adoption except by informant testimony. In order to capitalize on the prestige that goes with generous giving, some informants appear to have classified their 'loosely' adopted children as formal adoptees when asked if land had actually been promised or already allocated. It is more generous to take a person in as a formal rather than an informal adoptee because of the firm land allocation implicit in the former. Thus, the actual number of formally adopted children may be lower than people report and the number of informal adoptions in each community may be proportionately higher.

LAND HUNGER AND LEGAL CONTRACTS

Of all the adoptions with a stated (or demonstrated) land commitment in the three-island survey, most were not registered (80/127). If only the adoptions registered at the outset of the transaction are taken into account, then the number of unregistered adoptions increases to 104 out of 134 of the cases. These data are consistent with the adoption patterns expected under conditions of widespread land hunger.

An analysis of the amount of land per capita in the adopters' land groups and the type of contract negotiated reveals that land groups with adoptees who are registered tend to have more than twice as much land ($\bar{M} = 1.24$ acres per capita) than is held in land groups with adoptees who are not registered ($\bar{M} = 0.51$ acres per capita). These figures cluster respectively above and below the minimal average holdings needed where subsistence depends primarily upon the land (about one acre per capita). Thus, taking into account an intervening variable in the legal system—that the Lands Court will deny an adoption that, in its judgment, will cause a hardship on the adopter or his natural heirs—it appears that relative land hunger may have a direct effect on the type of contract negotiated.

The preferences for accommodating *taamafuataka* 'illegitimate children' also suggest that the type of adoption contract negotiated may be contingent in part on the relative land hunger of the principals. A man judged to be the genitor of an illegitimate child in a paternity suit before the Island Court must assume some legal responsibility for the child. The man can do this by formally adopting the child or, in the event the mother keeps the child as a member of her land group, by transferring at least one plot of coconut land and one garden pit to the child in permanent title. The first alternative allows a man to avoid increased plot fragmentation and land loss on his estate; the second alternative leads directly to fragmentation and loss of land. Men from land hungry groups generally prefer the first alternative. The distribution of 'illegitimate child' as a title in the lands registers also indicates that boys tend to be adopted by their genitors more often than girls under these circumstances. Whether or not the child is adopted by the father or stays with the mother, however, and irrespective of the sex of the child, the mandatory allocation of land rights to 'illegitimate' children concretizes and validates their kinship identity by adding land as ancestral 'substance' to what is already shared in terms of 'blood'.

SUMMARY AND CONCLUSIONS

Adoption is linked in a variety of ways to land tenure and land hunger. Kinship identities are calculated in large part by the manner in which 'strong' or 'weak' blood, active or latent rights to land, and appropriate conduct are shared with particular persons. Both land and blood symbolize solidarity, growth, nurturance, and communion with the ancestral past to the extent that shared access to either substance implies common kinship. These elements are joined "essentially" by the rule that provides access to land by birthright for Ellice people. It is this intersection, rather than just the 'natural' constructs of biogenetic relatedness, that forms the primary reference point for calculating relative kinship distance and for ordering social relations among 'kinsmen'. Adoption emerges, in this context, as a sociological and symbolic means for manipulating and transferring kinship identities that are normally assigned by birthright to persons in a particular matrix of shared land and blood.

Parallel to the rule that automatically entitles natural children to a share in their natal groups' estates, formal adoption obligates the adopters to assign some land in title to the adoptee. Moreover, this must be done without requiring the adoptee to forfeit usufruct and inheritance rights in his natal group. Adoption is presently jurally inclusive with respect to inheritance rights and incest taboo parameters in the adoptee's natal group, although there is some indication that more exclusive transactions prevailed in the past. The inclusiveness in inheritance also suggests that there is never a complete transfer of primary jural parenthood in adoption, except perhaps in a de facto sense in cases where the adoptees are orphans who have already inherited land from their deceased parents. Relative land hunger is also taken into account in deciding on whom the burden weighs more in the adoptee's double inheritance domain, so formal adoption does not necessarily double the adoptee's access to strategic resources in quantity. The minimal legal obligation at present is that adopters must provide at least one plot of coconut land and one garden pit for each formal adoptee. Adoption as a 'true child' exceeds this minimal stipulation by allocating jural rights in the adopters' estate that are equal to those held by the adopters' natural heirs of the same sex.

For a variety of reasons, some of which pertain directly to relative land hunger, there is a strong stated preference for adopting 'blood' kin, and most adoptions do in fact conform to this model by transpiring between persons who already share a 'parent-child' bond of one kind or another. Each of these transactions is thereby marked to some degree by the activation of existing entitlements to children on the principle of succession to primary jural parenthood. Perhaps the most ambiguous example of this kind of succession is the adoption of grandchildren as 'grandchildren'. Adoptive 'grandchild' transactions are intended to focus on a revision of interpersonal domestic relations with the least possible redefinition of existing land rights. Other succession transactions normally display a more conspicuous change in the kinship identity of the adoptees. The formal adoption of 'blood' kin of any type, however, supplements rather than replaces outright the existing kinship bonds, and the generosity associated with giving and receiving a close kinsman in adoption reinforces kinship solidarity among the participants.

The actual strength of obligations to give or to receive a 'blood' kinsman in adoption varies according to a number of contextual features. Priority rights for succession to primary jural parenthood are determined in part by the structural identity of claimants, and FZ and MB occupy especially important positions in this regard. But the actual ordering of priorities is calculated by taking into account the overall social, political, residential, and affective distance between the principals. To this extent, the outcome is situationally rather than structurally determined.

Fosterage transactions are differentiated from 'adoption' and 'formal friendship' primarily on the basis of differences in shared access to land, relative code for conduct features such as the applicability of incest taboos, and intended duration of the relationship. Fosterage explicitly does not mandate a reallocation of land; the sponsors assume only a temporary responsibility to provide subsistence and social welfare for their charges. Formal friendship also does not require a transfer of land, but, as in adoption, such relationships are intended ideally to last for the lifetime of the principals. Furthermore, whereas formal adoption represents primary membership recruitment to both households and land groups, fosterage represents recruitment on the household level only. Formal friendship is generally confined to recruitment on the level of interpersonal relationships, that is, it carries no mandate for broader reorganization of households or land groups. It does, however, qualify as "adoption" in the broad analytic sense insofar as a formal change in kinship identity is produced.

By far the majority of adoptions begin on an informal or ambiguous basis. Such prolonged fosterage or informal adoption contracts ideally allow sponsors sufficient time to determine whether or not a person loosely adopted at the outset will behave appropriately toward them in the long run, thereby earning the land allocation needed to transform the arrangement into formal adoption. This particular strategy increases individual mobility among various groups while it limits the risk of unwarranted or unnecessary property allocations from the sponsors. It is thereby especially adaptive as a strategy of recruitment in land hungry groups.

In general, the movement of people and resources through adoption and fosterage promotes a viable relationship between local populations and their environments by offsetting many of the adverse effects of infecundity, labor migration, old age, and real or presumed land hunger on household productivity and land group constitution. Adoption and fosterage function as transfer mechanisms for moving people to situations where they are needed to fill domestic work roles, to satisfy the demands of strong affective ties for close association, to provide heirs for estates, and, in many cases, to relieve indigent land groups of some of their members. Relative land hunger appears to have a direct bearing on the type of contract adopters negotiate, and an overall insufficiency of resources may preclude formal adoption altogether in some groups. Strategies for adopting illegitimate children appear to be influenced by similar concerns.

The most important contextual features of adoption and foster-age that have been considered in this chapter are: (1) kinship "in nature" versus kinship "in law"; (2) the symbolic and normative association of 'blood', 'land', and 'sharing' as kinship phenomena; (3) ground rules that provide land as a 'substantive' kinship construct in all formal adoptions; (4) the degree to which jural parent-hood is shared at the outset of a child's entry into the kinship system; (5) rights of succession to primary jural parenthood; (6) parental residence and tenure patterns; (7) traditional inherit-ance biases favoring males and seniority in age and generation; (8) contemporary land legislation; (9) levels of commitment and performance of adoptees and sponsors in the long run; (10) economic imbalance in households; and, (11) the land profiles of the principals in each transaction. The last may be embodied in a general proposition: Where property rights are associated with kin group membership, relative land hunger may affect directly the formulation, negotiation, and outcome of all types of alliance, affiliation, and recruitment decisions, including those of adoption and fosterage. The data presented in this chapter support this proposition, and the manner has been specified in which land tenure and land hunger—as kinship phenomena and subsistence conditions—are linked together with adoption and fosterage as determinants of group composition and performance.

NOTES

The Ellice Islanders recently voted (August 1974) to form a colony separate from the Gilbertese. It is anticipated that the new scheme will be implemented in 1976. Data for this chapter were gathered while I was conducting doctoral dissertation research in the Ellice in 1968 and 1969. Financial support was provided by a U. S. Public Health Service (NIMH) Research Grant (MH 11629) and Fellowship (MH 40529) and by the Department of Anthropology, University of Oregon. Additional information was obtained in 1971 on a Research Grant from the National Science Foundation (GS 29695). This assistance is gratefully acknowl-edged. I also wish to thank Vern Carroll, Mac Marshall, Michael Rynkiewich, Harold Scheffler, David Schneider, and Barry Isaac for their valuable criticisms of earlier drafts of this chapter. Special thanks are due to my field assistant in 1971, Telematua Kofe, for his help in gathering these data.

1. In order from north to south, the Ellice Islands are: Nanumea, Nanumanga, Niutao, Nui, Vaitupu, Nukufetau, Funafuti, Nukulaelae, and Niulakita. The last is owned as a copra plantation by the Niutao Islanders. Most of the research for this chapter was done during extended residence on Nukufetau, Nanumanga, and Funafuti. Shorter visits from time to time to the remaining islands in the group provided some overall impressions and some additional comparative materials, especially on land tenure patterns. Except where stated to the contrary, however, a close inspection of these other islands may reveal more variation than I have tried (or have been able) to account for here. My use of the phrase "in the Ellice Islands" should be understood with these limitations in mind.

2. The taro grown in the Ellice is *Colocasia esculenta*. A similar root crop, *Cyrtosperma chamissonis*, is known as *pulaka* in the Ellice and as *babai* in the Gilberts.

3. These land groups are not identified by the same term on all islands. For convenience in the past, I have used the southern Ellice term *puikaainga* 'line through the family estate' to refer to landholding groups generally (see Brady 1972, 1974, 1975). Evidently, this term is either not used or at least not popular on Nanumea (Keith and Anne Chambers, personal communication) or Niutao (Jay Noricks, personal communication). Whatever the local term happens to be, however, the information available to me at the present time suggests that land group structure and performance are similar throughout the district (see Brady 1974).

4. With the exception of Funafuti, the seat of the district government, and Nanumea (Keith and Anne Chambers, personal communication). Each of these islands has two villages, one of which is quite small.

5. *Soolonga* is a synonym for *ngafa* on Niutao.

6. A 'natural' child per se is an 'illegitimate child'. Except where specified to the contrary, the use of 'natural child' and 'natural heir' in this chapter is intended to convey the meaning of 'child' or 'heir' in nature and in law— that is, to refer to persons who share blood, land, and code for conduct by birthright in a particular kinship matrix.

7. My use of the term *jural* parallels Goodenough's (1970b:410) definition of a jural relationship: "... one in which one party can make a demand upon another and there is public agreement that the other is obligated to comply with the demand." Such agreement may derive from customary law (oral agreement), contractual arrangement, from statutory decree, or from written or unwritten precedent in a judicial decision. Both legal and customary sanctions for upholding such agreements are applied under colonial guidance in the Ellice Islands.

8. See Brady (1974) for a general discussion of the nature of fission versus segmentation in Ellice ramages, and the differential effects on primary land right distributions among cognate kinsmen.

9. *Kaainga* also has a wider referent as 'family' in general and a narrower meaning in the sense of 'immediate family', the latter implying coresidence, shared land, and regular interaction as in a household. On Nukufetau

matakaainga 'eye or center of the family' contrasts with *puikaainga* 'line through the family estate' in that the former is a bilateral concept that does not refer specifically to a property-holding unit as a corporate entity. *Matakaainga* refers to the bilateral complex of kinsmen aggregated as a category of 'own primary kinsmen', including 'own (rather than classificatory) parents' and 'lineal (maternal and paternal) grandparents', so long as all are alive. A still more inclusive concept is *kaukaainga* 'gathered family', which may be used to refer to kin who live in the same village or village section. In some contexts, *kaukaainga* is synonymous with *puikaainga* insofar as all active members of a landholding group are also 'gathered (and organized) kin'. *Kaukaainga* may also include as referents affines who share land formally with primary consanguines of the speaker. The broad concept of *kaainga* as 'bilateral kindred' is, of course, egocentric rather than ancestor-oriented as in the case of *ngafa* 'maximal ramage category' and *puikaainga* in the sense of 'landholding ramage segment'. The overall picture is one of a bilateral network of kin, segregated conceptually in terms of 'strong' and 'weak blood' descent lines, and subdivided into action groups according to shared residence, blood, land, and code for conduct profiles.

10. Cf. Brady 1972:303 concerning actual exchanges among less formal friends.

11. The only case known to me of "incestuous marriage" involving an adoptee is one that was engineered by a powerful and charismatic man who adopted a girl from his wife's family, divorced his wife, and then married the girl without formally negating the previous adoption transaction. This man and his adoptee now have three children of their own. The man's former wife complained bitterly about the marriage on the grounds that it was 'incestuous' and 'unorthodox' and therefore a violation of Ellice ground rules for both adoption and marriage. A variety of interested and disinterested parties have filed complaints with the district government over the years, but no one has actually tried with any degree of enthusiasm to bring the case to court. Few people are willing to risk a public confrontation with this man. Several informants also argued that there is greater tolerance in this case because the 'incest' violation pertains to kinship 'in custom only' as opposed to a relationship grounded by shared 'blood': the adoptee came originally from outside the man's 'kindred'.

12. Ellice kin terminology is Hawaiian-generational. In addition to the special label *fai* 'to make or create', as in *tamana fai* 'adoptive father' (which may also be used pejoratively), the qualifier normally used by adoptees to refer to their adoptive parents, *fakatau*, plus the appropriate core term, is the same as that used to differentiate referentially between 'real' and 'classificatory' kinsmen. An adoptive 'father', for example, is *fakatau tamana*; a classificatory 'father', such as FB, is the same. Thus, the terminology used to refer to adoptive 'parents' does not necessarily change from the original relationship when the adopters are already classificatory 'parents'. Personal names are normally used in direct address.

13. A man who decided to do so in the past allocated land to his stepchildren under the title of *tamana lua* 'second father'.

14. There was some debate among the Lands Courts I surveyed as to whether an adopted child who was named 'manager' in his adopter's will should or could by custom actually remain in that position against the wishes of the adopter's natural heirs. If the deceased manager's estate was held in individual tenure and the adopted children were properly registered, then the claims of adoptees for inheritance and succession were said to take precedence over those of any real siblings of the deceased 'manager'.

15. Ellice Islands regulations prior to 1954 contained a provision for the mandatory registration of adoptions on each island and a fine of 10 shillings for failure to do so. This provision was neither enforced nor, it seems, enforceable. It was ignored by the Lands Courts and the islanders, and many adoptions then and now continue to be negotiated outside the colonial legal system. The fine has been abandoned with new legislation, but customary adoptions still cannot be considered by the courts as legally binding unless they are registered.

16. The proportions may be left up to the landowner, provided that the Lands Court is satisfied that the distribution undertaken does not deprive natural heirs of their rightful share needed for subsistence. The desire to maximize agnatic alignments is more than an effort to be consistent with the descent bias for 'strong blood'. Since men generally inherit more land than women, maximizing agnatic alignments in residence tends to conserve landholdings and undermine estate fragmentation. The net result of these biases for residence and inheritance appears to have increased the number of strictly agnatic alignments in some land hungry communities (see Kennedy 1953: 350; also cf. Keesing 1970:1016; Meggitt 1962).

17. The actual number of court cases over adoption often is exaggerated by local people. For example, only about 8 percent (27/342) of the total Lands Court cases at Funafuti from 1957 to 1971 actually concerned adoption litigation, yet local discourse suggests that the percentage is much higher.

18. But, "At Nui, Gifts of Adoption will revert back to the donor or his issue upon the issueless death of the recipient or his issue irrespective of the number of generations after the gift. However, the land shall revert to not more than two members of the donor's issue to prevent undue fragmentation" (Ellice Islands Lands Code, 1956, Section 7, iv).

19. This pattern was instigated largely by an early administrator in the Ellice, Mr. G. W. B. Smith-Rewse.

20. There are plans on several of the Ellice Islands at present to pass new legislation that would allow the donors to disinherit their children securely adopted into other groups, as in the former system (see Brady 1974).

21. The largest aggregation of adoptees in a single household included five boys and four girls in a household at Funafuti, each of whom had been adopted jointly by the 'manager' and his wife over a period of twenty years. The adopters had no children of their own, and they have more than enough land to accommodate their adoptees.

22. Members of the island council at Nukulaelae stated that there were no 'foster' children on the island in 1968 and 1969. All children who might have been

'fostered' under other circumstances were classified instead as 'adopted children'. All of these informants agreed that it was more 'generous' to adopt rather than to foster a child; they also agreed that land hungry families often preferred to do the reverse. I cannot be sure that there were in fact no foster children on the island during these periods without a comprehensive census, but it is of some interest to note that Nukulaelae has the lowest estimated land hunger in the Ellice (see Brady 1974). Resource abundance may contribute to an actual precedence of formal adoption over simple fosterage, perhaps to the exclusion of the latter.

23. Some adults attempt to maximize the number of "employable" persons they take with them by adopting one or two of their own siblings as 'children'. These persons are then listed as "dependents," and their passage to the place of employment is usually paid. Adopting one's own siblings as 'children' is also done to keep other persons from adopting the younger children in a family of several whose primary jural parents have died. Keeping all of the children on the same estate helps to preserve the unity of the 'sibling set' and thereby to avoid unnecessary estate fragmentation.

24. The main employers at Funafuti are the Colony Wholesale Society, the Ellice Church headquarters, the district government, Air Pacific (formerly Fiji Airways), the local cooperative society, and the New Zealand Meteorological Service which has a weather station on the island.

25. All of the islands in the group have at least one cooperative society and a local cooperative retail outlet. The Funafuti Cooperative accounted for nearly 40 percent of the total sales in the Ellice in 1970–1971.

26. *Mataaniu* literally refers to 'center of the [joint] estate'. When extended metaphorically as a label for a role category, as in the text, it refers to the person in charge of diverting produce from the joint estate for wider social and economic ends.

27. This matter of consent is stated explicitly in the Ellice Islands Lands Code, 1956, Section 7, iv, as being particularly binding at Funafuti.

28. Sending large parties of visitors from one island to another is said to be an 'ancient' custom in the Ellice Islands that remains popular to the present. The purpose, ostensibly, is to extend the domain of friendship, to visit with relatives, and to compete in athletics and dancing. Marital alliances between islands are sometimes formed through these activities, and adoptions are also a common result of a 'good' visit.

8

ADOPTION, ALLIANCE, AND POLITICAL MOBILITY IN SAMOA

Bradd Shore

INTRODUCTION

In choosing the idiom of transaction to discuss adoption, Good-enough (1970:391) has implied the relevance of adoption for the creation of political alliances. Alliance theorists, notably Lévi-Strauss, have stressed the utility of systematic exchange between groups in the creation and maintenance of solidarity. Lévi-Strauss maintains that "Exchange can operate at different levels, among which the most important are food, goods, services and women" (1963:2). Samoan adoption practices suggest that children might well be added to this list.

While ethnographies from many other Polynesian societies emphasize that adoption practices generally occur only between groups considering themselves as biological kin (see, for example, Hooper 1970:58; Ottino 1970:90; Carroll 1970c:124; Lieber 1970:172), such is clearly not the case with Samoan adoption. Both Samoa and aboriginal Hawaii (Howard et al. 1970:27) possess complex and highly stratified political systems characterized by emphasis on alliances between chiefly descent lines and on the maintenance of the blood purity of any one of those lines.

At least two levels of analysis are important for Samoan adoption. Extensive fosterage and adoption within and between kin groups have multiple functions on the domestic level, while explicitly political adoptions create alliances between descent groups and maximize options for political mobility on another, structurally parallel level. Both of these levels will be treated in this chapter as complementary expressions of a single cultural system; however, political adoptions per se will provide the main focus of the study.

If, as Carroll suggests (1970b:15), the comparative study of adoption should provide answers to many crucial questions about the nature of kinship, it is because such a study leads us to examine the special place that adoption has often been accorded as an imitation of "real" kinship. The use of the term 'fictitious' to define the relationship between adopting group and the adoptee underscores this assumption, which has followed from the exclusive use of a genealogical grid in the cross-cultural comparison of kinship systems.[1] Recent studies in Oceania (Silverman 1971; Carroll n.d.) bear out the utility of analyzing the system of "symbols and meanings" (Schneider 1968a:8) by which a particular society defines kinship. Silverman's contention that "In the simplest cases of adoption certain values are obviously fulfilled by culture stepping in where 'nature' fails. . . ." (1970:231) suggests the best reason for abandoning the assumption that genealogical data exhaust the features that may be used to define kinship. To assume, for the sake of facilitating cross-cultural comparison, that societies are limited to the use of biological features in the elaboration of kinship relations is equivalent to denying a significant distinction between nature and culture, and to underestimating the creative and adaptive capacities of human groups (see Schneider 1965b; 1969:116).

This chapter offers a political and cultural analysis of Samoan adoption. My first goal is to provide a basic ethnography of both political and domestic adoption. Second, I examine the notion of adoption in light of Samoan categories defining kin relations to see if adoption in Samoa can be considered profitably as a legitimate variation on or an isolable aspect of kinship itself rather than a mere imitation.[2] Finally, adoption is analyzed within a larger context of alliance-forming transactions that create new or strengthen old kinship ties: both domestic level and political level adoptions are shown to be dimensions of a unified pattern of transactions, fully consistent with the general features of Samoan kinship.

DOMESTIC ADOPTION AND FOSTERAGE

An 'adopted child' in Samoa is a *tama fai* 'made child' or a *tama vavae* 'separated' or 'divided child'.[3] These terms are largely synonymous, but determining their precise referents is problematic. Many informants insisted that no blood relative could be considered as an 'adopted child', while others defined the term more generally to include all children transferred from the household or care of their biological parents to that of someone else, whether the other persons were blood relatives or not. Thus, several women were unsure whether or not to consider their 'true' (that is, biological) grandchildren for whom they were caring as 'adoptees'. Some insisted that the use of the term to refer to their true grandchildren was incorrect, while others insisted that the term was applicable.

For Samoa, therefore, it appears that Goodenough's distinction (1970:404–405) between true adoption and activation of prior jural rights or claims to the child (such as those of a grandparent) is not clearcut, presenting a problem in classification to Samoans themselves. Part of this confusion stems from the ambiguity inherent in the term 'made child'. In the section of this chapter that concerns political adoption, it is argued that a person's status as an 'adopted child' or 'true child' is not necessarily fixed; it may vary according to domestic or political context. For a given individual, the statuses of 'adopted' versus 'true child' are mutually exclusive only in reference to a given situation or occasion.[4]

My informants all distinguished between 'adoption' and 'fosterage'. While there is no explicit native term for fosterage, a 'foster child' is referred to as *tausia* 'cared for' by someone other than a biological parent in a household other than that of his birth. Residence patterns are important insofar as Samoan childcare emphasizes generalized responsibility for raising a child among all senior female siblings. Mead (1928) has discussed at length the pattern whereby older sisters 'mother' their *tei* 'junior siblings'. Because no change of household membership is involved, generalized childcare is not considered by Samoans to constitute fosterage.

Three major reasons are given for fosterage. First is the allocation of workers from a household with many children to one with few or none to help with household chores. Usually, such workers are recruited from among the kindred. A notable exception to this practice involves fosterage by the village pastor who usually has no kin in the village where he preaches. Village children are sent to the home of the pastor to help maintain his household, receiving in return schooling and care from the pastor and his wife. Some of these fostered children are eventually adopted by the pastor, while others return to their own families.

A second major reason given for fosterage is the temporary relocation of school children in a household close to their school. This results in a high degree of fosterage in villages located near district intermediate schools. Similarly, fosterage is frequent in households in the Apia urban area, due to the proximity of secondary schools and places of work. A final reason given for fosterage in Samoa is the ease with which children may change residence for extended periods in order to live with a friend or favorite relative, sometimes as a result of hostility or disagreement within the natal household (see Mead 1928:33). Even though such temporary changes in residence may last a year or more, they still do not constitute fosterage per se.

True adoption is distinguished from fosterage by an explicit acknowledgement of the transfer of primary jural authority over the child (see Brady, chapter 1). Traditionally, this acknowledgement took the form of customary property exchange in which the adopting party presented a gift of fine mats to the family of the child they were to adopt. The return gift in this exchange presumably was the child. Adoptions are rarely validated in this way today. Instead, the exchange is signaled by an explicit request by one of the parties and by the changing of the child's name on his birth certificate. There may also be an exchange of food between the two parties involved in the transaction. Although there are many adopted children today who have not had their birth certificates formally changed, most Samoans consider the legal name change as the validating act.

Samoan naming practices include the bestowal of a personal first name upon a child at birth and the use of the father's personal name or chiefly title as a second name. It is the change in this second name to that of the adoptive father that constitutes a legal change of the adoptee's birth certificate. This practice is not universally followed, however, and the actual choice of last name for the child often depends upon such factors as the relative status of the two fathers' names or titles and the age at which the child is adopted.

The minimal defining feature of an adoption is the explicit acknowledgment by both parties to the transaction of the transfer of primary jural authority over the adoptee. This acknowledgment is often manifest in the form of an adoption request by either the biological parent wishing to give up a child, or by the individual(s) wishing to adopt the child. Acceding to an adoption request is one of the most important manifestations of *alofa* 'sharing' or 'love' among kin and friends, and such a request is therefore hard to refuse.

An adoption is seen as a permanent transfer of jural authority over a child, and adoption is rarely terminated. The permanence of the adoptive relationship contrasts with the fragility of the rights that a biological parent has over possession of his own child. An adopted child is expected to remain with his adoptive family. A child may be taken away from his biological parents by a single adoption request.

Despite the emphasis on the permanence of the transfer of rights in adoption, it is important to stress the positive interpretation that Samoans give to adoption. What is emphasized is not so much the break between parent and child, or child and his natal kingroup, but rather the bond created or strengthened between two groups by virtue of the adoption. Thus, the permanence attributed to an adoption characterizes the new or strengthened alliance as much as it does the transfer of rights over a child.

Domestic adoption refers to transactions based upon local and personal interests within a particular household or minimal kinship unit rather than upon large-scale and long-term political considerations, such as the status of a descent group. Many different strategies are involved in adoption at this level. The following, in order of decreasing importance, are the primary motivations for adoption in Samoa.

A childless couple or woman will often request a child to raise to help maintain the household in later years. These adopted children are generally requested from close kin, usually from a real sibling of husband or wife.

Another type of adoption is that of an illegitimate or abandoned child, normally undertaken by a maternal grandparent. It should be reiterated here, however, that the 'adoptive' status of such a child in relation to a grandparent is anomalous.

Third is the adoption of a child whose real parent is sick, dead, or otherwise unable to properly care for the child. Again, the usual adopter in this case is a maternal grandparent. Often, grandparents will adopt a child at birth. The elderly are said to desire the company of young children, both because of the 'love' they bear for them and because these children will be able to care for them when they are too old to maintain the household themselves. Grandparental adoptions are most common when the elders have their own household within the residential compound.

A fifth form of adoption is the formalization of a long-standing fosterage relationship into one of 'true' adoption. In still another type, children whose biological parents have gone overseas to live are adopted. Such adoptions have become more common due to a recent New Zealand law limiting to four the number of children an immigrating parent or couple can bring. In one such adoption case, a boy's parents emigrated to the United States when the child was eight, leaving him behind with his maternal grandparents to finish his schooling and to look after the grandparents. When he was sixteen, the boy's grandparents died, and he went to live with a first cousin. He spent most of his time, however, with the family of his closest friend and soon decided that he would 'adopt' this family as his own. Although no formal request had been made for the adoption by either the boy's biological parents or the adopting family, he insisted that this new family was truly his 'real' family now. He referred to his friend's father as his own and used the proper kin terms when referring to the other members of the household. In this case, the distinction between adoption and fosterage is unclear, probably as a result of the unusual circumstances surrounding the incident.

A seventh type of adoption is that of a child taken by the pastor of a village. The pastor's paternalistic image within a village is often weakened by the fact that he seldom has local kin. Adopting village children provides one way of validating his role in the village: Having created local kinship ties, he is no longer a 'stranger' to the village, and he can count on kin support should any intravillage difficulties arise. In addition, the pastor gains workers to help maintain his household, and he enhances his reputation for Christian charity. In return, the family donating the child can rely on the economic support and social prestige of the pastor and his wife in time of need, such as during life-crisis celebrations.

Finally, children are adopted as a gesture that symbolizes and promotes solidarity among close friends. As in the adoption of a child by a pastor, this type of adoption exemplifies the *faiga 'aiga* 'creation of kinship ties'. The new alliance may lead to an extended series of reciprocal adoptions over several generations. It is in cases like this that adoption becomes a key mechanism for effecting political alliances. These political adoptions will be examined in more detail below.

The eight types of adoption discussed above are based upon statistical data collected in a census of adoption during my fieldwork in Samoa. The individual adult female was chosen as the basic unit in the census. The vast majority of women interviewed were over the age of 35 and about a third were grandmothers. Of the fifty-four interviewees, forty-eight were from a single large village comprising about 300 dwellings. This village was located about eighteen miles from town on the main road between the airport and the capital of Apia. The area is the most densely populated part of Samoa outside of the urban area itself, and the villages located along this road are rapidly urbanizing. Many of the residents attend school or work in Apia.

The census was designed to elicit information on (a) the total number of children born to each interviewee; (b) foster children residing in the household of the interviewee; (c) true children of the interviewee who had been given away in adoption; and (d) children who had been adopted by the interviewee from other households. Information was also collected on the age and sex of children adopted and fostered, as well as on the motivations for and circumstances surrounding each adoption.

While the focus of this chapter is not on domestic fosterage and adoption per se, several important inferences concerning adoption can be drawn from the statistical data collected. More than two-thirds of all adoptions were undertaken when the child was younger than the age of five. Given the difficulty of pinpointing the exact stage at which a casual visit of a child to a household becomes a case of fosterage, no information was collected on the age at which children were fostered. Yet it is my impression that the average age at which fosterage takes place is considerably higher than that for adoption. Since most foster children enter new households either to attend school or to help with household chores, their ages presumably would be higher than those of many adopted children who are taken at birth or in infancy. Infancy is also an easier time to adopt children than later childhood since emotional ties between children and their biological parents have not had as much time to develop.

Males outnumbered females in both fosterage and adoption events, but the imbalance in sex ratio was considerably higher among adopted children (males 61.2 percent; females 38.8 percent) than among fostered children (males 52.4 percent; females 47.6 percent). No single explanation accounts for these figures. Informants generally stated no sex preference when asked who was favored for adoption nor did they think that either sex was actually favored in adoptions.

Over one-half of the fosterage transactions involved school children, mainly those in intermediate school (ages 11–14). At this age, the number of girls and boys in school is roughly equal in Western Samoa. However, only 9.4 percent of the adoptees in this sample were adopted explicitly to relocate them for schooling. The marked preference for boys over girls in the adoptions might be due to the high value assigned to male labor both in households and on plantations.

Perhaps the most interesting pattern that emerged from the survey is the tendency of Samoans to adopt matrilateral kin. Of all adoptions reported, over 54 percent took place between matrilateral kin and only 27.1 percent between patrilateral kin. Maternal grandparents were responsible for 24.7 percent of the adoptions. This matrilateral bias in adoption statistics is accounted for by the fact that many adoptions involve children of unwed or abandoned mothers who choose to give their children to their own relatives. Among the adoptions by patrilateral kin, it is notable that almost one-half (representing 12.6 percent of *all* adoptions) involved a FZ as adopting parent. This statistic is consistent with the special status accorded to FZ in Samoan society. As in Tonga (see Kaeppler 1971), FZ is accorded the highest *fa'aaloalo* 'respect' in a kin group, and it is the duty of every male and his offspring to honor his sisters and her progeny. The *feagaiga* 'covenant of respect' between sister's and brother's descent lines was often sealed or enhanced by the 'gift' of a brother's child to the sister.[5] Although many of the more formal manifestations of this covenant have largely disappeared in modern Samoa, the adoption of a brother's child remains as a symbol of the brother-sister bond.

ADOPTION AND SAMOAN KINSHIP

In treating American kinship as a cultural system, Schneider (1968) eschews the exclusive use of kin terms or of genealogy and has demonstrated the usefulness of his more eclectic approach. His use of "shared (biogenetic) substance" and "code for conduct" as defining features of American kinship is, in one sense, an analytical truism and in another sense a powerful analytical tool. Insofar as recruitment principles for group membership can be defined by either achievement criteria (what one does; how one behaves) or by ascriptive criteria (what one is; one's substance), various combinations of substance and code for conduct features can describe membership criteria for all societies. Because of its general applicability, Schneider's scheme provides a convenient basis for both an emic description of any one kinship system and an etic comparison of different systems.

As a system, Samoan kinship exhibits a functional ambiguity. The function of this ambiguity appears to be its tendency to maximize options for social and political mobility (see Silverman 1971). Structurally, this ambiguity lies in the intersection of a strong genealogical tradition defining primary ascriptive descent categories with a cultural system of symbols whose interpretation can be manipulated to allow for the definition of kinship ties on a far more flexible basis than genealogy alone.

Ascriptive kinship relations defined by shared substance are classified in Samoa as *toto e tasi* 'one in blood'. Relationships defined only through code for conduct (behavioral features) are achieved rather than ascribed and are referred to as *tino e tasi* 'one in body'. The general description of a kinship relation is *tino e tasi ma toto e tasi* 'one in body and blood' since the genealogical relation is taken to imply appropriate kinship behavior as well.

Ground rules for kin behavior include resource sharing and moral and economic support in times of need as well as generous hospitality for visitors.

Although the conjunction of shared substance and proper kin behavior defines a model kinsman in Samoa, diminished kin relations can be defined by the total lack or weakening of either the code or substance feature. The limiting case of diminished kin relations occurs when either feature is lacking completely.[6] On the one hand are those relatives related genealogically with whom no behavioral relationship has been maintained. In these cases, the norms governing kinship generosity and support have been violated, and the kinsman is defined by shared substance alone. On the other hand, adopted kin define their relationship by stressing kinship behavior. In those cases where adoptive kin trace no blood relationship, the code for conduct appropriate to kin relations is their sole claim to kinship status. Adopted relatives are thus 'one in body' but not 'one in blood' with their adoptive kin groups.

Adopted children often are referred to as children of 'love', where love means not simply an abstract sentiment but also the behavioral manifestations of that sentiment in the form of the child's *tautua* 'service' to the adoptive group and the group's *tausiga* 'care' for the child. 'Service' consists of willing performance of household and plantation chores, while 'care' comprises feeding, general moral support, and economic responsibility for a child's welfare.

Purely adoptive relationships, defined as they are by behavior alone with no genealogical component, are inherently fragile. Their place in the kinship system rests entirely on shared code for conduct, with no reinforcement from shared substance. An ideal kin relation, defined by the conjunction of the features of shared substance and code for conduct, can survive minor breaches of kinship etiquette without serious consequences, since the ascribed status tends to offset the lack of appropriate behavior. In the case of a purely adoptive relationship, however, should either the adopting group or the child cease to demonstrate the expected behavior, the sole basis for the relationship is threatened and considerable tension results.

Informants often suggested that an adopted child would be

given better care by the adopting group than would the natural children of the family. This differential treatment was explained by the desire of the adopting parents to demonstrate to the child's natal family and to the child himself that they were fulfilling their behavioral obligation to the child. Similarly, adopted children are often expected (though tacitly) to be even more faithful in their service to their adopted kin group than natural children. This stress on proper behavior in an adoptive relationship follows from the lack of any other validating criteria for the kin relation. As one informant put it: "My real children can go roaming about and if we leave no food for them, it isn't so important. But for the adopted child, we always leave something, even if he goes roaming about [that is, and doesn't return for the common meal], for he must know of our love for him." Commensality and coresidence, in addition to the expected service to the kingroup, are the behavioral elements most commonly invoked in defining the kinship status of an adopted child. Clearly, adoptive relationships in Samoa are often fraught with anxiety and insecurity because so much stress is placed on continued demonstration of 'love' and thus on validation of the status of kinsman.

The validating criteria of mutual support and generosity for adoptive relationships are usually left implicit, and care is taken by all parties involved to stress their 'giving' roles in the relationship. Adoption is more commonly characterized explicitly by generosity than by expected generosity. Only in cases where normal etiquette has broken down and severe strains have occurred in the relationship will the reciprocal nature of the generosity become an open issue.

It is now possible to understand the permanence that is normatively attributed to adoptive relationships in contrast to the fragility of rights that a biological parent has over possession of his child. These two norms (that an adoption request ought never to be refused and that an adoptive relationship ought never to be terminated) work to offset the opposing tendencies of the biological and adoptive relationships as they operate in real life. Thus, the inherent stability of the biological tie of parent to child, a tie which no adoption can alter, is counterbalanced by the instability of the actual behavioral component of the parent-child relation, which can be severed by a single adoption request. On the other hand, the inherent fragility of purely achieved adoptive relationships is offset by the permanence normatively attributed to adoptions. The tension that might lead to the rapid deterioration of adoptive relations is relieved somewhat by the stabilizing influence of the norm that they are permanent.

All adoptive relations are not "purely adoptive" or behaviorally based. Only those where there is no genealogical link in addition to the adoptive one constitute "pure" adoption; in such cases the kin relation is characterized by code for conduct alone. However, in most 'adoptive' relationships, there is some genealogical link between adoptee and adopting group, and these adoptions represent an intermediate category of kinship. Rather than relying exclusively on behavioral features, adoption results from emphasizing the code for conduct; the genealogical link is not denied but simply held in reserve for recognition at other times and in other situations. Such polysemic relations make possible the situational or contextual definition of kin status, since in different situations either the adoptive or genealogical nature of the relationship can be invoked. This optional kinship status presents alternative kinship 'paths' and becomes extremely important in the case of explicitly political adoptions. The grandmothers in my sample who were unsure whether or not to classify their grandchildren for whom they were caring as 'adopted' were not expressing ignorance of their own cultural system. Their confusion resulted rather from the inappropriateness of the question, which demanded a single absolute status for children who actually had statuses that varied according to social contexts.

Of course, appropriate kin behavior is expected not only from adopted kin but also from blood relatives. To some extent, therefore, all kinship relations are behaviorally based and conditional rather than categorical.[7] This conditional aspect of all kin relationships is reflected by the case of a young man whose mother had emigrated to New Zealand. During the eight years this woman resided in New Zealand, her son had written her repeatedly asking for financial help in getting to New Zealand in order to find work. Yet the mother never replied. In a frustrated final letter, the son admonished her, saying that if she refused to answer he would know that she no longer wanted to be his mother. There was no attempt on the part of the son to deny his blood tie to his mother.

The implication was that since his mother had ceased to act like a mother, her maternal status had diminished considerably.

In another case, a boy insisted that his adoptive family was more his 'real' kin group than was his biological family, who all lived overseas and whom he had not seen in years. Once again, due to the extreme circumstances of the case, the behavioral features of kinship took precedence over the known genealogical facts. The relation between substance and code for conduct features in defining kinsmen, therefore, is complex and neither can be said to take absolute precedence over the other. Rather, both are in a continual state of tension, one being at times stressed over the other for situational advantage. Each actor continually reassesses his priorities according to the demands of social context, maximizing his social mobility and prestige.

In this sense, kinship distance is calculated with genealogical propinquity, the behavioral history of the relationship, and situational context as relevant variables. The maximization of options characteristic of kinship behavior is underscored by the insistence of adoptive parents that their adopted children know and maintain good relations with their natal families. Adopted children are often sent to visit their biological parents, and the alliance between the two groups is strengthened and maintained by continual reciprocity in food and other gifts. The adopted child is considered to have created a *fāiā* 'bridge' between the two groups (if no prior link existed) or to have strengthened an existing bond that may have joined the groups. This 'bridge' enhances the child's *āiā* 'claim' to economic and political rights in either group.

The conditional aspect of all kinship relationships in Samoa and the subordination of relationship to situational context are reflected in pronominal usage in the Samoan language. The pronominal system in Samoan is highly elaborated and includes as obligatory features inclusion/exclusion of the hearer in the first person dual (*ta'ua* [incl.]; *ma'ua* [excl.]) and first person plural pronouns (*tatou* [incl.]; *matou* [excl.]). These obligatory distinctions in pronominal reference indicate situational changes in grouping such that an individual is included as a group member in certain circumstances and excluded from the same membership in other situations.

In relations with my Samoan host family, the possessive form of the first person pronoun was constantly being manipulated, sometimes to indicate my solidarity with the kin group (as in *tatou 'aiga* 'our [incl.] family') when such identification was desirable or useful, and at other times to stress my exclusion from the kinship unit (*matou 'aiga* 'our [excl.] family') in the context of kinship obligations beyond the local group. When a contribution from me was desired for a funeral or wedding the use of the inclusive pronoun made it difficult for me to refuse aid to 'my' own family.

ADOPTION, ALLIANCE, AND POLITICAL MOBILITY

The *'aiga* 'bilateral kindred' is the generic term for Samoan kinship groups.[8] Its referent is far from precise. It may refer to an egocentric personal kindred, a single relative, a situationally relevant descent grouping as it is gathered together for a life-crisis event, or it may refer, by extension, to any familylike solidary group such as a teaching staff, who may be classified as an *'aiga faia'oga* 'family of teachers'. A body of kin tracing common allegiance to a given chiefly title and claiming a common right to assemble to elect a new holder of that title is called an *'aiga potopoto* 'assembling kin'. This term is also often employed in reference to an extended family as opposed to a simple nuclear family unit.

Samoan descent group organization is characterized by what Firth (1957, 1971) has called an 'optative' emphasis. There is, however, a lineal ideology stressing agnates and patrilateral links. The agnatic line is called *toto mālosi* 'strong blood' or *itū mālosi* 'strong side' while matrilateral links are *toto vaivai* 'weak blood' or the *itū vaivai* 'weak side'. Descent traced through the sister of an important titleholder or title-originator qualifies an individual for membership in the *tamafafine* 'sister's descent line' and a position of ritual respect in relation to the *tamatane* 'brother's descent line'. In spite of this agnatic bias in kinship ideology, there is an overriding principle of flexibility that operates in descent reckoning to maximize options for status and political mobility. Descent may be traced cognatically and, at times, through important affinal links to justify a claim to prestige or political power. An individual seeking such power has open to him as many *'auala* 'paths' as he can trace to significant contemporaries or ancestors.

Such paths provide an entree at political gatherings and possible claims to vacant titles. An individual intending to maintain or strengthen a kinship tie will *osi* 'seal the covenant' with an offering of mats, food, or money at a life-crisis event of the group with whom he wishes to maintain the bond. Such attendance at important life-crisis events, however, requires a clear statement of the precise path by which an individual claims the right to attend and thereby to validate and strengthen his kinship status.

In calculating their strongest paths, Samoans give precedence to patrilateral over matrilateral links, to male over female links, to lineal over collateral links, to consanguineal over affinal links, and, finally, to links through high-status individuals over those of lower status. Where criteria contradict each other, individuals must calculate their strongest paths according to the demands of the situation.

The political domain in Samoa may be defined in terms of a complex series of ranked political titles belonging to large political families. These kin groups are actually great alliances linked through ties of descent, marriage, adoption, and military conquest. Chiefly titles are usually said to belong to a descent group. But alliances of several types play an important role in increasing the power and prestige of the higher-ranking titles. The power and prestige of a given title reflect in part the geographical extent over which its authority is recognized. Holders of relatively insignificant titles may be accorded recognition only within a given village and within the minimal residential kin group. More important titles extend the domain of their holder's effective power to political districts comprising numerous villages. Persons holding the most important titles claim the allegiance of large political units comprising allied districts. Four titles are considered paramount "kingly" titles in Western Samoa and one (*Malietoa*) is often said to be acknowledged over all of Western Samoa. Associated with all but the most insignificant titles are tenure rights over parcels of ancestral land.

It would be impossible to rank all titles unambiguously on a single continuum. However, sets of titles related through common membership in a village *fono* 'council of chiefs' or belonging to a common descent group may be ranked. Characteristically, any title ranking is open to dispute. Yet the principles underlying all forms of title-ranking may be outlined as including: (1) relative genealogical seniority of the original holder; (2) the prestige of the title-originator achieved through acts of bravery or through his high-ranking genealogical connections; (3) the prestige associated with a series of previous holders of a title; and (4) military conquest of one local descent group by another and the consequent political ascendency of the victor's title over that of the vanquished.

Titles change in rank over long periods of time as a result of political and military vicissitudes. Changes in rank are reflected in institutions such as the kava ceremony where precedence in seating order or in the order of serving the kava are sensitive indicators of rank and rank changes. The *fa'alupega* 'village greeting' recited as a sign of respect for the village and its political organization by any important visitor is another barometer of rank changes. This traditional address includes a ranked listing of the important chiefs associated with the village, and the particular ranking given changes over time.

Succession to a Samoan title is extremely complex. As with ranking, no single principle of succession sufficiently accounts for what actually happens when a title is vacated by the death or ouster (by a decision of the assembled kin) of a former holder. Often, a title holder is 'elected' to the office of *matai* 'chief' in a series of lengthy meetings of the 'assembling kin'. Intense factional squabbling accompanies most such meetings, particularly when the title concerned is an important one.

A number of alternative mechanisms are important factors in title succession. They include:

1. *'aiga potopoto* 'assembling kin'. The body of kin claiming the right to speak for the title often have the right to choose a successor to fill a vacant title from their own number.[9]

2. *mavaega* 'the will'. The expressed will or dying wish of the incumbent in naming his own successor was formerly a crucial factor in title succession. It is rarely decisive today. Title claims in the Land and Titles Court often refer to the will of a former titleholder in supporting the particular claim, suggesting the residual influence of this mechanism today.

3. *suli moni* 'true heirs'. True heirs to a title (an ambiguous term generally taken to refer to direct descendants of former titleholders) have an important say in who receives the title.

4. *pule ma tūmua* 'body of orators'. For a few of the very highest titles, the right of selection of a successor is traditionally delegated to the body of men holding certain very important *tulafale* 'orator' titles. In these cases, the political 'families' that comprise the 'assembling kin' are too vast and perhaps too faction ridden to make direct election feasible.

5. Special traditional rights to selection were sometimes granted to a particular segment of a descent group, although these claims to privileged status in an election are often disputed by other factions of the 'assembling kin'.

6. Decisions of the Lands and Titles Court have become increasingly important in Western Samoa in shaping the political system.[10] In making claims to the court, hopeful contenders for a title employ as many of the competing criteria for succession as possible. The great number of these competing criteria, as well as the ambiguity inherent in any single criterion, serve to increase the possible options for acquisition of political power and, hence, maximize political mobility.

Informants' statements, records of actual succession disputes in the court, and Marsack's (1958) statement of Lands and Titles Court guidelines provide a basis for delineating the various criteria from which contenders may choose in making claim to titles in Western Samoa. These criteria may be divided into two general groups: those emphasizing achievement and those defining ascriptive bases for title succession.

The first group includes the criterion *agava'a* 'aptitude for and diligence in learning lore'. Titleholders should be well versed in family and village lore and history. They should be able to speak well in assemblies and handle themselves with skill and grace in council, and they should be able and energetic leaders and providers for their constituency. Persons possessing these qualities tend to be favored for entitlement over those without them.

A second criterion emphasizing achievement is suggested by the Samoan saying '*o le ala i le pule o le tautua* 'the path to power is through service'. 'Service', defined somewhat broadly nowadays in Samoa, most commonly refers to the service that a *taule'ale'a* 'untitled man' renders to his chiefs by providing them with daily food and other care. Such service is seen as a test of the loyalty and worthiness of an individual and is essential for an aspiring chief.

This norm can also act as a powerful socializing force by winning the loyalty of the potentially rebellious young men of the society. Acceptance by the untitled men of the authority of the chiefs, and ultimately of the chief system itself, is rewarded through promises of future chiefly power.

The important role that this ideal of service to the chiefs in power has played in Samoa is suggested by the history of the paramount title *Tamasese*. In a recent court case over succession to this title, the following explanation was offered of the title's origin:

> After the death of King I'amafana's only son, Safeofafine, there was a terrific scramble for succession. It was in the midst of the seemingly endless scramble ... for succession, that *Tumua* [the body of orator chiefs given authority of succession to certain kingly titles] called together the political families ... in the hope that exhaustion might inspire the various champions to settle the issue by negotiations.
>
> In those days, a man's breeding was assessed by his diligence and efficiency of the service he rendered (*tautua gasese*). In this, Titimaea repeatedly excelled himself. . . . The political families could not agree [on a successor]. . . .At this critical point in the discussion, the Tumua "took the bull by the horns" and approached the house of the *Aloali'is* [the noble line of descendants from King Galumalemana]. Arriving there, Alipia enquired for Titimaea. The *Aloali'is* replied that he was preparing the food for their house. Alipia then said, "Bring forth the man who serves so well"—*Tama-gasese-mea-lelei*, abbreviated [as] *Tamasese*. He shall be our chief. (Sā Tamasese n.d.)

The humble origin of the first holder of the *Tamasese*, earning his title through exemplary service to the chiefs, is a matter of pride to the heirs of this title. It is notable in this account how the relative clarity of rights to title succession through service contrasts with the ambiguity and squabbling surrounding rights through descent.

While the foregoing set of succession criteria emphasize achievement, the following criteria reflect an alternative emphasis on ascription to political power and provide alternate paths to power through birth.

One ascriptive feature of title succession is sex. While women may and sometimes do hold political titles, political ideology defines chiefly power as a masculine prerogative. Occasional ascendance to political power by a woman is often resented by men, who claim that women as 'the weak side' are stepping out of their proper domain. Despite the norm that men hold political titles, however, it was a woman, Salamasina, who first held the legendary *Tafa'ifa* or kingship over all of Samoa.

Another of the ascriptive criteria governing political succession is primogeniture. The eldest child of a chief, called the *ulu matua*, is accorded special respect within the kin group and is often given special consideration for title succession. Primogeniture, however, cannot be considered the crucial criterion for political succession since other factors are far more important in the actual choice of successors.

Of greater importance than primogeniture is *nofo soso'o* 'direct succession' to titles from father to son. Although there are many examples of indirect succession, Samoan genealogies reveal a strong tendency for titles to pass directly from father to son. Direct succession, then, can be viewed as an optional strategy rule for succession rather than a fixed ground rule.

Despite the statistical importance of direct father-to-son political succession, there is another, conflicting norm for chiefly succession that specifies the right of the remaining brothers of the incumbent to the title, in order of seniority. This 'right of the brothers', called in Samoan *toe'o le uso* is justified on the grounds that generational group should take precedence over descent line and that only when the senior generation has had its chance for political power should the junior generation rule. Given this norm, it is interesting that it has so little effect on the actual disposition of titles. This discrepancy between theory and practice is the result of a combination of factors, not the least of which is the competition among brothers of a titleholder who desire their own titles. Another effective consideration here is the great number of political titles in Western Samoa. A group of brothers may all hold their own titles without impinging on each other's authority. It is reasonable to assume, therefore, that the norm of succession by the remaining brothers has become less and less important in Samoa as the number of available political titles has increased.

The last ascriptive criterion for succession is membership in the *tamatane* 'brother's line'. Claims through descendants of a former titleholder's brother, or of the descendants of that title-holder himself, take precedence over claims through a sister of a former titleholder. The effectiveness of this norm has weakened today, although the right of the 'brother's line' is still recognized as a legitimate succession principle by the Lands and Titles Court.

There is still another set of succession criteria, a set characterized by neither clear achievement nor ascription. For example, it is often stated that a chief should be good-looking, strong, and healthy. It is doubtful, however, that such personal characteristics have ever been of more than secondary importance in determining actual choices of title-successors.

More important is the criterion that a successor ideally should be a member of a high-ranking descent line. A titleholder with distinguished forebears brings added *mamalu* 'dignity' as well as new blood into other descent groups in which he may acquire a title. Considerations of descent status include the number of important connections (whether through actual descent, marriage, or adoption) that an individual brings to the title to enhance its dignity. It is in this sense that 'descent' becomes as much an aspect of achieved status as an ascribed one.

The two classes of ascribed and achieved criteria for title succession have as their bases the substance and code features that define the parameters of Samoan kinship. The parallel between criteria for political succession and those for membership in kin groups is no coincidence. The ideal successor to a political title is the one who has both "proper" genealogical connections as well as a record of faithful service to the chiefs. The conjunction of these two criteria is identical with the conjunction of 'one blood' and 'one body'—that is, the substance and code features that define the model kinsman in Samoa. The political and kinship systems are thus alternative expressions of a unitary cultural pattern. The distinctive features of both of these systems are summarized in table 17.

In the kinship system, it is the adopted child whose status is defined in terms of a code for conduct appropriate to kinsmen in the absence of any shared substance. This code for conduct is manifest in expectations of service to the kin group. In the domain of politics, a claim may also be made for title succession through behavior alone. Here, 'service' refers to any help rendered to the chiefs by anyone. But the term *tautua* also has a more specialized meaning and may be used to refer to an adopted child who makes a claim by virtue of his service to the kin group and the chiefs.

TABLE 17. Distinctive Features of Kin and Political Status

Validating Criteria for a Given Status

| Social Context of Relationship | Disjunctive Sets | | | | Conjunctive Set | |
| | Code for Conduct | | Shared Substance | | Code for Conduct + Substance | |
	Criteria	Status	Criteria	Status	Criteria	Status
'Kinship'	*tautua* 'service' *tausiga* 'care' *alofa* 'love' *tino e tasi* 'one body'	*tamafai* 'adopted child'	*toto e tasi* 'shared blood'	*tama moni* 'real child'	*tino ma toto* 'one body and one blood'	model kinsman
'Politics'	(a) *tautua* 'service' (b) *agava'a* 'diligence' (c) *gafa maualuga* 'high ranking descent'	(a) 'adopted child' (b) 'adopted child' (c) *tama si'i* 'transferred child'	*gafa* 'descent'	*suli moni* 'true heir'	*tautua ma le toto* 'service and blood'	model title-successor

SOURCE: Author's field notes, 1971.

Thus, a person who validates his kinship role through service to the household also validates his political claims through service to the kindred and the chiefs. This is an 'adopted child' status.

A person who validates his kinship status primarily through genealogical links defined by shared blood validates his claim to political power in the same way—that is as a 'true heir'. In the domestic sphere he is a 'real child', as illustrated in table 17. There is thus a tendency for persons of high-ranking descent to emphasize the ascribed criteria of blood in their definition of the proper path to political power, while persons with weak descent links or with no useful genealogical connections at all commonly invoke notions of service as the valid path to political power. Both paths are culturally approved alternative strategies that widen options for political mobility.

ADOPTION AND ALLIANCE: SOME CASE HISTORIES

Adoption as an alliance mechanism that unites previously unrelated groups operates both on the relatively small scale of domestic and local interests and on a larger political and supralocal level. Small-scale domestic adoptions involving persons who trace no biological relationship strengthen affective bonds between friends by transforming a tie of *faigā uo* 'friendship' into one of *faigā 'aiga* 'kinship'. These adoptions are usually recognized only among a limited group of localized or actually coresident kin. An adoptive relative within a household might not be recognized as 'kin' by that group's more distant relatives, unless he were to 'prove' his kin status by his generosity in descent group affairs. Political adoptions, on the other hand, are explicitly undertaken to unite larger groups and enhance their political options.

The following case history of domestic adoption concerns persons in two previously unrelated households who created kin ties between themselves by a carefully balanced series of transactions in children and in personal names. Figure 5 illustrates the extensive series of adoption transactions that took place between these two local family units over three generations. Family A is that of a distinguished village pastor who was a resident 'stranger' in his congregation's village. The family and its name are well-known throughout Samoa for distinguished public and church service.

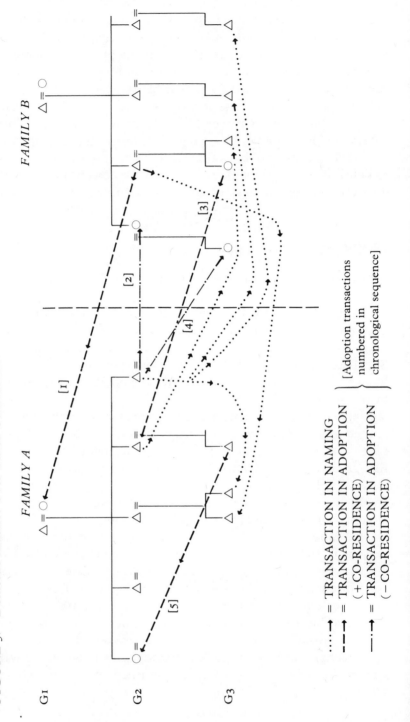

FIGURE 5. Domestic Alliance Over Three Generations.

The members of family B were residents of the village. The media in these transactions included both children and names for children. Naming transactions refer to the bestowing of the personal name of one individual upon another so as to create bonds between the individuals and also between their respective kin groups. A second kind of naming transaction is implicit in adoption itself, since an adopted child normally assumes the name of his adoptive father as his own second name.

The adoption-alliance pattern shown in figure 5 was begun by the senior male in generation 1 of family A, who adopted an elder son of family B (adoption 1) at the request of the latter group. The reciprocal exchange pattern begun by this adoption has continued to the present through three generations between the two sibling groups of the second generation (G2) with personal names and children providing alternative media of exchange. It may be noted that family A has tended to take children from and donate names to family B. This asymmetrical exchange is consistent with the status difference between the two families since both the taking of a child and the donating of one's name imply status superiority. The status superiority of family A to family B is further indicated by the fact that all of the adoptions of family B children into family A included a shift in residence for the child to its adoptive family, and each transaction also included changing the child's second name to that of family A. Conversely, of the two children adopted by family B from family A, neither resided permanently with his new family, and both retained their old (and high-status) family name. In the long run, while members of family B increased their status by their new kinship links with family A, the pastor's family gained strong supportive kinship ties in the village in which they had been resident strangers.

POLITICAL ADOPTION AND ALLIANCE

The preceding section described how an adoption alliance is created through an exchange of people and names. At a higher level of adoption undertaken for explicitly political purposes, the same equivalence between person and name is operative. Here, a political title may replace a person in an adoption to create a political alliance.[11] Thus, two individuals may claim relationship through a title rather than through a common ancestor, but they are 'kin' nonetheless.

Two kinds of genealogical reckoning in Samoa underscore this equivalence between persons and names or titles. In the 'personal descent line', an individual traces his consanguineal relations to others through common ancestors. The focal point in this descent line is an apical ancestor chosen either for his historical prominence or because he provides the link between two individuals wishing to trace common descent. The *auga nofo* 'title-succession line', on the other hand, is the history or 'descent' of a particular title, and it is the title that provides the focus for the path traced. Only to the extent that the principles governing political succession correspond to those of descent will an individual's descent line replicate the title-succession line. The two types of genealogical reckoning do not generally produce identical results.

Table 18 shows the formal equivalence of persons and names as exchange media in kinship transactions. As this table illustrates, a political alliance may be effected either through the transfer of a political title between two previously unrelated groups or through the adoption of the son of a high chief from another descent group.

Chiefly titles are subject to subdivision and, in unusual cases, to alienation from the descent group in which they originated. The most common reason for the alienation of a title is to repay an

TABLE 18.   Transactions in People and Names

| Transaction | Synchronic | | Diachronic |
	Domestic	Political	
In people	*tama fai* 'adopted child'	*tama fai* 'adopted child'	*gafa* 'personal descent line'
		tama si'i 'transferred child'	
In names	*igoa* 'personal name'	*suafa* 'chiefly title'	*'auga nofo* 'line of title succession'

Source: Author's field notes, 1971.

outsider for a service rendered to the descent group. The following case history illustrates this sort of title transfer—that is, one that establishes links of kinship through a title rather than through descent per se.

Figure 6 shows a title-succession line for the title *Tofilau*. The genealogy illustrates two *itū paepae* 'title-divisions'. For the first fifteen generations, the succession continues directly along the main agnatic line reaching the present *Tofilau* titleholder: Matagalu *(Tofilau 1)*.[12] Recently, this title was subdivided and awarded to Eti in generation 15, who traces his descent through Lanuola, sister of *Tofilau* Tanoa'i in generation 2. Traditionally, such descent through a 'sister's line' would have given rights to a veto over a choice of the successor made by the 'brother's line' but not the right to actually succeed to the title. Today, claims by a member of the 'sister's line' are sometimes recognized—often by the clever political maneuvering of succession criteria.

Affinal links to the title in figure 6 are shown in lowercase type and consanguineal links in uppercase type. Actual titleholders are underscored. Generations 1–3 illustrate the evolution of a stable title from a personal name. By generation 4 the title *Tofilau* has been established. Brackets enclose the names of the high chiefs whose daughter was involved in a marriage alliance rather than the name of the girl herself. The names marked with asterisks in generations 9, 12, and 13 are those of daughters through whom descent is traced in the absence of any male siblings. These girls are considered equivalent to 'brother's line' links since there are no brothers.

In addition to the two *Tofilau* titles related through descent links (*Tofilau I* through direct agnatic descent and *Tofilau II* through a sister line), two other title divisions have arisen through adoption alliances. In these cases, the title is said to have another *maota* 'home', but the descent groups involved are considered to have a *fāiā* 'connection' through kinship though not through common 'blood'.

The history of *Tofilau i Poesea (Tofilau III)* is as follows: A high-level political marriage was planned between a girl from Iva and a boy from Leulumoega village. The body of orator chiefs came from Leulumoega to Iva to arrange the wedding and discovered to their dismay that the girl was the daughter not of the high chief Tofilau but of the unimportant chief Tia. This news

FIGURE 6. Succession Line of the *Tofilau* Title.

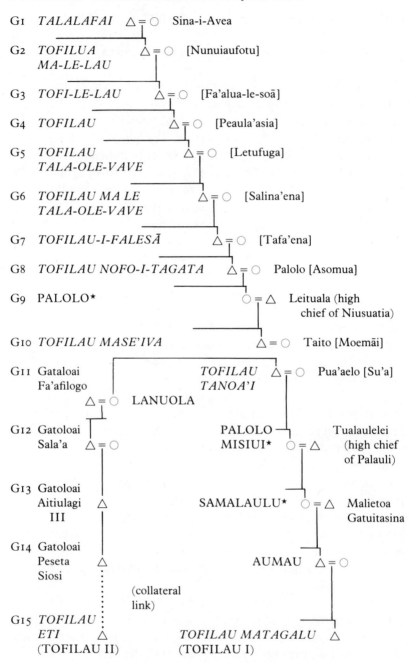

*Daughters through whom descent is traced in the absence of male siblings.

came as a severe blow to the hopes of the orators, who considered that their personal dignity as well as the dignity of the village had suffered. They made their feelings known to the chiefs of Iva village who decided to give a *Tofilau* to Tia so that his daughter would bear the proper status for the wedding alliance. The *Tofilau* title was thus split again, and Tia's descendants still possess it today.

In both of these cases, the alliance mechanism was the transfer of a political title rather than the adoption of a child. In the first case, the title was given in recognition of services rendered. Thus the kinship tie was achieved through 'service' just as the status of an adopted child is validated. In the second instance, the title was given to justify a political alliance through marriage, suggesting a structural parallel between alliance mechanisms through marriage and those through adoption or title transfer. In other words, women, children, and names (titles) are interchangeable media in Samoan kinship transactions.

Title-splitting would seem to be an effective mechanism for creating political alliances without losing either women, children, or titles. The problem is, however, that subdivision dilutes the prestige attached to particular titles. None of the four paramount titles in Western Samoa has ever been split in this way.

TAMA SI'I: ALLIANCE TRANSACTIONS IN CHILDREN

The *tama si'i* 'transferred child' is the most elaborate form of Samoan adoption; its role in Samoan political history has been significant. This form of adoption complements marriage insofar as it expands important kinship links. According to one informant, there are two distinct classes of 'transferred children': those adopted into a descent line to which they already have genealogical links and those with no prior kinship ties with the adopting group. The second form is especially important because it adds new (and presumably prestigious) 'blood' to the adopting group's descent line. There are many examples of this latter kind of adoption in Samoan history. The following case history, presented here in the form of a verbatim account by an informant, is typical:

> Leātaua Lesāfinaumaleata was the high chief of [the Island of] Manono. His wife comes from Faga [on the Island of] Savaii; her

name was Tofoaipupu'u. Her father was Fuaifagalilo who was the
brother of Toleafoa. The canoe fleet went over to take this lady to her
village in Faga, since there was a custom that the first child had to
be born in the lady's family. This fleet took her over to have her
family. That could have been done on purpose, since the high chief
Namulaulu of Fagapoa had no son. Fagapoa was a village lying on
the way to Faga. The chief Namulaulu of Fagapoa saw that she
would have the baby on the way and told this lady to go on the beach,
where she had the child. This baby was called Ietuma. . . . This chief,
Namulaulu, told his people to bring this child over to his house—
because this is the son of the high chief [that is, the chief of all
Manono]. This is the *matua o pule* ['highest authority']. So they
took the child over to him and he said, "this is my son," and he took
the [signs of sacred authority], put them over the infant and said,
"now you are going to be the *pule* ['authority'] over this village, the
people, the lands, and all." So then this couple to whom the baby
belonged asked if they could raise the baby for a few years and then
bring him back; and so when the child was 5 years old—and all
during those 5 years Namulaulu kept going over to Manono and
brought over some fine mats—that is the proper way of adopting a
child—a high way. No papers, but a gift of fine mats. This high
chief who wanted the son of the chief of Manono took the fine mats
over as a dignified way of making this adoption. . . .This child,
Namulaulu Ietuma now, is the *pule* ['authority'] over this village.

The essence of this high-level adoption is illustrated in figure
7. The motive for this adoption is advantage gained by Namulaulu
as a result of the high rank of the child, whose father was virtually
"king" of Manono Island. Not only does Namulaulu add this high
'blood' to his own line, but he has created a link between the
descent groups of the child and his own group, a connection which
gives him potential *āiā* 'claims' to political and economic power on
the island of Manono.

Requests such as this for adoption of a child by a high chief
are considered flattering and difficult to refuse. Where high rank
of a child's forebears is the motive for an adoption request, it is
common for political power to remain in the hands of the descendants of the 'transferred child'. Where an adopted son gains a
title only through his personal merit or service, it is common for a
title to pass back to the heirs of its original holder after the adoptive
holder dies or otherwise loses the title. Thus, the fragility and

FIGURE 7.   *Tama Si'i* 'Transferred Child'.

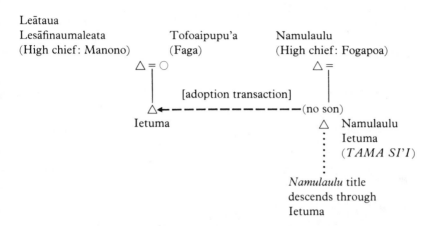

Leātaua
Lesāfinaumaleata   Tofoaipupu'a   Namulaulu
(High chief: Manono)   (Faga)   (High chief: Fogapoa)

instability of the behaviorally defined claims on a title are in marked contrast to the enduring power of the residual rights of the blood line.

The second example of 'transferred child' adoption occurs where there are residual claims to a title through descent that are ignored in favor of a claim through a high-level adoption alliance. The most famous instance of this sort of adoption in Samoa involves the *Tupua* title of the descent line of Tamasese, one of the paramount chiefs.

Figure 8 is a genealogy of the Tamasese line, derived from data found in Krämer (1902). From generations 1 to 6, succession in line A is by 'direct descent'. At this point in Samoan history, it might be noted, there were no political 'titles' as such, only the personal names of powerful chiefs. The point at which a personal name stabilizes into a title is difficult to specify because of the common practice of passing a personal name from father to son (see, for example, line B, generations 2–3). In generation 6, chief Muagututi'a of line A married twice. His first marriage was to a lowborn woman and produced the heir Fepulea'i. He then remarried, this time to the daughter of a high chief, hoping to produce an heir with strong patrilateral and matrilateral ties. Fenunuivao proved barren, however, and rather than allow the power to pass to Fepulea'i, Muagututi'a 'brought over' Fuiāvailili from line B and

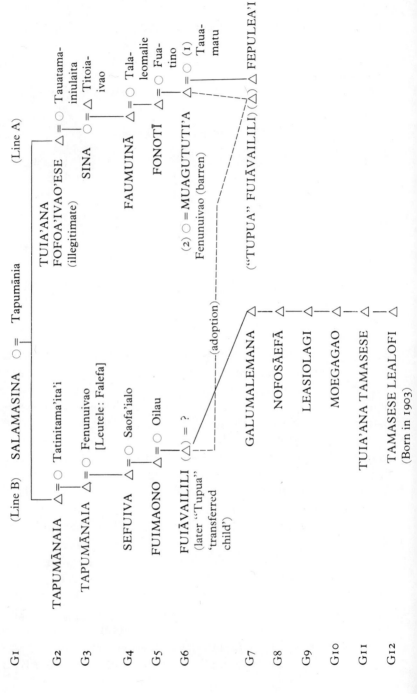

FIGURE 8. 'Transferred Child': The Origin of The Tupua Title: A High Level Adoption.

adopted him as a 'transferred child', thus giving him power and creating the special honorific *Tupua* for him. The chieftaincy then passed to this adopted son's descendants, where it rests today in the modern paramount title *Tamasese*.

While most Samoans with any knowledge of traditional political history consider Fuiāvailili as the prototypical 'transferred child', the son of the last *Tamasese* insisted that his claim to power was not in fact as an adopted son, but rather through direct descent. He explained that the status of 'transferred child' applied to him and his line only in reference to Muagututi'a. However, in relation to Salamasina, the founding ancestress of both lines A and B, he is a direct descendant and thus a 'true heir' rather than a 'transferred child'. Furthermore, he insisted that his claim to descent took precedence over that of Fepulea'i, since his line (B) descends through a legitimate offspring of Salamasina (Tapumānaia) and contains only agnatic links, whereas line A traces its descent from Salamasina through her illegitimate son Fofoa'ivao'ese (literally 'bred in the bush') and through a female link (Sina).

Here, then, is one example of how a person may manipulate the various criteria for succession and descent so as to place himself in the most advantageous position for pursuing a claim to power. My informant in this instance clearly had a choice of 'paths' that he could invoke in defining his kinship and political status. Only one path may be used on any single occasion, but the alternative 'paths' do not simply disappear. They assume a residual status, with the potential for being activated according to the situation at hand.

There are many occasions when a claim through a 'transferred child' link would supersede one through direct descent. Many informants insisted that the claim of a 'transferred child' would always outrank that of a 'true heir' since the adopted child in this instance performs the valuable 'service' of bringing his prestigious blood to the title line and to the group that the title represents.

SUMMARY AND CONCLUSIONS

The object of this chapter has been to expand Goodenough's (1970b) notion of adoption as "transactions in parenthood" and to develop a framework for the analysis of adoption as part of a system of alliance-forming prestations. In a polity such as that of Samoa—characterized by political and social mobility and a strong emphasis on validating political status through ascriptive, genealogical links—adoption becomes a powerful mechanism for transforming an achieved alliance into secondary 'descent' status. The parallel between adoption and marriage alliance is clear: both transform alliance into descent.

The analysis suggests that adoption can be viewed less profitably as a class of "fictive" kinship relations than as one among several alternative sets of behavioral criteria for defining 'kinsmen'. Similarly, the data suggest that alternative sets of criteria for legitimate political succession are identical with those defining the parameters of kinship relations and that the same ambiguities and analytical problems characterize both domains.

Mary Douglas (1966) suggests that pollution and danger beliefs protect structure from anti-structure at those points of greatest ambiguity in cultural classification.[13] If pollution or potential cognitive chaos lies in ambiguous classification, what must we conclude about societies like Samoa, where a high degree of structural ambiguity keeps options open for mobility? I have suggested that the ambiguity of the Samoan system is problematical only if we approach concepts such as *status* as fixed, structural points of absolute orientation for individual actors.

If our model for kinship classification includes not only a set of possible statuses and individuals, but also a set of situational variables, then it is possible to make some sense out of the "sliding scale" system of overlapping statuses found in Samoa (cf. Goodenough 1965) without being forced to view the entire social system as "polluting" or cognitively "dangerous" in Douglas' sense.

Carroll's assertion (1970b) that, properly studied, adoption can provide many important insights into the nature of kinship has proven accurate. An understanding of adoption practices in Samoa has necessitated a more general analysis of the nature of Samoan kinship. One of the more significant issues in kinship theory has been the debate between descent and alliance theorists. Alliance and descent have been viewed as competing general theories of kinship and social organization, as complementary perspectives relevant for all kinship systems, and as processes that characterize the social organization of different sorts of societies (see Leach 1961:16).

The nature of Samoan adoption can be delineated from the perspective of both alliance and descent theory. It has been demonstrated that alliance and descent exist in Samoa as complementary cultural strategies for maximizing political mobility. The adoption of an outsider into a kin group as a 'transferred child' transforms simple alliance into the idiom of descent since the title line passes to the adopted child and usually to his heirs. Descent in this case is derived from adoption as an alliance mechanism that is parallel to that of a marriage alliance: both will produce heirs.

However, in the case of a 'transferred child' adoption involving a child already linked genealogically to the adoptive kin group, descent and alliance must be viewed as logically alternative rather than as sequential statuses. Here, descent and alliance exist simultaneously as culturally approved, alternative strategies. Either descent or alliance (but not both) can be invoked by this kind of transaction on any occasion to justify the adoptee's right to political power. The more paths to power an individual has, the greater is his potential sociopolitical mobility. Samoan kinship permits and even encourages such mobility by allowing descent and alliance to operate as concurrent strategies. Moreover, in 'transferred child' transactions, either strategy may refer to the same relationship. The 'transferred child' may be a relative both by adoption and by descent. Incestuous marriage would produce a comparable ambiguity (Shore 1971).

Blood in Samoa is seen as shared substance in two ways. It is either a medium of descent, shared vertically between parents and progeny, or a medium of exchange horizontally, as in marriage or adoption. The blood of a 'transferred child' may be both a medium of exchange and of descent, providing the Samoans with a culturally approved alternative to incestuous union.

Transferring political power vertically through descent links alone preserves the integrity of the descent line at the expense of horizontal alliance relations. Emphasis on adoption and marital ties strengthens horizontal political relations at the expense of the integrity of the blood line (unless incestuous marriage is permitted). Adoption of a child already related by blood solves both problems at once—much as incest would, creating as it does a political alliance where a prior bond of descent exists. As an alliance mechanism that promotes integration both between and within kin groups, adoption occupies a structural status similar to marriage. Viewed from this perspective, it is possible to see the utility of adding children, and possibly also their names, to the list of goods, services, women, and messages that constitute media of exchange in Lévi-Strauss' (1967b:60) total communication system.

NOTES

The fieldwork upon which this chapter is based was conducted from June to September 1971 on Upolu, Western Samoa. The research was partially supported by grants from the National Science Foundation and the National Institute of Mental Health. Their support is gratefully acknowledged. The main burden of my task was shouldered by my many informants, whose cooperation and eagerness to share what they knew made my job far more exciting and fruitful than it would otherwise have been.

Special thanks must go to Pesetā Siō, Uelese Petaia, and the Honorable Tupuola Efi for the many hours of stimulating conversation they provided and for the trust they demonstrated by freely providing important personal histories.

This chapter has also benefited from extensive and helpful comments on an earlier draft by Felix Wendt, Ivan Brady, and Shepard Forman. I am grateful for their assistance. While I alone must bear the responsibility for what I have done with his ideas, my intellectual debt to Professor David Schneider is evident throughout the chapter.

1. See also Firth (1971:65) where he refers to adoption as "quasi-kinship—the simulation of kinship."
2. On the notion of 'permitted ambiguity' in membership criteria for Polynesian descent groups see Firth (1971:75).
3. The reciprocal forms of *tama fai* are *tinā fai* 'foster mother' or 'adoptive mother' and *tamā fai* 'foster father' or 'adoptive father'. The morpheme *fai* 'make' or 'do' may be appended to any kin term to indicate adoptive status, although such usage is rare.
4. For an interesting theoretical discussion of the relationship between status and social context see Goodenough (1965). An attempt to apply this contextual approach to status is found in Kaeppler (1971).
5. Basing his information on Turner (1884), Mauss suggests that Samoa is an example of a society where "[bilateral] cross-cousin marriage is the rule. . . ." (1967:7); that a man gives his son to be raised by his own sister; and, finally that the sister's husband is also the boy's maternal uncle and his future father-in-law. This suggestion is patently wrong since the primary definition of incest in Samoa involves sexual relations between cross-cousins and the treatment of a girl residing in one's household as a sexual object instead of as a 'sister' (see Shore 1971). A claim that a boy is raised by his FZ, however, would make sense as an alternative to cross-cousin marriage in binding the sister's line with her brother's.

6. Cf. Schneider 1968a:28 for a similar analysis of American kinsmen in terms of the distinctive features 'nature' and 'law'.

7. Levy (1970:84) suggests that the 'psychological message' implicit in Polynesian adoption is that "relationships between all parents and children are fragile and conditional," a notion fully supported by the Samoan data.

8. For more detailed accounts of Samoan social organization see Gilson (1963, 1970:chapters 1 and 2), Mead (1930), and Freeman (1964).

9. Traditionally, the 'assembling kin' comprised both the 'brother's line' and the 'sister's line', the former group having rights to election and succession, the latter group maintaining a veto over the selection. This distinction has lost some of its force today.

10. Since 1902, disputes over title succession have been adjudicated in the Lands and Titles Court, presided over by a chief justice, three Samoan justices, and a panel of five "assessors." These nine men examine competing claims for title and land tenure and pass final judgment on the disposal of the titles and land. A definitive history of the effect of this court system on the structure of Samoan politics has yet to be undertaken, but it seems clear that the court has had the following general effects on the political system:

   a. Traditionally private and carefully guarded genealogies have been subject to public recitation and rigidification through being recorded as written claims and careful scrutiny by neutral authorities;

   b. There has been some limitation placed on the flexibility of traditional criteria for succession by the court's demand for a clearly written statement of each claim and by court decisions that have set precedents for favoring some criteria over others;

   c. The traditional autonomy of descent groups in settling their own internal political differences has been restricted by the creation of a fully 'national' court system;

   d. The wars that often accompanied succession disputes have been nearly eliminated, since hostilities have been restricted to oratorical contests on the courtroom floor. For a detailed discussion of the Lands and Titles Court in Western Samoa see Marsack (1958).

11. The commonly used word *igoa* 'name' becomes in chiefly speech *suafa*, which also means 'title'.

12. Although he traces his title claim through a female link, Matagalu's position is still orthodox since this female connection, lacking any male siblings, is still considered 'brother's line'. This situation is in contrast to that of Eti (*Tofilau II*) whose claim is through a sister to a former titleholder and therefore counts as a 'sister's line' claim.

13. For an earlier statement of an essentially identical view see Leach (1964).

9

ADOPTION AND PARENTHOOD ON YAP

John T. Kirkpatrick
Charles R. Broder

INTRODUCTION

This chapter presents data on Yapese adoption beliefs and practices, placed in the contexts of Yapese symbols of identity and relationship and of the range of variation in parent-child relationships found on Yap. These contexts are employed to account for certain features of Yapese adoption and to simplify comparison of adoption on Yap with transactions in other Oceanic systems of relationships.

Carroll (1970c), Levy (1970), and Goodenough (1970b) all have isolated important aspects of adoption for study. Carroll treats Nukuoro adoption as an information system that encodes messages about kinship solidarity and the interdependence of kinsmen. Working in a similar vein, Levy stresses that kin relationships may be conditional and that they may require continuous maintenance. Such relationships may lapse if they are not enacted regularly or they may be contingent on other relationships for their quality and existence. Where many relationships are conditional, the creation and rupture of bonds in adoption need not be viewed as exceptional by the observer. Goodenough urges the study of adoption as a transaction in the rights and duties of parenthood. He views change in a child's relationships by adoption as a transaction to be located within a continuum of types of transaction permissible or proper in a society.

Our examination of Yapese adoption is primarily concerned with underlying cultural premises and the conditionality of relationships. We present short case studies and examples of some prevalent types of transaction and negotiation in relationships. These data can be used to discover what might be gained from an ethnography of the range of transactions in the rights and duties of parenthood on Yap.

ETHNOGRAPHIC BACKGROUND

The population of Yap has varied from a maximum estimated at about 40,000 for the early 1800s (Schneider 1955; Mahoney 1958) to a minimum in 1946 of 2,582 (Hunt, Kidder, and Schneider 1954). The June 1972 population was 4,790 (Office of the District Administrator 1972).

Yap is divided into some 120 villages, of which about a tenth are now uninhabited. The modal population per village is about forty persons. Whether or not a village is populated today, the land surrounding it is owned and often worked.

In the traditional Yapese political system, villages were ranked. Villages of different ranks were linked into networks in which the higher-ranking villages received tribute and ordered their subordinates to participate in activities involving many villages, especially warfare. Intervillage contact was infrequent and tense, being largely limited to activities established by relations of dominance and dependence (Schneider 1962:17–18).

Yapese mingle today in the town of Colonia, and many traditional political duties go unperformed. But Yapese still orient much of their interaction in terms of traditional ranking and alliance patterns. People are known by their village of origin, even though they may never visit it. There are, consequently, 'people of Rumung' municipality who are never to be seen there while there are no 'people of Colonia' even though nearly one-half the population of Yap lives in the town and its environs.

Within the village, plots of land are ordered into *tabinaw* 'estates'. The resources of the estate include taro patches, fishing grounds, house sites, political offices, and personal names. A person's membership in an estate is gained with naming. Elders of the estate confer these names and can take them back. Membership rights are maintained so long as a person bears a name given by the elders of the estate. At marriage, women are said to be members of their husbands' estates, but they do not lose membership in their natal group. A woman is active in her natal estate and is 'over' her brother's wife and children. Her authority becomes stronger after her brother's death, and she has rights over his heirs, whether or not they are genealogically related to her.

A senior male usually speaks for the people of his estate in village affairs and makes decisions as to allocation of the resources of the estate. Should other members of the estate inherit land, the senior male takes responsibility over their land. Vigorous men may be suspected of trying to take full control of land inherited by others in their estate. When land is inherited by siblings, their lands may be said to form one estate or two, depending on the context. Leadership should pass to the eldest male, but this depends on the personalities involved: a leader has a right to ignore his brother and to give his lands and authority in the estate to his son or anyone else he might choose.[1]

The rights and duties of a leader and other elders of the estate are spelled out in detail only with regard to a few contexts, such as village councils and situations in which disgrace threatens the estate. Many estate matters are discussed by all the people with seniority in the group. Relationships among these elders vary, of course, in different estates. It may be clear in one case that a certain man alone made a decision, while, in another group, decisions are reached through a complex set of compromises among elders.

Yapese live in conjugal family households. Young men live apart from their families to avoid sleeping in the same house with their sisters, although such young men do eat their meals at the family house. Traditionally, Yapese were ranked into eating grades, so that each male of an estate had a rank and did not eat with males of other ranks. Few follow the eating rules today, but the stress placed on seniority through these rules remains important in village and estate affairs.[2]

FREQUENCY OF ADOPTION

Early reports (Müller 1918; Furness 1910) stress that adoption is prevalent on Yap but provide no numerical data. Studies done in

1947 and 1972 are more helpful. They differ in an important respect: in the 1947 census, persons were listed as *pof* 'adopted' or not (Hunt, Kidder, and Schneider 1954). In our 1972 fieldwork, we asked a more open-ended question: "Were you born or adopted or what to this estate?" In the two villages studied, few cases could not be subsumed under the rubrics of 'birth' and 'adoption' in 1972. At an earlier date or in other villages, this might not be the case. Hence the 1947 and 1972 figures are not strictly comparable, and we can only draw tentative conclusions from them.

The 1947 census showed 16.5 percent of the Yapese population to have been adopted. If "not known" responses in this census are excluded, we find an adoption rate of 24.3 percent in a sample of 2,011 persons. This figure includes those whose adopters had died but presumably not those whose adopters had rejected them in the long run. The 1947 data show no preference for either sex among adoptees. Adoption appears to be more frequent among higher-ranking people, but this may be because more complete returns were gathered in high-ranking villages. Table 19 indicates the distribution of adoption in 1947 by age of adoptee.

A survey of people in two villages on Rumung Island in 1972 shows an adoption rate of 15.4 percent in a sample of seventy-eight people (table 20). Only 11.3 percent of those under age thirty are adopted. The change in the adoption rate varies inversely with the population increase, although the sample used in our adoption survey is too small to attempt exact correlation.[3]

THE SYMBOLIC ORDER

Labby (1971, 1972) has shown that traditional Yapese understandings of identity and relationship form a system of knowledge geared for survival on Yap. In this section we draw selectively from his work.

Yapese ideology stresses the interdependence of land and people for social continuity. The land would be neglected and valueless without people to maintain it; people would starve without the land to support them. The land is organized into estates and the people into matrilineal clans. Survival is assured, in this theory, by the clans' moving to new estates in each generation.

At marriage, a woman gains access to new resources for the people of her clan. She works to earn the land for her children:

TABLE 19.   Adoption Frequencies by Age of Adoptees, 1947

Age	Adopted No.	Adopted Percent	Not Adopted No.	Not Adopted Percent	Not Known No.	Not Known Percent	Total No.	Total Percent
0–29	201	15.4	946	72.6	155	11.9	1302	100.0
30–49	130	18.7	454	65.2	112	16.1	696	100.0
50–69	87	16.2	322	63.7	96	19.0	505	100.0
70+	14	17.7	52	65.8	13	16.5	79	100.0
Age not Known	0		3	9.4	29	90.6	32	100.0

SOURCE: Adapted from the 1947 census data in Hunt, Kidder, and Schneider (1954).

TABLE 20.   Number of Adoptions in Two Rumung Island Villages

Age	Adopted Male	Adopted Female	Not Adopted Male	Not Adopted Female	Total
0–14	1	4	20	16	41
15–29	1	0	6	5	12
30–49	4	0	8	1	13
50–69	1	1	2	4	8
70+	0	0	2	2	4

SOURCE: Authors' survey, 1972.

she must match with her work the value of the land. This value comes from previous work. A man passes land to his children in recognition of their labor and that of his wife. The children profit by their mother's labor since they are of 'the same blood' as her. Clan identity always has connotations of sharing on Yap: within an estate it implies that a woman's children all have claims to land she has earned.

Authority results from work that has not been matched. When land is transferred, work has been done for the previous land-holder, but his sister's share of the labor done to gain the land has not been met. As a result, she and her children have an important voice in the estate. Over two or three generations, their involvement diminishes as their work is matched with gifts and obedience.

These *m'fen* 'trustees' should see that the current landholder maintains or increases the value of the land. The sister of an immediately previous landholder and her children—the trustees closest to the current landholder—may exile people from the land for failure to respect them or the dead landholder.

Such understandings of the relation of land and people through work have consequences which are important in the study of parent-child relationships. Most relationships are symbolized with reference to work and land, and these terms form a foundation for additional symbolizations of particular relationships.

Parenthood is understood as a combination of work on the land and a long-term exchange between parents and children. A father holds land or is closer to the landholder than are his children and will pass it on in recognition of labor. A mother is of the same clan as her children and has made a place for them on her husband's lands. Parents and children engage in a long-term balanced exchange—the parents working to support their infants and the children caring for the parents in old age. This exchange distinguishes parenthood from other relational categories. While people aid grandparents and grandchildren, the exchange of care is spoken of as a feature of parent-child relations. This feature alone is not sufficient to define parenthood, if only because care for anyone in need is enjoined on all Yapese. Rather, it is the combination of estate, clan, and exchange ties that defines parenthood within the ideology.

The definition of parenthood in terms of the exchange of work, estate, and clan ties is congruent with the rules informants offer for the use of kin terms on the death or divorce of parents. On a man's death, his brother alone is *citamangin*, 'father' to his children; on a woman's death, no one becomes *citiningin* 'mother'. Ideally, the father's wife, if anyone, becomes 'mother' in the event of divorce while the father remains 'father'. Frequently, in a case of divorce (which ignores clan ties), the rule for the 'mother' is ignored (Schneider 1953).

A person's social identity[4] is defined in terms of clan membership and progress through relations on the estate. While Yapese may speak of a clan's gaining a higher place in society through marriages or political action, clan membership has little to do with the perceived social worth of a person. Clan membership is secret, while a person's estate affiliations are well known. An estate has rank in the village, and a person takes his rank from his estate and his position within it. Work transforms a person's social identity from child to elder and eventually to estate ghost. A person's initial tie to the estate—through his name or, for women, marriage—is fragile, since names may be taken away by authorities of the estate and marriages often break up. Social identity develops as a person becomes a parent, leader, or 'trustee'. A man who lives on his own land is an adult in his village while one who is much older but who is under a landholder in his estate may still be considered an irresponsible young man.

Political offices and seniority in the eating grades may be gained only through succession to authority in particular estates. Only cumulative work for an estate assures prominence in traditional Yapese society. Estate rank and personal worth are seen as interdependent. Moreover, such characteristics as generosity or slyness may be broadly ascribed to the people of particular estates.

This ideology provides terms in which relationships between people living on different lands may be understood. It allows for a complex system of political offices. The thrust of the ideology, however, is not on these relationships but on the estate as a discrete unit of land and people. The only relations between persons or land units, including villages, that are stressed are hierarchical ones in which authority is explained as deriving from past work. The message of the ideology for an individual is clear: hierarchical relations on the land endure while relations between people of different estates do not. The estate endures partly because work there is done under the authority of elders whose position derives from past work. Clansmen may be called on for aid and friends may be found outside the estate, but ties to these people are, in the end, supplementary to estate ties in assuring a person's identity and survival.

The interdependence of clan and land implies a person's dependence on the elders of the estate. It also implies that the elders' first and last duty is to 'keep the estate together' so that the value of the land and the survival of the people on it are assured.

UNDERSTANDING OF BIRTH AND ADOPTION

Yapese ideology delineates the way in which a person rises to authority, but it says little about becoming a child in an estate.

Birth into an estate is not taken as a precondition for membership; rather people say that a child 'is formed on the estate', stressing residence and activity over recruitment.

There is general agreement about adoption procedures and expectations of adoption outcomes. Since these understandings are widely shared, while there is general uncertainty concerning other modes of recruitment, it is clear that they form a cultural model. In this section, we compare the model of adoption with the traditional explanation of conception. An examination of the distinctions made between natural and adopted children leads us to the conclusion that the contrast between birth and adoption simply is not highly significant for Yapese understandings of relationship. Birth and adoption differ, but the difference does not make one an imitation of the other.

Schneider's (1968b) informants denied coitus any causal role in conception. They said that a woman became pregnant when the ghosts of her marital estate decided that she was worthy of having a child. Promiscuous women were rightly infertile while hard-working women had many children. To clinch the argument, they cited the case of a woman so ugly that no man would think of approaching her. Being a good woman, she had two children. The ghosts of the natal estate granted offspring in her case.

Labby's informants stressed that the roles of husband and wife are complementary: a man works his wife's reproductive 'garden' just as she works his food-producing land (1972: 54–55). Both a woman's work—in bearing a child and making a place for it on her husband's land—and a man's work are bases for relationship to the child.[5]

The ghosts of the estate delegate a spirit to form the child in the womb. Should the parents break certain prohibitions during pregnancy, the ghosts will make sure that the child is stillborn or deformed. The parents present a stone valuable as a prayer to the ghosts. Traditionally, the mother and child went to the village menstrual area immediately after birth and stayed there about five days. Ideally, their return to the estate followed or coincided with the naming of the child (Furness 1910: 154; Mangefel, in Defngin 1958).

Yapese explain that 'adoption' is arranged before the birth of the child. The would-be adopter or adopters—any adult or married couple can 'adopt'—get permission to 'adopt' from the elders of their estate and seek out a woman who has children. They ask for her next child and present a stone valuable to the ghosts of her marital estate. They may request a boy or a girl. While the woman is pregnant, they provide food and, nowadays, pay her medical expenses. After the birth, more gifts go to the natal mother and child. The child goes to live with its adopters at weaning or, should they be too old to care for an infant, the child will move later. If the child is not of the sex desired, they may take the child anyway or wait for the woman's next child.

An adopted child is named by the elders of the adoptive estate. The child takes the clan affiliation of both natural and adoptive mothers. An adopted girl transmits only the affiliation of her adoptive mother to her children.

In terms of the ideology described above, the relation of parent and child is the same for children born or adopted into an estate. In both cases a claim of relationship is established with a gift to ghosts and the child's name comes from the parents' estate.[6] However, in seeing birth and 'adoption' as equivalent, we ignore the relation to the natal estate of the adopted child and the adopters. This limited view of the situation is the one implicit in the message of the ideology that systematically devalues ties between people not connected by clan identity or shared claims in land. Similarly, Yapese explanations of the term for 'adoption' emphasize separation between adoptive and natal groups. We heard three folk etymologies:

1. 'To slowly take a leaf or branch from a tree. To adopt a child you patiently separate it from others and make it your own through good discussion'.

2. 'To change from warm all the way to cold: the child begins as one thing and ends as another'.

3. 'To relieve another of a burden: so people with too many children do not have to take care of a child adopted from them'.[7]

It is not an easy matter to break ties, even purely symbolic ones. When an adopted child is named, the work done to produce it is recognized as contributing to the continuity of the adopters' estate. Hence the natural parents work for the adoptive estate, and a few Yapese even say that natural parents are 'of the same estate' or 'of the same land' as the adopters. Such a situation is anomalous in terms of the theory, and Yapese stress that the natural parents' claim on the adoptive estate must be extinguished. The adopters accordingly are expected to make gifts to the natural parents but should do so secretly so that the child will not know of any relationship with its natural parents.

The ideology and the model of 'adoption' are similarly phrased. Despite this similarity, they cannot be in agreement in every detail, since the model of 'adoption' deals with a situation that is disregarded in the ideology, and this omission is hardly accidental. The ideology, in presenting estates as discrete and authority in estates as following from work, presupposes that estates are self-sufficient in production and reproduction, that authority is distributed in a simple hierarchy, that all the lands of the estate are held by the leader, and so on. 'Adoption' is one of a number of situations in which such presuppositions are wrong, and the use of the ideology's terms in this context could lead to contradiction of its message.

The model of 'adoption' is aligned with the ideology through the isolation of difficulties in adoptive relationships. The problems that Yapese expect to occur in 'adoption' arise at exactly those points where the application of the symbols of the ideology contradicts its message. 'Adoption', as Yapese speak of it, serves in part as a cautionary tale of what may happen if the message is not heeded.

Two features of 'adoption', in addition to the work of the parents, are usually seen as problematic: the clan identity of the child and natural mother, and the child as 'thrown away' by the natural parents.

A child is expected to establish relationships with its natural parents as a result of clan identity and their work. A child is not told of its 'adoption' until it reaches puberty but, no matter how well the 'adoption' is concealed, the child eventually will discover his natural parents and establish an ongoing relationship with them.

Yapese note that in order to carry out their agreement with the adopters, natural parents must treat their child as being of little worth, as something that can be given away. This conflicts with the stress on the value of a person. Yapese do not adopt just any child, but rather one of about the same rank as the adopters. Thus the child's value is affirmed by the adopters but denied by the natural parents. Following up on the importance of exchange to parenthood, informants assert that since the natural parents rejected the child, the child will treat them unkindly in return and may steal from them or fight them.

These expectations identify strains arising from 'adoption' while making no assertion that the relation of adopter to child is an imitation of, or less than that of, parent and natural child. It is better, so people say, to have a child born to the estate than to 'adopt' one because of the above-mentioned difficulties. Some people expect children born to an estate to ally against adopted children. They do not say that an adopted child has weaker rights or is not worthy to inherit land or leadership. They point, rather, to the fact that children born to the 'estate' have a common solidarity, which they may call on in order to oppose an adopted child.

The last expectation, that some members of the junior generation of the estate will combine against others, applies to other situations as well. For instance, at a man's death, his children come under his brother's authority. With the transfer of authority goes a change in terminology: for the dead man's children, his brother becomes the only person who is *citamangin* 'father'. All the children under this man should be treated alike and should treat each other as 'siblings'. Yapese do not, however, expect all such 'siblings' to share as they should.

An explicit contrast between natural and adopted children is thus made at one point in the cultural model of 'adoption', but it occurs in a context where other criteria for alliance within the sibling set could be used to the same effect. In this context, people emphasize that 'siblings' may well unite under some pretext to exclude others when they escape parental guidance. The problem is seen as greed, not as any inadequacy of adoptive parent-child relations.

Various dyads may be the foci of interpersonal tensions in 'adoption', but the possibility of conflict between adopters and children is barely hinted in the expectations discussed here. The assumption that an adopted child will return to his natural parents suggests that the child may well break with its adopters. Different Yapese draw different conclusions: some see 'adoption' as a thankless effort; some expect an adopted child to try to get resources from both sets of parents; others hope that the child will realize that its best chances lie with the adopters.

A recurrent theme is that adopters are exemplary parents. Adopters go to considerable effort to get a child, showing care and love. Other parents have children without forethought.

The cultural model of 'adoption' dovetails neatly with the central message of Yapese social theory. If adopters were seen as less adequate or proper parents than natural parents, the message would be flatly contradicted, since care for the child is emphasized over procreation. Both adopters and natural parents start off as parents in Yapese terms, as both work to bring the child to life and to raise it. Given the Yapese stress on work, which persons remain a child's parents depends on continuing action to maintain the relationship.

CASES OF 'ADOPTION' AND 'HELP'

Cases of adoption may diverge widely from the details of the model. To an extent this is inevitable: no model predicts the exact outcome of the transactions it represents, and, as shown above, the model of adoption serves to warn as well as to predict. Shared expectations cannot encompass the details of particular relationships. The problem goes deeper, however, for the details of many cases contradict the shared understandings. While the breaking of ties between 'estates' is stressed time and again, Lingenfelter notes correctly that "The effect of adoption is not to cut off relationships, but to reinforce and extend them for both the parents and the children" (1971:60).

There is rarely any disagreement on the question of whether someone was 'adopted' or not. In the following cases—selected to illustrate the range of relationships labeled as adoptive—informants had no trouble deciding that 'adoption' occurred.

Case 1. The adopters had no children and asked a woman in their village for her next child. She was one of two women in the village who gave birth to more than one child in the period 1930–1940. The child, a boy, lived with his adopters and took over the estate at the death of his adoptive father.

Case 2. A boy born to the woman mentioned above was 'adopted' by another couple in the same village. The adoptive father gave the boy two names, J and K, from his estate. He divorced his wife when the child was still young, 'threw away' the child at the same time, and took back both names. The child went to live with his natural parents and his natural father gave him a new name, again K. All these names were properly given; those chosen by the adoptive father were those of men who had been in his estate, and the name given by the natural father referred to a different K who had lived on lands held by the natural father. At this point, K was no longer 'adopted': his adopter broke their relationship in taking back the names. His adopter's sister, however, had lands in the village that she could not oversee, as she lived some distance away. Some years later, this sister sent her son with stone valuables to be given to K's natural father. He accepted the stone valuables, and informants agreed that this meant that K was no longer a member of his natural father's estate. When asked, people hesitantly said that K had been more or less 'adopted' in this transaction. K is seen as having his own estate, although he lives on land lent by his natural father. He has not been given any land by the people who separated him from his natural father's estate.

Case 3. An old man whose children were grown asked for a girl in 'adoption'. He said that he wanted a girl because most of his daughters had died. He named the child, and, although she resides with her natural parents, she visits her adopter daily. The adopter is confident that she will take responsibility for his care when she finishes school.

Case 4. An unmarried woman was pregnant. Her lover did not wish to treat her as worthless, but he would not marry her. A friend of his adopted the child. The child lives with her adopters and neither visits nor, we were told, knows her natural mother.

Case 5. A village chief had only one daughter who married a man from another part of Yap. Since political offices cannot be held by women, the chief needed a son and so he 'adopted' his daughter's child. The boy was named by the adopter, but he has lived mainly with his natural parents, far from his adopter's home. His mother explains that the boy is her 'sibling in name and child in person'. Now that the adopter has died, the boy is acknowledged as chief in his village although—perhaps because—he is rarely there.

FIGURE 9.   Adoption Cases 6 and 9 Diagrammed.

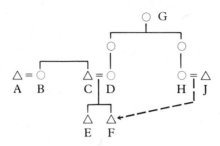

Case 6. This adoption as well as other data which are discussed later, is shown in figure 9. H and J asked for F before his birth. F was born in a village ranking just below J's village. His name comes from C's estate; he says that this was at A's request. J may not have wanted to give a name from his own lands because his claim to them was irregular. F stayed with both his adoptive and natural parents during his youth. He inherited land from all four of them. He has given a name from his adoptive father's land to his first son and has named his second son for C, his natural father. He currently lives on land in his natal village although he holds political office in his adoptive village.

Case 7. A boy grew up with his natural parents until they separated and his father was killed by his mother's brother. His older brother was taken in by a man related to his father, but he was 'adopted' by a relative of his mother's. His mother has married again elsewhere. He lives with his adopter but visits his mother. Although he stays with his mother's relatives when in his natal village, he considers his natural brother to be his 'brother' and still bears a name from his natal estate.

Case 8. A married woman had no children of her own, although her husband had a child by a former wife. She wanted a child in order to commemorate her father. She asked a distant relative on her father's side—the precise genealogical relation is not certain— for a boy. She has given her adopted son her father's name. The child has lived with his natural parents in town, rarely if ever visiting his adopter. We were told that he would be allowed use of estate lands if he came to live in the area but could not expect to inherit since his adopter's natal estate was held not by his adopter but by another man, her FBSS.

When we pressed a group of informants to explain why the above are cases of 'adoption', they separated cases of 'adoption' from *ayuweg* 'help' and other, unremarkable relationships. They had difficulty, however, in pointing to features which distinguish the three. They could offer no model of 'help' like that of 'adoption' discussed above. Their 'adoption' model did not hold in its details for all cases of 'adoption': in discriminating between different cases, Yapese do not appear to be treating a gift of stone money, say, or a child's naming as a necessary condition for 'adoption'.[8]

Conceivably, given enough cases, rules might be generated to account for the divergence of particular cases from shared expectations. Our informants discussed the particulars of each case in terms of the personalities involved and their individual relationships to estates. In looking for a syntax of 'adoption' transactions, we would have to posit very similar motivations and understandings on the part of the actors involved if our informants' discussion of cases is relevant. We see no reason to assume that all Yapese are alike in outlook and knowledge and, instead, look for similarities in the cases designated as 'adoption' which are absent in 'help' and other cases.

Our informants explained that adopters are *gafagow* 'destitute', as is the child in cases of 'help'. 'Destitution' cannot be operationally defined. However, two cases of 'help' and one in which neither 'help' nor 'adoption' was found illustrate some of the circumstances in which people may be called 'destitute':

Case 9. In figure 9, E was helped by A and B. People explain that E's mother, D, could not care for E when she was pregnant and so A and B took him in. He grew up in the homes of both his helping and natural parents and inherited from both. Informants explain that A and B cared for E but had a relationship with him above and beyond nurture. Relatives may take care of children without any change in public perception of relationship, but, we were told, B was *cegow* 'greedy' and took advantage of D's situation in order to get the child.

Case 10. A girl went to live with an elderly relative. She took care of the old woman and inherited a plot of land 'in exchange for work'. We were told that the gift of land showed that she, and not the old woman, was 'destitute'.

Case 11. People say that this case, shown in figure 10, is neither 'adoption' nor 'help'. D was unmarried when she bore A2. We do not know whether A1 or C gave stone valuables to ghosts as prayer. The child was given A1's name, but this was not understood to indicate 'adoption': B had access to the name from her husband's estate and gave it as an elder of C's estate. The child lived with all his 'grandparents' as he grew up. It appears that A1 and B decided that A2 should inherit both their estates. Neither had a son, and they preferred to merge their lands rather than to 'adopt' or otherwise find heirs. A2 grew to be a well-liked man and duly inherited from all his 'grandparents'.[9]

Adopters and helped children thus appear to be 'destitute' by definition in hindsight, rather than because of facts always visible before 'adoption' or 'help' transactions are negotiated.

We cannot distinguish types of cases in terms of the formality of transaction. In Case 7, a boy was 'adopted' without any gift of stone money. Conversely, a number of cases of 'help' arise when a father seeks out another man to act as *taceyalen* 'guardian' of his estate after his death. The 'guardian' raises the children and watches over the estate until they can work the land. A man is not considered a 'guardian' unless he was chosen by the father and was publicly known to have accepted this duty. In Case 2, the natural father formally 'helped' his child by giving it a new name.

We find that no features in the parent-child relationship neatly separate 'adoption', 'help', and other situations but that they may be distinguished in terms of the status of the estates concerned. The sets of elders interested in the child as potentially or actually a member of their estates and the amount of agreement among the elders vary with the types of transaction.

FIGURE 10.   Case 11 Diagrammed.

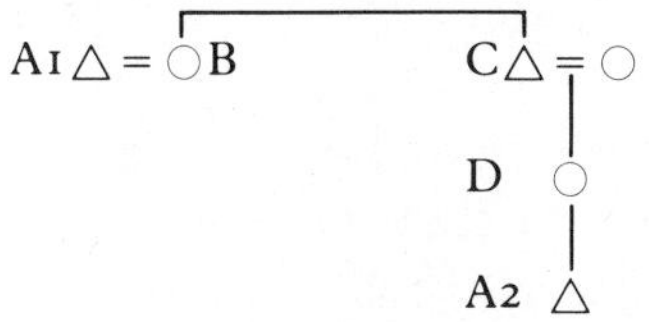

In 'adoption', two estates are necessarily involved in the transaction. Both estates continue as separate units, the child being affiliated to one yet having ties to the other. In all cases of 'adoption', a possibility remains that the child may be taken in by his natal group. What is most crucial is that the adopters have little or no control over the natal group and vice versa. The adopters have no guarantee that the natural parents will not try to entice the child to stay with them, and the natural parents cannot be certain the adopters will provide for the child.

In cases of 'help', two estates are involved, but only the elders of one estate can enforce decisions about the child's future. In Case 10, the old woman was about to die when she 'helped' the child. She gave the child land but had no power over the girl. The woman who 'helped' the child in Case 9 eventually became 'trustee' over her brother's lands: he could not oppose her in estate matters without risking that she would, later, take the land from his heir.

Cases 9 and 11 show that 'help' and other parent-child relationships may have great similarity. In both cases, the child's FZ recruited the child. The difference between the two cases rests on the willingness of the women to use authority in the estate. In Case 9, a 'greedy' woman took her brother's son, even though his other son was to be adopted. In Case 11, the two sets of 'grandparents' were friendly and agreed to treat A2 as their mutual child. In this case, as well as others that seemed to us to border on 'help' or 'adoption', we were told that exercise of 'trustee' authority was out of the question.

The labeling of these parent-child relationships rests not on aspects of the parent-child dyad but on the ability of the various elders concerned to agree to cooperate. In 'adoption', two groups of elders have ties to a child, and neither can depend on the other with assurance. In 'help' one set of elders imposes its decisions without any worry about opposition. In situations that go unlabeled, elders show that their interests with regard to the child need not cause conflict, and matters can be settled amicably: 'their word is good'.

These distinctions rest on the negotiation of relationships, not on rights and duties. As a result, they are congruent with the Yapese emphasis on work and worth since they stress the conditional qualities of relationships. Occasional care of a child may be construed as 'help', if relations in the senior generation go sour. An 'adoption' exists so long as all parties involved do not work to disrupt it, and all involved can, if they choose, try to end it. The labels for relationships are applied with regard to the entire complex of relations that center on parent-child ties, and not just the links between the child and any or all parents.

Given the situations of elders in the three types of relationship, a child's opportunities for negotiation differ according to type. Adopted children can try to develop their ties to one or two estates. They can risk the displeasure of their elders since they can activate their ties to the natal estate even if they are rejected by their adopters. Children who are 'helped' may have land that they may use as they wish when grown, but they have less chance of finding support from people outside the group that 'help' them, since those who 'help' in most cases replace the children's original support group. The variety in parent-child relations not coded as 'adoption' or 'help' is great, and we cannot easily generalize about children's opportunities in them. We shall return to this subject below.

RANK IN ADOPTION

We can now deal with a question we have skirted so far: from whom can people 'adopt'?

Yapese say that a child once had to be of about the same rank as its adopters but that this requirement has been relaxed somewhat. If, in the past, a high-ranking man liked a low ranking child, he could not 'adopt' it; the best he could do would be to get a man of intermediate rank to 'adopt'. He would then oversee the child's growth and give it things. He might take the child into his household on the adopter's death. He could never 'adopt' the child, for the difference in rank was simply too great.

The rank of a child is not, however, the only political consideration involved. Adopters must be able to maintain a relationship with the natural parents. Minimally, they have to hope that the natural parents will abide by the 'adoption' agreement. If only for this reason, there is no point in 'adopting' from people who might become overt enemies.

All of Yap is divided into two *baan* 'sides'. This division has complex political implications, but on Rumung Island it separates villages into two groups with different relations to higher villages elsewhere. Repeated skirmishes—as opposed to wars arranged by the highest chiefs of Yap—occurred between villages of the two sides before the German occupation in 1895, and rivalry remains. Among 'adoptions' initiated from about 1860 to the present, we know of only one case on Rumung—dating from 1940—which was across 'sides'.

The difficulty of negotiation would seem to account for the restriction of most 'adoption' transactions to a small local area. From our Rumung data and fragmentary evidence from elsewhere on Yap, we can estimate that traditionally about 60 percent of 'adoption' transactions were in one village, 15 percent between nearby villages immediately superordinate and subordinate to each other politically—and hence on the same side—and most of the remainder between persons recognizing distant ties but who lived in widely separated villages. Since 1940, these three classes of 'adoptions' seem to have occurred with equal frequency. 'Adoptions' since 1940 have also included situations such as Case 4 in which distant adopter-natural parent relations do not imply that the parties are of about the same rank. As our evidence is from limited informant reports and genealogies, these estimates are only rough approximations.

The interplay of the Yapese stress on worth and the negotiation of 'adoption' can also lead to serial 'adoption'. Yapese term this practice 'new' and 'bad'; it has occurred a few times in the lowest-ranking villages. In the case we know, a child was 'adopted' from a village slightly higher in rank than the adopters' village and then 'adopted' again by covillagers of the adopters. The adopters had children born to them after the 'adoption' and others asked for them. To keep the adopted child while giving away children who are initially less worthy would be 'greedy', but giving away the adopted child would alienate only people with whom the adopters need not interact daily. Informants claimed that whatever gain was involved in having a higher-ranking child was not lost to the initial adopters when they gave the child away. Instead, rank distinctions within the village were obliterated, and the village as a whole profited.

In serial 'adoption', village solidarity outweighs the responsibilities owed by adopters to natural parents. In this disapproved form, 'adoption' is negotiated in terms of rank and is uncertain because people can neither count on nor enforce a desired turn of events. In this light, it is not an exceptional case but only an extreme one.

ESTATE TIES

Thus far we have concentrated on transactions labeled as 'adoption' or 'help', discussing other situations only to highlight features shared by such transactions. The data that have been presented show that a child's life situation, the exclusivity of the adopter-child tie, and the relations between sets of parents may vary greatly within the classes of 'adoption' and 'help'. The transactions involve continuing activity and are hence open to change. Since the classes of transaction are separable in terms of relations among elders, and not among parents alone, it seems worthwhile to ask whether they are extraordinary in this regard: Is a wider range of relationships than 'adoption' and 'help' contingent in definition on the activities of elders?

The greatest rewards and sanctions that adopters offer to children involve the estate. Children get land and eventual authority or are denied land and names. This is true for all parents, just as the reasons offered for 'adoption' are the reasons given for desiring any child: people want children as workers, heirs, and—a reason rarely mentioned—good company.

Whether or not a child is 'adopted' or 'helped', responsibility for and interest in it may be widely shared. Similarly, other people may replace a child's parents in caring for it. The most striking case occurs when a man becomes 'father' to his dead brother's children. Children may live with any member of their natal estate or with close relatives without much comment being generated. On the other hand, struggle over a child's loyalties, refusals to care for a child, and, on the child's part, attempts to cultivate the favors of people of different estates are noted and discussed. Yapese seem to be far more concerned in all relationships with the level of conflict and concurrence than with the punctilio of who feeds whom or whether every detail of a relationship is executed properly.

As estate affairs, 'adoption' and 'help' can affect large sets of relationships. Once again, this is not distinctive of 'adoption' and 'help' alone. In recounting Case 2, we mentioned K's questionable second 'adoption'. He was chosen as probable heir to lands in his village. He called on his relation to the old woman who holds these lands in naming his daughter for her. Matters did not end there, for the old woman seemed to have become dissatisfied with him. She arranged that a child in K's village bear the name of one of her ancestors and gave land to this boy. K can no longer be certain of gaining any of her land.

Since naming and gifts of land may be used to affect the behavior of a number of people at the same time, no relation is absolute and certain during its existence. Elders may search for new dependents, and workers may search for estates with less demanding elders. The large majority of people do not desert their estates, and few elders cut workers off from estates entirely. Nonetheless, such extreme acts occasionally do happen. Workers who desert their elders find others to give them use of land while elders who exile people from their land cannot be overruled by people outside of the estate—the possibility that a relationship may be broken can never be ruled out.

The uncertainty of relationships to estates is indirectly demonstrated by the way people's actual relationships to estates diverge from Yapese ideology. In theory, people have a tie to an estate, are given a name from the estate, work on the estate lands, come to exercise estate authority, and finally become ghosts of the estate. It is possible to measure several features of estate relationships that indicate that succession to roles may be much more complex. In these marked relations, there is public recognition of the possibility of a person's changing estate allegiance or having multiple estate ties or having a less worthy tie to the estate than others.[10]

A person may receive a name given by elders which is not held by his estate. Elders may further distinguish names from the highest-ranking lands, names previously held by people who died there, and names from less worthy lands. Such naming may be cited to account for the choice of an heir or the division of property among heirs. For any person whose name is not from the highest lands of the estate, the name may serve to justify lack of authority or limited access to land.[11]

An individual may have a recognized relationship to persons outside his estate that may or may not result in inheritance or 'help'. As in Case 9, the relation is seen as consisting in more than care, coresidence, or genealogical connection. We also include relations marked by gifts of land in this category.

A survey of two villages was taken in 1972. The sample included only persons for whom evidence on naming and current estate relationships could be obtained. As a result, women from distant villages and village women who had married elsewhere are excluded from the sample.

We found that a substantial part of the population was involved in marked relations: 'adoption', 'help', marked naming, or extra-estate ties. Six people were in two different types of marked relation. The distribution of types of marked relation was as follows:

current 'adoption'	10
current 'help'	1
marked naming	15
extra-'estate' ties	11

Table 21 shows the incidence of all marked relations in the sample. It indicates that not only are 'estate' relations open to change but that such change is publicly recognized in many cases.

In the long term, persons in marked relations seem no more likely than others to change estates or to get land from more than one estate. The data in table 21 do not show which relationships are manipulated so much as they show the extent to which manipulations of estate relations may be visible at one time.

The incidence of marked relations results from the actions taken

TABLE 21.   Incidence of Marked Relations

Age	No. of Persons in Sample Population	No. of Persons in Marked Relations*	Percent of Persons in Marked Relations
0–14	41	18	43.9
15–29	12	3	25.0
30–49	13	8	61.5
50–69	8	2	25.0
70+	4	0	0
ALL AGES	78	31	39.7

SOURCE: Authors' survey, 1972.
*Each relation is listed only once, according to the age of the junior party: adoptee, person 'helped', and so on.

by elders to maintain the whole set of relationships in an estate in order to 'keep the estate together'. Naming provides the most salient examples of the opportunity of adjusting relationships with the use of a marked relation. When elders meet to choose a name, each may wish a particular name given, and the name may be chosen only after lengthy discussion. Elders may simply want to name a child, but they may also wish to commemorate particular ghosts, to see a name given from particular lands, to honor some-one inside or outside the estate, to threaten others with the possibility of disinheritance, or to oppose other elders. Conversely, of course, elders may accede to others' wishes for various reasons. Even unexceptional naming may be the outcome of compromise or attempts to reorder all relationships in the estate (Kirkpatrick 1973:24, 27–29). Elders may also change a person's name to indicate disapproval of his conduct.

Marked relations point to past manipulations and the possibility of future adjustments in estate relations. Even where they are absent, relationships need not be certain; it is perhaps only with the dead that Yapese can be sure that a relationship stays constant.

CONCLUSION

In this chapter we have reported Yapese 'adoption' beliefs and practices and placed them in the contexts of cultural under-standings of relationship and the variety of parent-child relation-ships found on Yap. A cultural model of the nature, process, and outcome of 'adoption' meshes with general cultural premises. Shared expectations of 'adoption' outcomes allow for tensions in adoptive relations and predict the emergence of these tensions in such a way as to reinforce the central cultural premises.

The continuity of the estate as discrete, the importance of estate rank and personal worth, and a stress on work as over-shadowing consanguineal ties are affirmed in the model of 'adop-tion'. 'Adoption' is seen as less desirable than birth as a mode of recruitment because of the complexity of the relations established. Any hint that birth confers a more rightful claim to parental attention or estate resources than 'adoption' is avoided; on the contrary, adopters are seen as exemplary parents because of their work to obtain and raise a child.

The cultural model of 'adoption' is not of great help in predicting the details of actual relationships. In labeling particular relationships, Yapese distinguish between types of control and cooperation among estate elders. They thereby acknowledge that parent-child relationships are mutable and contingent on wider sets of relations, while stressing the continuity of the estate.

There are important similarities in Yapese understandings of 'adoption' in general and of particular 'adoption' transactions. In both, relationships depend on activity to maintain them. Among people's motivations, the search for land and workers for the estate is given high priority.

Data on parent-child relationships show the Yapese stress on the contingent quality of relationships to be well placed. Transactions are not neatly classifiable in terms of the rights and duties of parenthood. 'Adoption', 'help', and other relationships differ not in the allocation of rights and duties so much as in *the possibilities for reallocating them*. In 'adoption', all parties involved may work to dissolve or develop ties between the child and his various parents; in 'help' one group of elders can impose its will, but the child usually has its own resources. While young, the child is dependent on those who 'help' him, but later he usually can act independently of their wishes. The prevalence of marked relations demonstrates the frequency with which Yapese act within particular relationships to affect other ones.

Because of the conditional quality of relations, 'adoption' and 'help' should be seen as types of transaction between estates. They cannot be explained without taking into account the interdependent relationships of the various estate members.

We do not mean to imply that an ethnography of transactions in the rights and duties of parenthood on Yap would be impossible or fruitless. Any study concerned *only* with rights and duties would, however, fail to pinpoint the sorts of distinctions being made when Yapese speak of 'adoption' or 'parents'. In a similar vein, it might be difficult to decide whether 'help' establishes jural relationships. For instance, we are far from sure whether any rights and duties were involved in Case 10. The old woman might scold the girl who cared for her, she might threaten not to give the girl land, but neither of them had any definite duty to the other beyond the duty of any person to aid those who are 'destitute'.

Goodenough's (1970b) focus on the transactional component of 'adoption' is to the point, but the Yapese evidence indicates that our concepts of what is transacted need to be broadened or redirected. It may be more useful, for instance, to concentrate on the cultural allocation of freedom of action among the parties to transactions. Such an emphasis would give due regard for both contingency in relationships and factors such as rank that help to shape different possibilities for and outcomes of transactions for people in different positions in the social order.

Goodenough (1970b:409–410) reproached the authors of chapters in *Adoption in Eastern Oceania* for failing to investigate the entire set of transactions in parenthood in particular societies. Such an investigation would supersede externally derived contrasts between, say, adoption and birth, bringing out the features that distinguish types of relationship in societies. Our criticism is parallel: Goodenough's emphasis on rights and duties obscures the fact that decisions not to exercise rights, the scope of duties imposed on persons due to relationships outside the parent-child link, and other factors may be the basis for important cultural discriminations. Such factors, which might be handled as strategies with regard to rights and duties, cannot be treated as secondary to other distinctive features—rights and duties in the abstract—if a comparative perspective on transactions in parenthood is to be achieved.

In conclusion, an explanation for the separation between Yapese accounts of 'adoption' and of particular transactions may be suggested. Yapese tend to view villages, estates, and persons atomistically, attributing rank and other characteristics to large and small units. For instance, serial 'adoption' takes its name from a village where, we were assured, other despicable acts are normal. An estate's generosity may be apparent to people in its history of land dealings. The estate that people strive to continue is not simply a group but a unique entity, and a person's own individuality tends to be seen in terms of the way he adapts his estate's qualities.

It seems reasonable that a general explanation of Yapese 'adoption' that would account for most cases would be unsatisfactory in Yapese culture. Such an understanding would ignore the histories of work that distinguish each estate and person. Instead of treating estates and people as reducible to simple formulations,

Yapese recognize a general code for conduct that cannot be applied point for point in every case. The symbolic order that is incorporated in shared understandings of 'adoption' is highly flexible and can be accommodated to many contexts without necessarily contradicting its central premises. Yapese do not say one thing and do another in 'adoption' so much as they do the same thing in two different modalities. They perform a complex cultural task while concurrently preserving the estate as a continuing individual unit and the person as an independent actor.

NOTES

Our fieldwork was conducted in 1972. We concentrated on the higher-ranking villages of Rumung municipality at the north of Yap. Generalization from our data to the situations of people living permanently near the town of Colonia or people low in the traditional ranking system may be hazardous. We also rely on census data collected by Edward Hunt and Nathaniel Kidder as part of the Peabody Museum expedition of 1947–1948 and processed by David M. Schneider with the assistance of the Center for Advanced Study in the Behavioral Sciences. We would like to acknowledge the financial support of the National Institute of Mental Health through its grant to Schneider as well as support by the Lichtstern Fund of the Department of Anthropology, University of Chicago. Comments on earlier drafts by Ivan Brady, David Labby, Susan Montague, and David M. Schneider have improved this chapter considerably.

1. The term *leader* is used here to refer to the man who inherits the highest-ranking lands of the estate. This does not gloss a Yapese term, although 'landholder', 'elder', and 'chief' may be used to designate such a man. A case illustrates the complexity of relations among elders in an estate: A man told his younger brother to 'speak for the land' in village affairs even though they were on bad terms. The younger brother hence acted as chief while the elder brother was the actual leader in their estate. The elder brother gave all the estate lands except for one outlying plot to his son. The new leader allowed his father's brother to continue to act in village affairs even though the old man held no land in the village. The old man had no recourse in the matter of inheritance: this is an estate matter and no appeal to norms or village authorities can be used to overrule the decision of a leader.
2. For much greater detail on these matters, see Lingenfelter (1971) and Schneider (1953, 1955, 1957, 1962).
3. The 1972 survey was made to obtain the data shown in Table 21. For more data and analysis on Yapese population problems, see Hunt, Kidder, and Schneider (1954) and Underwood (1973). The contemporary population increase may be partly attributed to improved medical control over disease, especially low-grade infections that the abovementioned authors see as important in explaining depopulation on Yap.

4. We use the phrase *social identity* in a wider sense than Goodenough (1965) does. He defines *social identity* with regard to rights and duties in relationships, while we wish to leave open the possibility that "James of Riy village" may be a social identity, ideally definable in terms of all of James's relationships to his associates (see also Brady, chapters 1 and 7).

5. Labby (1971, 1972) and Schneider (1968) disagree in evaluating the evidence on whether coitus is a necessary condition for conception in Yapese theory. Our data offer some support for both views. Yapese have been mocked by Germans and Japanese on account of belief in estate ghosts. Most Yapese today are Roman Catholic. We see no way to be certain whether or not Yapese today hold traditional beliefs about conception: Schneider's informants at first told him "that the Japanese had explained everything, and that they were now quite well informed on the whole subject" (1968b:127).

6. The giving of stone money to ghosts in 'prayer' is not diacritical of parenthood to our knowledge; it is a leader's task to 'pray' to the ghosts, and we suspect that the leader of the child's estate rather than the child's father, usually gives the stone money.

7. *Pof* in the second usage differs phonemically from the other cases in northern Yapese dialects. The third etymological explanation ignores the syntactic difference between *pof e bitir* 'to adopt a child' and *pof e chaanem* 'to relieve that person (of a burden)'. Such facts do not detract from the value of the analogies in explaining matters to foreigners and children.

8. The distinction between 'adoption' and 'help' was taken as categorical by a small group of informants. Others from northern Yap also made this contrast in speaking of actual cases. Very few people recognized 'help' as a clearly defined type of relationship although there was wide agreement in the villages we studied as to whether someone had 'adopted' or 'helped' a child. Many contrasted the two in discussing cases and agreed in the labeling of particular cases. Awareness of this distinction is not great and answers to questions such as "What types of adoption are there?" vary widely. For example, some of Lingenfelter's informants clearly separated 'adoption' from *cowiy* 'plucking' and discussed cases of 'plucking' (1971). All our informants—and some of his—agreed that 'plucking' no longer exists, and few people understand the distinction. They said that people 'plucked' the children of close relatives and 'adopted' from others or vice versa but disagreed as to precisely who might 'pluck' whose child. Müller (1918) lists *pof* and *cowiy* as distinguishing between 'adoption' of younger and older children. Informants were uncertain or disagreed on the details of 'plucking' or 'raising' children, while they knew the cultural model of 'adoption' well.

9. In Case 11, A2 was in a situation that is often unfortunate: he was the child of an unwed mother. Such a child may be called 'child of a thief' since the mother does not marry and earn lands that the child might inherit. In this particular case, we do not think this factor is of importance. None of A2's 'grandparents' had other heirs. A2 was born at a time of declining population, and we suspect that all children were welcome, however irregular the way in which they came to estates.

10. The phrase *marked relations* is used in analogy to marking theory in linguistics. Informants expected that marked relations needed particular explanations in terms of personalities or histories of interaction. An exemplary contrast is provided by Cases 9 and 11; Case 11 was seen as unexceptionable, needing no comment in particular, while Case 9 occasioned smiles and lengthy explanations. This is congruent with Greenberg's suggestion that an unmarked category is analogous to the Gestalt "ground," with its character of being taken for granted (1966:94).

   We do not claim that what we call "marked relations" are precisely equivalent to examples of marking in phonology, syntax, or semantics. We simply note that "marked relations" give evidence of complex strategies at work—and often in conflict—in the senior generation of an estate. If we take the exercise of strategies for affecting multiple relationships as the property underlying all "marked relations," our usage is in line with Jakobson's definition: "The general meaning of a marked category states the presence of a certain property A; the general meaning of the corresponding unmarked category states nothing about the presence of A and is used chiefly but not exclusively to indicate the absence of A" (1957:5).

11. We do not count namings as marked if informants were uncertain from which lands a name came. An elder could, however, easily change his mind and decide that a name came from unimportant land; it is unlikely that his statement would be disputed. Elders are the keepers of historical knowledge in their estates, so they can manipulate the provenance of a name. For further data on elders' control and use of information about names and land histories, see Kirkpatrick (1973).

10

ADOPTION AND SISTER EXCHANGE IN A NEW HEBRIDEAN COMMUNITY

Robert Tonkinson

This chapter has a twofold purpose: first, to provide some data on Melanesian adoption which, with the exception of Scheffler's analysis (1970:369–389) of certain practices in the northern New Hebrides, was lacking in the previous ASAO monograph on adoption (Carroll 1970a); and, second, to discuss the implications of certain features of adoption practices among South East Ambrymese people that are not characteristic of the Oceanic communities reported on thus far. Specifically, I refer to the connection between bridewealth contributions and subsequent adoption claims and also to the link between such claims and the practice of sister exchange marriage. This adoption-marriage interrelationship is unusual and is noteworthy because it bears on certain general problems pertaining to the study of kinship. While it can be shown that adoption at Maat village conforms in many respects to the situation in much of the rest of Oceania (see Carroll 1970b:5–7), the Maat data provide additional insights into the dimensions of kin solidarity, which is one of the concerns of this volume.

Contrary to the situation in much of Oceania, the reallocation of resources such as land is not closely linked to the practice of adoption at Maat, and, in the case of female adoptees, economic considerations are likewise of little relevance. To understand the significance of adoption among Maat people, it will be necessary to examine both the actual situation, in which some children are living with adoptive parents, and the long-term implications of adoption claims. As Ottino (1970:116) notes: " ... adoption must be studied as a sequential process. Its pattern cannot be grasped by focusing on the events of only a brief moment." Unless adoption at Maat is studied both synchronically and diachronically, a distorted picture of the practice will inevitably emerge.

A diachronic approach is most useful in situations where the term *adoption* connotes a wide range of transactions and practices and where adoptees may have considerable say as to whether or not they will live with their adoptive parents. For Maat, if consideration is given only to adoptions involving residence change on the part of the adoptee, little is revealed concerning the wider significance of the institution. Only by an examination of adoption claims, which most often do not entail a change of residence and may be activated in the long run without reference to residence at all, can the ethnographer hope to understand their rationale.

The main body of this chapter begins with a description of certain aspects of the cultural background of the people of Maat, as a necessary prelude to the later treatment of adoption. I then present what I consider to be the most relevant statistics on adoption practices and attempt to interpret them. In conclusion, the distinctive features of adoption at Maat are reviewed and compared with Oceanic adoption patterns in general.

CULTURAL BACKGROUND

Maat village was established near the town of Vila in 1952 by a group of South East Ambrymese, following their evacuation from Ambrym in the wake of prolonged volcanic ash falls. Unlike their Ambrymese neighbors, who returned home after the ash falls had ceased, the people of the Ambrym village of Maat chose to stay on Efate, where they worked as laborers on nearby plantations and in Vila. They have retained their land interests in Ambrym, and many of them return there from time to time. While visiting their homeland, they usually stay in Maat, Ambrym, one of fifteen villages in the southeastern region of the island. Thus, despite their relocation, they have maintained close links with Ambrym.

Their village on Efate is physically and culturally more Ambrymese than Efatese in character.[1] For this reason, a study of adoption at Maat must take into account the cultural background of its Ambrymese inhabitants, especially since relocation itself appears to have had little effect on basic values and behaviors (cf. Tonkinson 1968, 1974). In assessing the effects of relocation, therefore, it is more appropriate to speak of continuities than of change.

South East Ambrymese villages consist of several residentially contiguous patrilineages, named in terms of one of their earlier locations when they were separate hamlets. They are characterized by a high degree of virilocality. Traditionally, the scattered hamlets, which consisted of one or more closely related lineages, tended to be exogamous. Today, the incidence of village exogamy ranges from about 44 percent in the largest village, to 100 percent in the smallest; within all villages, the rule of patrilineage exogamy still holds. This suggests that traditionally the patrilineage functioned strongly as a corporate group, since its members were coresident and held land in common. Largely as a result of cash-cropping for copra, there is now considerable fragmentation of lineage holdings into family-held units, and, although strong solidarity between men related agnatically is less obvious, it is still the ideal.

Despite the absence of named or recognized moieties, clans, marriage classes, or descent reckoning through the matriline, the kinship system in South East Ambrym is nonetheless similar in basic structure to that of the controversial 'six class' system of North Ambrym. Marriage should take place with real or classificatory MBDD, FZDD, ZSD, MFZD, MMBD, FMBSD, or any other person called by the term for 'spouse'. 'Wrong' marriages, that is, between people not related to each other as 'spouse', were apparently as common traditionally as they are today and simply entail an adjustment in the terminology used between relatives of the couple. The practice of sister exchange marriage remains an integral part of the kinship system. Traditionally, there was a marked tendency for marriage alignments to be regularized between the various hamlets or village segments in the form of cyclical exchange. Thus, a woman of Maat Holeru, whose natal hamlet was Peas, would endeavor to marry her daughter to a Peas man; and her DD, would marry a Holeru man if possible, and so on. Because of sister exchange, a man's wife's brothers were often also his sisters' husbands, and this strong affinal tie was frequently exploited to obtain various kinds of assistance.

The provision of bridewealth was an essential part of the arrangement of marriages between patrilineages, and the intended groom relied heavily on his agnates to help him amass the necessary pigs and foodstuffs for presentation to his future wife's family. This remains true today, for despite the ceiling of twenty dollars bride-wealth payment imposed by the Presbyterian Church, a man's kin must collect large amounts of money, food, and pigs to pay for the cost of the wedding feast and for gifts that go directly to the family of the bride. An intended groom can expect financial assistance from his classificatory agnatic kin in other villages, with whom he shares, ideally, bonds of friendship, hospitality, and mutual aid. But the largest share of the necessary money and gifts generally comes from his own or coresident patrilines.[2] He in turn will be expected to reciprocate on later occasions when other members of his patrilineage are preparing for marriage.

With respect to sister exchange marriage and bridewealth contributions, both of which relate to adoption practices, the situation in the relocated Maat community is slightly different from that obtaining in the homeland. Since relocation, the local church elders have been more successful in playing down the practice of sister exchange marriage in favor of free choice of a spouse. Most elders do not oppose sister exchange per se; they object only when the practice involves the coercion of a girl into a marriage she does not want. However, the ideology of sister exchange remains strong among many of the inhabitants, who continue to view the practice as a sure way of securing marriage partners for their sons. Several attempts at sister exchange between Maat and Ambrym families since relocation have failed when either one or both of the proposed partners decided that they were not interested in such a marriage. Likewise, several attempts to oppose marriages because the prospective groom had no real or classificatory sisters available to exchange with his future wife's kin ended in failure when community sentiment favored the marriage.

The system of bridewealth contributions has likewise been altered since relocation, in favor of the entire village (except for the wife's immediate family) giving financial support to the groom's kin to pay for the wedding feast. Although gift-exchanges occur between the immediate families of both bride and groom, the cost of the wedding celebration is borne by the entire Maat community on the basis of voluntary contributions. Nevertheless, in every case many of the necessary funds are donated by real and classificatory agnatic kin of the groom.

CONNOTATIONS OF ADOPTION

The South East Ambrymese use the noun *hurxauen* to refer exclusively to adoption; the verb is *-hurxauni* 'to adopt'. In much more common use, however, is the phrase . . . *nguri bei nan* ' . . . takes to be his/her own', which can also allude to nonhuman beings and objects, but when used in reference to people can mean much the same as *mingurxaun tuvava tei* 'he/she adopts a baby'. When someone says *natehurxaun tuvava*, they mean that they have actually taken the child from its parents to live with them, whereas the phrase *natehuri tehei navan* 'I took it as mine' could mean this, or it could indicate that the person has initiated an adoption claim on someone else's child and that the claim has been agreed to by the child's natural parents. This phrase suggests that the claim is initiated by one person, and this is what happens in most cases. If the claimant is married, his or her action is taken on behalf of both partners (and perhaps one of their children). Since almost all adoptions involve one of the husband's patrikin, a wife who initiated a claim would be doing so as an agent of her husband. The transactions described in this chapter center mainly on adoption claims because it is through a study of claims that the institution as it exists among South East Ambrymese can best be understood.

Adoption claims may be made before a child's birth or, in many cases, before its conception. If the request is made prior to birth, the prospective adopters may specify the sex of the baby they want and may indicate that their claim will lapse if the child is not of the desired sex or will transfer automatically to the next born until they get a child of the sex they desire. This procedure indicates that different motives lie behind the initiation of many adoption claims.

The presentation of gifts for the child, necessary to validate adoption claims, need not take place until after the birth. As among the Nukuoro (Carroll 1970c:124), gift-giving is an important element in the claim and is proof of the sincerity of the claimants. Acceptance of an adoption claim is acknowledged by the parents by telling the adopters that the child in question is promised to them. In most cases, it is not the intention of the adopters to take the child from its parents while it is still a baby, but this has happened in at least two cases at Maat.

Ideally, the adoptive parents continue to give presents to the child, or to the parents on its behalf, since it now 'belongs' to them. The Maat people commonly use the Pidgin term *lukaut hem* 'look after him/her' to describe the adopter-adoptee relationship. From the time that it can move about confidently, a child is sent to visit the household of its adoptive parents, and it eats meals with them periodically. Most adoptive parents actively encourage the child to visit them, and, since they typically live in the same village, they urge it to sleep at their house. Encouraged by its natural parents, the child will often comply if it likes its adoptive parents. However, if the residence change entails the child leaving its natal village, its natural parents are generally reluctant to urge it to go and live with the adopters. Although young children are made aware at an early age who their adoptive parents are, that is, who they 'belong' to, they are never forced to reside with them against their will.

THE DISTRIBUTION OF ADOPTION

Maat is a village of about 300 people (July 1973), some 50 to 70 of whom at any given time are visitors from South East Ambrym in temporary residence. Fifty families, totalling 243 people, were listed as 'belonging' to Maat in January 1967, and it is this population (which includes both resident and nonresident Maat people) that forms the basis for the following statistics on adoption.[3]

The people of Maat number 143 males and 100 females, which indicates an extremely high masculinity ratio (that is, there are many more than 100 males per 100 females), even when compared to that of South East Ambrym, which at 125:100 is approximately double the New Hebridean average.[4] Largely as a result of differential birthrates, which favor male babies, females are outnumbered by males both in Maat and South East Ambrym.

A majority of Maat people (166/243 or 68 percent) have been

subject to adoption claims that were recognized as such by their parents; about 31 percent actually resided with adoptive parents at some time. More males are claimed for adoption than females (102:64), a discrepancy in part due to the sex imbalance among Maat people. About 70 percent (52/75) of the adoptees who changed residence at some time did so before the deaths of their natural mothers. Not all of these people lived permanently with their adoptive parents until marriage; at least sixteen of them returned to their natural parents for varying periods.

An examination of kinship relations between natural and adoptive parents reveals a very strong bias in favor of agnatic linkages: women rarely adopt consanguineal kin. About 94 percent of adoption claims were initiated by the adoptee's patrikin; in 72 percent of the total (119/166), the claimant was a 'F' or his wife or an actual FB of the child; 16 percent (27/166) of the claimants were 'FF' or his wife; and about 6 percent (11/166) of the claims were by 'B'. In only twelve cases were claims initiated by people who do not belong to Maat, and five of these claims were made by the father's agnates in his natal village; that is, the fathers concerned were Ambrymese who live uxorilocally at Maat.

Kinship terminology is not normally altered by an adoption, and, even in the case of adoption by a 'FF' or his wife, the child concerned continues to call its grandparents by the correct term, whether it goes to live with them or not. Only six such adoption claims involved a change of residence at some stage, because most 'FF' who claim a grandchild do so on behalf of one of their younger sons, who may not be old enough to make a claim himself. The concern of the grandparents is not so much for removing the child from its natural parents as it is simply to claim the child for one of their other sons.

In January 1967, eleven families belonging to Maat had fourteen adoptees (ten males, four females) living with them or—in the case of five adult adoptees who are unmarried—eating meals with them and identifying principally with their household. Seven of the ten males were adopted into families that had no sons of their own. One boy and one girl were adopted by a childless couple; the wife is said to be the only barren Maat woman.[5] Twelve of the adoptees lived in the household of a 'F' or 'M'. One boy had been living with his MB since 1965 when his parents sent him to Vila for hospital treatment.[6] One small girl, whose mother is dead, was living in Maat Ambrym with a 'B' and his wife, whose only child (a girl) was away at school most of the year. Eight of the adoptees had changed residence after the deaths of their natural mothers, although in all cases their adoptive parents had prior claims on them. Only two adoptees, both boys, were taken by their adoptive parents when they were still quite small; in fact, one of them was unaware that he was adopted until his older natural siblings told him, after which he spent much time visiting his natural parents' household and playing with his siblings there.

By July 1969, some changes had occurred in these adoption patterns. One boy had run away to Santo and was living there with relatives from his natal Ambrym village. A girl whose parents left Maat in 1967 to return to the father's village in Ambrym remained behind with her widowed MM. The small girl who had been living with her 'B' in Maat Ambrym had returned to her father's village and was again living with him and her older sisters. The adopted son of the childless couple died in 1967 so they took the wife's ZS to live with them. The adopted son of a Maat girl went with her to Ambrym when she married and was living in her huband's natal village. A Maat man activated his claim to a ten year old 'D' and took her with his family to another island where he was working. This couple already had one other daughter and three sons, one of whom had been adopted by this FB and was living in Maat. In the period from 1967 to 1973, no very small children were taken to live with adoptive parents, and there were no plans afoot for such changes of residence.

Between mid-1969 and mid-1973 further changes occurred. Three Maat couples activated existing adoption claims and took two 'S', aged ten and sixteen, and a 'D', aged seven, to live with them. Two boys, aged fourteen, had returned to live with their natural parents, and the small girl who was back with her father in 1969 was again living with her adoptive 'B' and wife. The boy who had been living with his MB since 1965 returned to his natal Ambrym village in 1970. The remaining adoptees were still with their adoptive parents.

MAAT ADOPTIONS AND ADOPTION CLAIMS: INTERPRETATION

Several clearly distinguishable features of adoption at Maat emerge from the foregoing summary. Judging by the changes that occurred between 1967 and 1973, adoption viewed in terms of change of residence is a rather flexible, fluid arrangement. With the possible exception of children adopted while babies and those whose natural mothers are dead, adoptees are likely to change residence— either to join adoptive parents or to return to their natural parents —at any time. Although children have no say in the initial adoption claims that are made on them, the later decision as to whether or not they go to live with adoptive parents, and for how long, is largely theirs.

The incidence of adoption involving changes of residence is quite low among Maat people and is much lower than in any of the communities described in Carroll (1970a).[7] Having occurred in eleven families out of fifty, this means that only 22 percent of Maat households contained adopted children in 1967. Since eight of the fourteen adoptees changed residence after their natural mothers' deaths, the incidence of adoptions entailing change of residence occurring while the natural mothers are still alive is very low indeed. According to informants, had the mothers of the eight adoptees not died, the adoptive parents would not have taken them away from their natural parents. This fact points to one important function of adoption at Maat: it provides alternative parents in the event of the death of natural parents, particularly the mother. Since this function of adoption exists in virtually all societies, it does not warrrant further discussion here.

The statistics on adoption claims and adoptions involving residence change indicate that adoption at Maat is definitely an intravillage institution.[8] Almost all the principals involved are coresidents in the village, and, more than this, the adoptions include in almost all cases people who are closely related in the male line—that is, adoption transactions at Maat are predominantly between, or initiated on behalf of, members of closely related patrilineages and their affiliates.[9] As among the Kapinga (Lieber 1970:174), virtually all adoptees are either classificatory children, classificatory siblings, or real or classificatory grandchildren of their adopters. Adoption operates within a group of people who are, or who consider themselves to be, related consanguineally.

Since adoption transactions take place between parties already closely linked by kinship, the commonly held view that adoption is an expression of kin solidarity (see especially Carroll 1970c:153) is fully supported by the Maat data. But at Maat, adoption is closely linked to a particular manifestation of solidarity among closely related agnates: bridewealth contributions. In the event that conflicting claims are made on the same child, its natural parents should give the highest priority to the claimant who has contributed the largest proportion of the bridewealth amassed on behalf of the child's father for the benefit of its mother's family. Such contributions are in effect more than manifestations of the network of obligations and responsibilities that bind patrikin together in this society. These gifts are investments in the outcome of the proposed marriage, and the possible investment return is a claim to one of the children that it is hoped will result from the union. Since actual or closely related siblings of the adoptee's father generally contribute the largest proportion of the bridewealth, they are favored over lesser contributors and claimants who do not contribute anything.[10] Any substantial contributor, or his wife, may feel that his claim has a good chance of succeeding, especially when no rival claims have been made, or when he has been unsuccessful in claiming a previous child of the marriage. Natural parents, both of whom have a say in the promising of the child, feel obliged to agree to such adoption claims, and they often do so with little hesitation because they are confident that the claimants do not intend to actually take the child away from them.

Any person, married or single, male or female, can make an adoption claim. Any child can be claimed for adoption, regardless of its position in the family. For example, in 1967 two of the Maat boys living with their adoptive parents were the firstborn of their natural parents. There appears to be a cultural preference for adoption claims to be made on males, even after Maat's high masculinity ratio is taken into account. Of the eighteen adoption claims made by actual FB of the adoptees, fifteen were made on BS and only three on BD, which suggests that 'true' FB have a strong preference for claiming sons of their brothers, particularly older brothers (thirteen of the eighteen claims were made by younger brothers of the adoptees' fathers).

Parents with or without sons of their own appear equally likely to initiate adoption claims to male children. But, judging by the situation in 1967, families without sons are more likely to take the adoptees to live with them; 70 percent of male adoptees in 1967 who were with adoptive parents were living in families that had no sons of their own. Short-term economic factors appear to have little to do with this desire of families to have sons living with them. Children at Maat are much more of an economic liability than an asset while being reared, because they must be fed, clothed, and educated, but contribute relatively little in the way of labor for gardening, household tasks, and so on. This is especially true of boys, who enjoy more freedom from childminding and menial tasks than do all but the youngest girls.

In the long run, however, most informants see a definite economic prospect in the adoption of males. In return for having been reared, boys are subsequently expected to give both physical and financial support to their adoptive parents. In this sense, the adoption of boys provides economic insurance for aging parents. The desire to have male heirs for the eventual inheritance of land and coconut groves may also be a motivating factor in the case of couples without sons of their own, but even in Ambrym this is rarely cited as a reason for initiating an adoption claim on a boy.[11]

The absence of land as an important topic of conversation among Maat people in connection with adoption and inheritance must be accounted for in view of its central importance in so much of Oceania. For the Ambrymese, as for many other Melanesians who practice swidden horticulture in land-plentiful areas, the symbolic load carried by land is small compared to that of most Polynesians and Micronesians, especially those living on atolls where survival depends greatly on what is often less than one-half square mile of land. In the case of the Maat people, the circumstances of resettlement also explain the minor importance of land issues in internal politics. The relatively small amount of Efate land owned by the villagers is held communally in the village name. There is no individual ownership per se, only shared usufruct rights to garden plots. The people of Maat have not renounced their land rights in Ambrym, but these occasion little discussion at Maat because the immediate concerns of the villagers center on their life in Efate. In addition, the younger people consider Efate to be their home, and they show much less interest in, or enthusiasm for, Ambrym than do their parents, all of whom were born there. It could also be argued that to the extent that Ambrym land is still held communally by patrilineages, within which most adoptions take place, adoption constitutes no threat to the alienation of this land from the patrilineage and is thus not an important mechanism for redistributing resources.

Consideration of the adoption of Maat females reveals a clear distinction between the on-the-ground situation of adoptions involving residence changes, seen at a given point in time, and the long-term significance of adoption claims on females. Three of the four females cited in the 1967 statistics had lived with their adoptive parents only since the deaths of their natural mothers. One of the four, an adult, is financially independent and works in Vila; the other three girls are all dependent on their adoptive parents (and older siblings, in one case). None of these girls contributes much to the household labor force. This suggests that economic motives similar to those which may underlie the adoption of males are much less relevant to female adoptions. This is especially so in view of the strong patrivirilocal nature of Ambrymese residence, which means that, in many cases, a girl leaves her natal village at marriage and is thus not at hand to assist with daily tasks in her family of orientation. Judged solely on actual adoptions involving residence change, the adoption of females at Maat is predominantly a function of the responsibility of closely related kin to activate their prior adoption claims and to take care of girls in the event that the girls' natural mothers die.

The primary significance of the majority of adoption claims on females can be discerned only when marriage practices, particularly sister exchange, are taken into account. The combination of a persistent excess of males over females among the people belonging to Maat, plus the institution of *exoles* 'sister exchange' (wherein two men from different lineages exchange their sisters in marriage), make it difficult for a man without sisters, or without claims to 'Z', to find a wife among South East Ambrymese women. Villagers themselves attest to this, and the bachelor status of several Maat men in their late twenties and early thirties is attributed by many to their lack of sisters for exchange or to the reluctance of their sisters to marry the brother of women with whom they or their families sought to arrange a marriage.[12]

It is largely because of sister exchange that parents initiate adoption claims on female offspring of their patrilineal kinsmen— so as to ensure 'Z' for their sons. They are far less intent on actually removing the claimed girl from her natural parents than they are on establishing a right of bestowal in marriage. If they later have daughters of their own, or if their sons manage to marry without resorting to sister exchange, they may never need to activate their claim to the bestowal of the girl concerned. Nevertheless, in this event, they must be consulted before 'their' girl can marry anyone, since she 'belongs' to them. Many adoptive claims placed on females are, in effect, a form of insurance, initiated on behalf of the sons or the son's sons of the adoptive parents. If the adoptive parents should die, their claims automatically pass to their sons, who thenceforth have the major say in the bestowal of their 'Z' in marriage. The continuity of such claims further suggests that long-term interests are paramount in the practice of adoption at Maat.

CONCLUSIONS

It was noted earlier in this chapter that in some of its features adoption at Maat resembles many other Oceanic areas described in Carroll (1970a). Some specific examples can now be mentioned. Maat children are never put up for adoption, and most parents would rather not part with their children, no matter how many they already have. All adoptions are customary in that no legal transactions are involved in implementing adoption proceedings. Anyone, apart from small children, can initiate an adoption claim. All adoption transactions take place within the context of existing kinship networks, among or on behalf of principals who are almost always related as patrikin, generally as brothers or 'B'. Although the children who are claimed have no part in the initiation of adoption claims, they later have much influence regarding whether or not they will visit or live with adoptive parents. The consent of both natural parents is necessary before an adoption claim is recognized as valid. People can initiate claims on behalf of others; real or classificatory father's fathers often do so on behalf of their younger sons. Adoptions at Maat do not entail changes in kinship terminology, since the large majority of adopters already stand in a 'parental' relationship to the adoptee. Concomitantly, there is also no serious alteration of patterned kin behavior as a result of adoption. Adopters generally have children of their own and are not concerned with the physical attributes of the child they claim.

Natural parents find it difficult to refuse adoption claims made upon their children by kinsmen.[13] Among Maat people, such claims rarely occasion parental anxiety because so few adoptions result in the adoptee changing domicile.

Turning to the distinctive features of the transactions that I have been referring to as 'adoption' among South East Ambrymese, it is clear that if the institution were to be defined in part by a change of domicile by the adoptee, then adoption is uncommon at Maat. This is particularly true if one were to consider only those cases where a child goes to live with its adoptive parents while its natural mother is still alive. One obvious function of adoption at Maat is the provision of surrogate parents in the event of the death of a child's natural mother. It appears that if no women died while their children were still growing up, few children would change residence and live with adoptive parents. In the past, though, adoptions entailing residence change were more common.

What else is distinctive about adoption at Maat, besides the low incidence of adoption involving residence change? For one thing, the connection between adoption practices and the reallocation of resources, particularly land (see, for example, the chapters by Brady and Rynkiewich in this volume), is either unimportant or nonexistent. Traditionally in South East Ambrym land for gardens and tree crops was apparently never in short supply and population pressures were slight. Long-term factors are undoubtedly of crucial importance in assessing the significance of adoption practices at Maat, but these relate to human rather than natural resources. Economic factors appear to be of some importance in the adoption of boys, since they are eventually expected to support their aging parents in return for having been raised and educated. This explains in part why families without sons are likely to adopt boys and take them them into their households.

Most adoptions at Maat take the form of claims on other people's children, supported with gifts and a willingness to give the adoptee meals and a measure of financial assistance, especially for education expenses. Most such claims do not necessitate relocation of the adoptee with its adoptive parents—that is, with the family it is said to 'belong' to and which 'looks after' it. Claimants are, for the most part, only those kinsmen who have given financial support to the father of the adoptee by contributing to the bridewealth he and his family amassed to enable him to marry. An examination of the adoption claims made by Maat people bears this out as a criterion of eligibility to make adoption claims; other claims are likely to be politely ignored. Those patrilineally related kinsmen of the intended groom who contribute the most bridewealth have the strongest claims to any children resulting from the marriage. Generally, it is the father and the siblings of the groom who contribute most and therefore have the strongest claims. Even within families, the right to bestowal of an otherwise unclaimed daughter is given to whichever brothers have given the girl the most financial support. In other words, the same general principle applies as with adoption.

This suggests that, among the people of Maat, the existence of a consanguineal kinship link is not in itself sufficient justification for the exercise by one person of control over the affairs of a close relative. Such a link must be demonstrated and supported over time in repeated acts of assistance. It could well be that 'kin' are defined as those who show their allegiance and commitment to the relationship concerned by providing such support.[14] Adoption transactions take place between people already closely linked to one another by generalized bonds of obligation and responsibility. By gift-giving in support of their adoption claims, they demonstrate their sincerity as kinsmen and their willingness to evince this sincerity in a concrete, socially desirable fashion. This is why Maat people do not take adoption claims seriously if they remain at the verbal level and are not followed up with tangible evidence (in the form of gifts and visits) that the claim is genuine.

The initiation of adoption claims on girls has been viewed in the Maat context as an attempt by kinsmen to secure rights of bestowal over 'D' in a society where the practice of sister exchange marriage, plus a persistent shortage of females, causes anxiety among parents who have sons but not enough daughters to exchange for wives for their sons. Through his contributions to his brother's bridewealth, a man 'buys into' the latter's family and may as a result claim a BD as his own, as a form of long-range insurance in the event that he needs girls to exchange for wives for his sons. In Maat society, everyone is expected to marry, and children are highly valued, so family and lineage continuity depend on the ability of members to find wives for all males of marriageable age. The initiation of adoption claims on the daughters of 'B' enables parents to equalize sex ratios within their own family and thus increase the chances of marrying off their sons.

To generalize, briefly, the South East Ambrymese case can be seen as an interesting permutation that bears directly on a central problem in kinship studies—that of the interrelationship among consanguinity, marriage, and adoption-fosterage. The correspondences between adoption and marriage at Maat are noteworthy in view of the overwhelming evidence from Oceania that adoption is predominantly evidenced by consanguineal transactions in kinship and has no direct or close connection with affinal ties and alliances. Lambert (1964), however, has pointed out close parallels between the practice of fosterage in the northern Gilbert Islands (which is similar to adoption at Maat in that residence change is rarely involved) and prescriptive matrilateral cross-cousin marriage. He concludes (1964 : 232–258) that both institutions are similar in that they connect certain descent groups on a semi-permanent basis; are asymmetrical because they entail an irreversible flow of persons, goods and rights; and are consistent with a system of social stratification. In the Ambrymese case, where such asymmetry and social stratification are absent, the situation is different again. The institutions of marriage and adoption are interdependent elements of what is essentially the same unitary structural system. Each aspect is contingent to a large extent upon the other and each feeds into the other. For example, the legitimacy of adoption claims rests heavily on the contribution of wealth in order to secure a wife for an agnate. Likewise, an important reason why Maat people marry is to produce children, and a primary reason why they make adoption claims is to assure the marriages of these children.

Informants say that adoptions were much more frequent in Ambrym in the old days, and more children were taken to live with their adoptive parents. The same informants maintain that this practice seems to be declining in the new village. There are several possible reasons why this could be so in spite of the great increase in the number of children who now survive infancy.[15] For one thing, community financial support of weddings appears to have lessened the burden on the groom's agnates in providing bridewealth, and this may have had an effect of weakening individual claims to the children of these marriages. More importantly, pressures against sister exchange marriage, in favor of 'free choice' among the young, inevitably lessen the necessity of claiming extra girls as marriage insurance for sons. There is now a greater opportunity for young Maat men to find wives outside the village or in Ambrym because of their new environment. (Maat is one of several large peri-urban villages surrounding Vila, and the town itself has a large population of Hebrideans from all over the country).[16]

However, the practice of initiating adoption claims on the children of close kin no doubt will continue, since the claim itself as well as the gifts that follow demonstrate the kinds of kin solidarity and reciprocity that are still highly valued by Maat people, despite their increased involvement, economically and socially, in the wider society. In the past, in Ambrym, a much smaller proportion of children survived to adulthood so the promising of a child to relatives was, and still is, the ultimate act of unselfishness in response to those whose previous generosity made possible the marriage of the parents. A successful claim on someone else's child is the expected return on an investment in their marriage. This kind of reciprocal obligation is typical of Melanesian society but rarely does kin solidarity entail such claims on the offspring of a relative's marriage. Lieber (1970:203) concludes that among the Kapinga: "The cultural models of kinship relations and behavior in general and of adoption in particular afford an ideal framework within which, and by means of which, people can manipulate their social relationships to their immediate or future advantage." The Maat case supports this contention, with the important difference that the motivations underlying adoption transactions are predominantly generated by long-term considerations, for the eventual 'payoff', if it occurs, is often fifteen to twenty years in coming.

NOTES

This study is based on fieldwork conducted in the New Hebrides between July 1966 and August 1967, July and August 1969 and July to September 1973. The first period of field research was supported by the University of Oregon on a grant from the National Science Foundation; the second period of fieldwork was undertaken while I was a Graduate Fellow of the University of British Columbia, and fieldwork in 1973 was supported by a Summer Research Award from the Office of Scientific and Scholarly Research, University of Oregon. I wish to thank Professor H.G. Barnett, director of the 1966–1967 project, Ivan Brady, Mac Marshall, Mike Rynkiewich, and Martin Silverman for their helpful criticisms of an earlier draft of this paper. I wish also to thank teachers Abiut Donald and Yoane Iereta of South East Ambrym for their invaluable comments on the penultimate draft.

1. Between 1969 and 1973, however, a number of large, substantial cement and corrugated iron houses were built and, as a result, the village has taken on more of an Efatese physical appearance.

2. For example, the contributions to a wedding feast at Penapo village in South East Ambrym in May 1967 were as follows: the groom gave $60, his father $20, seven Penapo patriline relatives gave a total of $54, and twenty-two patriline relatives from nine other villages in the area and Maat Efate gave a total of $116; thirteen of his mother's Penapo patriline members gave $60 in all, and four Penapo people related to him as 'wife's patriline' gave a total of $24. No one outside Penapo who was not a patrilineal relative contributed. (All sums are in Australian dollars; $A1 = $US1.42 in July 1973.)

3. Those considered here as 'belonging' to Maat are all people born in Maat Ambrym, married or adopted into the village, born of Maat parents since relocation on Efate (a total of 187), plus 56 people who come originally from South East Ambrym villages other than Maat but have lived in the Efate village for at least the previous five years on a permanent basis. Some of these people have been at Maat Efate since its founding in 1952.

4. According to the official New Hebrides census of 1967 (McArthur and Yaxley 1968), there were 37,429 males and 33,408 females, which gives a masculinity ratio of approximately 112:100 for New Hebrideans. According to my census of South East Ambrymese in 1967, there were 862 males and 692 females.

5. Male infertility is also recognized by Ambrymese, and the term *lumalum* is used to refer to members of both sexes who are unable to beget children.

6. This case is best regarded as 'fosterage' because the couple concerned had no prior claims to the boy as regards adoption. Besides, he returned to Ambrym in 1970 and has not been back to Maat Efate since.

7. See Smith (chapter 11) for a convenient summary of adoption statistics from Carroll (1970a).

8. When adoptions are intervillage transactions, as is sometimes the case in South East Ambrym, the principals involved usually are linked closely by ties of kinship or friendship, or the adopting man has contributed a substantial part of his 'B's' bridewealth payment.

9. By 'affiliates' I mean men whose village of origin is not Maat, but by means of kinship or friendship links have come to identify more closely with members of one residentially based kin group (known as a 'small-name') within the village, near whom they reside. Such 'small-name' divisions still exist to a certain extent at Maat, but, because of numerous cross-cutting links and multiple affiliations and the increasing geographical spread of the village, they are not discernible by observation alone. The precontact equivalent of the 'small-name' would have been the hamlet.

10. Since the 1913 Ambrym volcanic eruption, when the population of the southeastern region was evacuated to nearby Paama and was hosted for some time by Paamese families, fictive kinship links have been maintained between many Ambrymese and Paamese families, who describe themselves as being of one line—that is, as 'brothers'. Gift-exchanges, reciprocal visits, and adoption claims have been undertaken over the years to bolster mutual feelings of 'kin' solidarity between the families so linked. No such adoption claims, however, have resulted in a change of residence on the part of the adoptees.

11. One Ambrym informant, a widower with no sons, said that he had activated an adoption claim on a 'S' specifically to obtain a male heir to his land and coconut holdings. However, he chose not to adopt a son of his brother (who has four), claiming that the brother already had ample land and coconuts for all his sons. Instead, he chose one of the sons of a village 'B' because this 'B' had contributed generously to the bridewealth payment for the informant's mother.

12. Maat is not characterized by a high level of overt conflict among its members, but, since relocation, when there have been disputes involving relations between families and lineages, these have arisen over sister exchange and marriage arrangements. What usually happens is that a girl's patrilineal relatives and parents object to her proposed marriage because the prospective groom has no sister or 'Z' available in exchange for the bride. In at least one case where the village elders overruled parental objections and allowed the marriage, members of the bride's patrilineage and affiliates stayed away from the celebrations in protest. Sister exchange thus remains a bone of contention at Maat.

13. South East Ambrymese parents would never voice an outright refusal, but there are strategies for discouraging people from persisting in unwanted or unjustified claims to the children of others. The parents may simply refuse to take the claim seriously, or they may lie and say that the child is already spoken for. Informants say that a claimant would be entitled to ask the parents who they have promised the child to, but people can tell by the speech and facial expressions of the parents whether or not they are lying and would never persist in case the parents became angry and told them exactly why they did not want to accede to their claim.

14. Cf. Schneider (1968a:117) who discusses the notion of commitment as being a vital element which makes 'solidarity' really solidary.

15. Only 54 of 111 children born to women in Maat Ambrym before relocation survived past childhood. This is in marked contrast to the post-relocation period, to 1967, when 102 of the 120 children born in the new location were still alive. This represents a fall in mortality rate from 51 percent to 15 percent.

16. These greater opportunities are being increasingly exploited by young Maat men; since about 1969, seven have married South East Ambrymese and seven have married women from islands other than Ambrym. Only two of the marriages with Ambrymese women involved sister exchange.

11

ROTANESE FOSTERAGE: COUNTEREXAMPLE OF AN OCEANIC PATTERN

J. Jerome Smith

INTRODUCTION

The point of departure for this chapter is the volume on *Adoption in Eastern Oceania*, edited by Vern Carroll (1970a). In his introduction (1970b), Carroll discusses a number of problems relating to the conceptualization of adoption and to various explanations of adoption within the Oceanic context. I shall address the issue of functional explanations of Oceanic adoption patterns in the light of data gathered on Rota, an island in the Mariana Islands District of the U.S. Trust Territory of the Pacific Islands.

Rotanese fosterage will be presented as a counterexample of a general Oceanic pattern of adoption. Specifically, Rotanese fosterage will be compared with the patterns of adoption in communities treated in Carroll's volume mentioned above (1970a). Keeping in mind Brady's definition of adoption as "... any positive and formal transaction in kinship, other than birth or marriage, that creates new or revises existing kinship bonds to bring them into accordance with any other kinship identity set customarily occupied by two or more persons in that society," fosterage is "... a temporary change in kinship identity through kin group and perhaps residential realignment ..." (Brady, chapter 1). The fact that adoption on Rota may be characterized more precisely as fosterage is an important aspect of its value as a counterexample of the general pattern of Oceanic adoption.

Throughout the present chapter, the term *adoption* is used in its generic sense (as defined above) unless specifically treated in direct contrast with fosterage. Use of the two terms in juxtaposition is not uncommon. Note, for instance, Ward Goodenough's argument that "... adoption and fosterage involve transactions in which rights and duties are transferred or delegated from one party to another as parents ..." (1970b:391–392) and Carroll's observation that "in most of the societies examined in this volume [*Adoption in Eastern Oceania*], the natives clearly distinguish, terminologically and conceptually, between 'fosterage' (temporarily taking care of others' children as an obligation of kinship) and 'adoption' (permanently assuming the major responsibilities of natural parents)" (1970b:7). Any potential terminological confusion may be clarified by the following tree diagram:

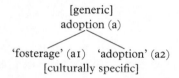

In the present chapter, 'fosterage' (a1) refers to a type of transaction in kinship, other than marriage, that is manifested on Rota to the exclusion of 'adoption' (a2). General use of the term *adoption* refers to (a) rather than (a2), unless otherwise specified.

The data presented in this chapter indicate that Rotanese fosterage transactions are limited in the number and kind of rights and duties transferred as well as in the duration of the fosterage arrangement. Furthermore, the overall frequency of transactions is low compared to the frequency of adoption transactions in the communities treated in Carroll's volume (1970a). In these two senses—'fosterage' (a1) to the exclusion of 'adoption' (a2), and the overall low frequency of adoption (a) transactions—Rotanese fosterage presents a useful counterexample to the general pattern of adoption reflected in many Oceanic communities.

Rotanese fosterage also provides comparative data for the investigation of adoption transactions viewed as recruitment strategies. From this perspective, adoption transactions have often been explained functionally as expressions of kinship solidarity and as procedures for the redistribution of property. Explanations of this sort presented in Carroll's volume (1970a) will be reviewed below, but it may be stated at the outset that the Rotanese case, although a counterexample in substance, does not contradict these explanations. The data from Rota do suggest, however, that alternate strategies may exist that serve the same functions, and, further, that frequency and other measures of the relative imporance of adoption are inversely related to the number and relative importance of these alternate strategies.

ADOPTION FREQUENCIES IN OCEANIA

Oceania has long been recognized as an area where adoption is frequent and widespread: "In some regions of the globe . . . adoption is practiced on a scale wholly disproportionate to any rational ground, therefore . . . Oceania as a whole represents a main center for adoption carried to unusual lengths" (Lowie 1930:460, quoted in Levy 1970:71). The anthropologist's interest in Oceanic adoption is succinctly stated by Carroll: "The extremely high incidence of adoption in many parts of Oceania requires an explanation. What is the motivation for practicing it on this scale?" (1970b:11).

As table 22 illustrates, the frequency of fosterage on Rota is about one-half that of adoption occurrences in a sample of Pacific communities.[1] The average frequency of households with one or more adopted children for the sample, excluding Rota, is 37 percent. More significantly, the Rotanese frequency of 17 percent is the extreme low point in the range, the extreme high point being 67 percent on Nukuoro Island and on Romónum, Truk. Furthermore, the next higher frequency after Rota is that of Waimanalo, Hawaii (19 percent), about which it is said, "The probable reason that the Waimanalo rate is significantly lower than the other three [Hawaiian] homesteads is because it is a newer community and has a lower proportion of women over thirty-five years old" (Howard et al. 1970:31).

Frequency figures of this sort are no more than a crude descriptive measure of the relative importance of adoption in Oceanic communities. It is only because the frequency of Rotanese fosterage stands out so clearly from the other frequencies of adoption

TABLE 22. Frequency of Adoption in a Sample of Oceanic Communities

Community	Number of Households	Households with one or more Adopted or Foster Children		Source
		No.	Percent	
Rota, Mariana Is. District	160	27	17	Author's field research, 1970–1971
Waimanalo, Hawaii	210	40	19	Howard et al. 1970:31
Rotuman households in Suva, Fiji	206	46	22	Howard 1970:353
Rotuma Island, Fiji	416	97	23	Howard 1970:353
Papakolea, Hawaii	51	13	25	Howard et al. 1970:31
Nanakuli, Hawaii	265	86	32	Howard et al. 1970:31
Kewalo, Hawaii	155	49	32	Howard et al. 1970:31
Rangiroa Atoll, Tuamotu Archipelago	74	26	35	Ottino 1970:93–94
Rambi (Gilbertese), Fiji	291	101	35	Silverman 1970:214
Maupiti, Society Islands	102	39	38	Hooper 1970:63
Piri, Society Islands	54	25	46	Levy 1970:75
Nukuoro, Ponape District	48	32	67	Carroll 1970c:154
Romónum, Truk District	Two out of three households with children		67	Ruth Goodenough 1970:314

that the data are presented. In some communities, such calculations are not feasible due to the structure of adoption arrangements. On Kapingamarangi, for instance, adoption situations are so complex and fluid that a simple statement of the number of adoptees in a household is virtually impossible to make and would have little relevance to the adoption pattern if it were made (Lieber 1970:171). From the cases surveyed, however, it is evident that Rotanese fosterage is an exception to the generally high incidence of adoption in Oceania.

FUNCTIONAL EXPLANATIONS OF ADOPTION

A review of the conclusions of contributors to Carroll's (1970a) volume indicates two basic functions served by adoption in the communities examined: (1) the expression of kinship solidarity; or, (2) the redistribution of property, or both. To be sure, form and function differ from island to island. Nevertheless, there is a striking uniformity in the explanatory statements of the several authors.

Adoption operates everywhere to create new or rearrange existing kinship relations. At the very least, new parent-child or other dyadic relations are established, and in many societies the range of new kinship relations generated by adoption is extensive. In this sense, adoption may be considered a primary mechanism for the recruitment of personnel into kin groups that complements other recruitment mechanisms such as marriage and procreation. The economic and integrative functions of marriage and procreation have long been recognized; that adoption serves similar functions is therefore not surprising.

The functional significance of Oceanic adoption lies in the fact that it takes place almost entirely within the context of existing kinship networks. All but one of the authors in Carroll's volume (1970a) report this to be the case in the communities studied.[2] In effect, the recruitment system is closed and involves the redistribution of kinsmen rather than the addition of non-kinsmen. Since adoption strategies are limited in this fashion, the expression of kinship solidarity is assured in that the recruitment of every foster or adoptive child must call attention to and rely upon the complex set of rights and duties associated with kinship.

A particularly clear example of adoption as an expression of kinship solidarity is found on Tamana Island in the Southern

Gilberts. Here, adoption ultimately involves a transfer of property: "If this transfer of property takes place within the family it simply serves to consolidate an ancestral estate and reaffirm reciprocal obligations between kinsmen" (Lundsgaarde 1970:256). Departing from this norm by refusing to adopt a sibling's child or by adopting a non-kinsman conveys a strong message: "Such an act is interpreted as an insult against one's siblings, and it most effectively serves as a warning signal to one's natural heirs that, unless they prepare to take better care of their aging parents, their inheritance share will be markedly reduced" (Lundsgaarde 1970:256).

Robert Levy sees an entirely different message being conveyed by Oceanic adoption in general, and, on the surface, it appears to contradict the argument that adoption expresses kinship solidarity: "The message in the Polynesian and Micronesian adoption is that *relationships between all parents and children are fragile and conditional*" (Levy 1970:84). However, the message may be rephrased with regard to all children's kinsmen, in which case it reads: *In the face of adversity, including the absence or death of parents, security and support are to be found among kinsmen* (see Brooks, chapter 3). Accordingly, adoption in Oceania occurs predominantly as a transaction among kinsmen.

It is generally agreed that adoption plays an important role in the redistribution of property in Oceania, although statements to this effect vary more than do those concerning adoption as an expression of kinship solidarity. As I shall demonstrate from the data on Rotanese fosterage, this variability is at least partially dependent upon the variable role of kinship in the flow of economic goods and services in Oceanic communities.

In addition to Levy's (1970) treatment of adoption as a psychological message, several other of the authors in Carroll (1970a) do not cite economic functions for the practice. Hawaiian adoption, for instance, "... combines personal gratification with social reward in a most compelling fashion ..." (Howard et al. 1970:50). Others point out specific economic functions but caution against overestimating their significance. Thus, Lundsgaarde concludes that adoption on Tamana Island "... reinforces family solidarity by establishing additional ties between kinsmen, and it is not to be regarded solely as a convenient way to reallocate rights and privileges to scarce natural resources among destitute members of the family" (1970:256).[3]

For the most part, however, the economic function of property redistribution is viewed unambiguously as a reasonable functional explanation for the prevalence of Oceanic adoption. On Ponape, for example, "... it appears clear that adoption serves important socioeconomic functions in bringing about a rough redistribution of land in each generation, and in providing a form of personal care for the aged" (Fischer 1970:310–311). Also, in the Western Tuamotus, "Together with ... other practices it [adoption] facilitated the allocation and redistribution of people among small localized descent groups ..." (Ottino 1970:88).

What this examination of recent studies of Oceanic adoption reveals is, first, that the expression of kinship solidarity and the redistribution of property are indeed two basic functions served by adoption on Pacific islands. A second conclusion reached through this review is that there is certainly a wide range of variability in the degree to which adoption serves these functions in Oceania. At one extreme is Romónum, Truk, where

> adoption is not used by the adopting parents as a pretext for extracting favors from the real ... parents, nor ... were there reports of the real parents trying to wangle subsequent favors from the adopting parents.... Children are not exchanged by families to ensure that mutual obligations are lived up to. Adoptions are not used to strengthen weakening social bonds caused by absence or indifference. Donor parents do not give an accompanying piece of land or goods with their child to establish for him a social base independent of the adopting parents (Ruth Goodenough 1970:317).[4]

At the other extreme is Kapingamarangi, where "adoption and fosterage are behaviors exclusive to the relations among kinsmen" (Lieber 1970:159), and where, furthermore, "the cultural models of kinship relations and behavior in general and of adoption in particular afford an ideal framework within which, and by means of which, people can manipulate their social relationships to their immediate or future advantage" (Lieber 1970:203).

Having described the variable functional significance of adoption in several Oceanic communities, I will discuss that variation as it applies to Rotanese fosterage by means of a descriptive model currently being developed for the analysis of decision-making. Before doing so, however, a brief description of the ethnographic setting is in order.

ROTA, MARIANA ISLANDS

Rota is the southernmost island of the Mariana Islands District of the U.S. Trust Territory of the Pacific Islands. The island has an area of 32.9 square miles and rises to a height of 1,612 feet on a series of limestone terraces. The population of 1,062 is located in a single community, Songsong Village, on a narrow peninsula at the southwestern end of the island.[5]

Since Magellan's discovery in 1521, the Mariana Islands have been successively dominated by four colonial powers (Spoehr 1954:34–91; Thompson 1945). During the Spanish period, the native Chamorro population was decimated, converted to Catholicism, and had its social organization restructured from that of a stratified and probably matrilineal system to an egalitarian and cognatic one. The Germans and Japanese, especially, established formal colonial systems of government, law, and education. Under American control since World War II, modernization has proceeded rapidly on Rota, and the traditional subsistence base of swidden agriculture has been largely overshadowed by the economics of entrepreneurship and wage labor.

Rota today has all the material trappings of a peasant community embedded in postindustrial civilization. Songsong Village boasts an administration building, a small hospital, a library, a post office, a power plant, a slaughterhouse, and a sixteen-room hotel and restaurant, all of which were built between 1968 and 1970. There are, in addition, numerous family-owned stores and bars, a movie theater, two gas stations, an elementary school, and the recently refurbished Catholic church of San Francisco de Borja.

The following outline of Rotanese economics and social organization should be considered in the context of three current demographic realities. First, the population density of the island is thirty-one persons per square mile. This density is quite low relative to other Micronesian islands (Hainline 1965:1176–1177). Second, an examination of land registration records in the Rota Office of Land Management shows that only 31 percent of the island is controlled by Rotanese (exclusive of the village), while it is estimated that 41 percent of the island consists of arable land (Bowers 1950:126). All land not otherwise registered is held in public trust by the Trust Territory government. Third, emigration is a significant variable in Rotanese population dynamics. A comparison of my 1971 village census with the family list maintained by the municipal government revealed that thirty-four families had moved away from the island since January 1970. Only one family immigrated to Rota from Guam during this period. These data suggest that the intense pressures of population on available land resources characteristic of many Pacific islands do not obtain on Rota. As will be seen in the discussion of economics below, this bears directly on the functional significance of Rotanese fosterage.

ECONOMICS AND PROPERTY

The Rotanese cash economy is based on local employment by the Trust Territory government and the export of beef and vegetables to Guam and Saipan. Income derived from these two sources and a growing tourist industry stimulate a smaller private commercial sector. As noted above, a subsistence base of swidden agriculture underlies the highly developed cash economy.

Land remains the basis of economic security on Rota, despite the fact that the average biweekly government payroll of nearly $7,500 is distributed among more than one-half of Rota's 160 households. The importance of land is partially inflated by the great demand for beef and agricultural produce in the markets of Guam and Saipan. Basically, however, land is the source of daily subsistence. Wages may be insufficient and employment limited, commercial crops may fail and market demand may be uneven, but the production of traditional foods for direct consumption is constant and assured.

Land is controlled primarily by individuals and, to a lesser extent, by sibling corporations in the name of a trustee. Control of land is validated through legal procedures established by the Trust Territory government and takes the form of government–individual contracts pertaining to village lots, private agricultural parcels, village and agricultural homesteads, and grazing leases.

Except for grazing leases, real property may be transferred among individuals through direct exchange of parcels, sale, or inheritance. In addition, usufruct arrangements are commonly allocated among kinsmen, as are arrangements for sharing subsistence items among related households.

KINSHIP AND HOUSEHOLDS

The Rotanese kinship system is cognatic and essentially the product of Hispanicization. As indicated in figure 11, kin terms are Spanish cognates, with the exceptions of those for spouse (*asagua*, not shown), offspring, and sibling. Collateral and lineal relatives are distinguished terminologically. Agnatic and uterine linkages are not differentiated, although the custom of agnatically-passed surnames provides identity for a diffuse patrilateral "family" entity.

FIGURE 11. Rotanese Consanguineal Kin Terms for *Parientes* 'Kinsmen'.

	Lineal		Collateral	
Generation	Male	Female	Male	Female
+2	*guelo* 'grand-father'	*guela* 'grand-mother'	*tio* 'uncle'	*tia* 'aunt'
+1	*tata* 'father'	*nana* 'mother'		
0		*chelu* 'sibling'	*primo* 'male cousin'	*prima* 'female cousin'
−1	*lahi* 'son'	*haga* 'daughter'	*sobrino* 'nephew'	*sobrina* 'niece'
−2	*nieto* 'grand-son'	*nieta* 'grand-daughter'		

The principal unit of kinship is the nuclear family, headed by a male who functions as husband and father. Village social structure may be viewed in this respect as a network of nuclear families, linked through both spouses. However, these links are predicated less on formal ties than on sentiment and affect. Such bonds are generally peripheral as a mechanism for the organization of production units.

Beyond the nuclear family, it cannot be said that an individual's personal kindred comprises a primary interaction sphere in the conduct of his daily affairs. Numerous other social units, especially occupational peer groups and neighboring households, play more important roles in the continuing cycle of work and leisure activities. The personal kindred, through the structure of linked nuclear families, operates most importantly during scheduled and unscheduled life crises to pool moral support and economic resources in aid of the affected individual and his nuclear family.

I have alluded to the incorporation of siblings for the purpose of land control. The significance of this will become apparent in the treatment of Rotanese fosterage as an activity system. Briefly, siblings may inherit land from their parents as a unit under conditions where it would be inappropriate to distribute the land to them as individuals. The corporateness of this unit is limited strictly to the use and control of land assigned to it.

A final socioeconomic unit, the household, must be described in order that Rotanese fosterage may be viewed in its proper setting. The household is the basic economic unit on Rota. Members share a common roof and table and routinely pool their labor and resources in cooperative support of the unit. The household developmental cycle may be conceptualized as a continuum, beginning with a married couple's establishment of a new household and ending with the transfer of leadership from the original couple to other members or to household dissolution through the death of its members. An analysis of Rotanese households reveals five distinctive states or types defined through time by the arrival and departure of members and by the status of members relative to one another (see table 23).

The nuclear family ordinarily constitutes a household by itself, or it may be combined with generationally linked families into an extended household. It is within the composition of households,

TABLE 23.   Household Types on Rota

Type	Composition	No.
Young Nuclear	Consists entirely of a newly married couple with no children over six years, the age at which schooling begins.	27
Established Nuclear	Consists entirely of a married couple with children of school age or older.	66
Extended	Consists minimally of a household head in the senior generation, with married offspring and/or other relatives in residence.	23
Residual Extended	Consists minimally of a household head in the junior generation, with the former household head still in residence.	18
Residual Nuclear	Consists minimally of a married couple or surviving spouse, with all offspring residing elsewhere.	20
Other	Consists primarily of young bachelors temporarily residing alone.	6
TOTAL		160

SOURCE: Author's field notes, 1970–1971.

and not families as such, that the presence or absence of dependent children contributes to delineation of both the responsibilities and capacities of nuclear families. The question of personnel recruitment through fosterage, then, is pertinent to households rather than to nuclear families, even when the two are equivalent in membership.

I have presented the preceding outline of Rotanese social organization in an effort to depict the sociocultural context within which Rotanese fosterage takes place. By most measures, it is clear that Songsong Village on Rota is rapidly modernizing and Americanizing. New values, new technologies, and a new variety of economic alternatives all are having an impact on this small, kin-based society. Many features of modern Rotanese society compete with fosterage as a means of allocating kin-group personnel in relation to economic resources, with a consequent reduction in the importance of fosterage and other transactions in kinship as expressions of kinship solidarity.

ROTANESE FOSTERAGE

The Chamorro term *poksai* is a root form that refers to 'raising' or 'caring for' an animal, such as a pig or a cow. Through metaphorical extension and nominalization, the term *pineksai* refers to a 'foster child'.[6] As a transaction in kinship, Rotanese fosterage involves at least a temporary transfer of a minimal set of parental rights and duties among kinsmen. These include rights of discipline and domestic labor and duties of socialization and nurturance with regard to the foster child. The child is considered an active participant in the transaction to the extent that he is old enough or interested enough to assert his will in the matter.

The status of foster child is congruent with the status of offspring only to the degree that both occupy positions as immature members of households. Specifically, a foster child does not give up rights to property in his natal family, nor does he gain rights to property in his foster family in any way that usurps the property rights of the natural children of that family. Formal distinctions between foster and natural children are maintained within the household. A foster child retains the surname of his natal family. The expression of kinship relations through address terms is similarly maintained as it existed prior to the fosterage transaction. In the case of fostered infants, instruction in these prior relations is an element of enculturation.

In terms of role expectations, a foster child becomes a full participant in the fostering household's domestic affairs. He assumes no more and no less than the typical prerogatives and obligations of childhood. With the exceptions discussed below, there is nothing in the status of foster child that lends itself to special parental attention, either positive or negative.

A foster child's status is distinctive in that he continues to maintain an identity with his natal family's household. Ideally, a foster child will receive incidental economic support from his natural parents in the form of small gifts such as money, clothing, and toys.

Rights and duties allocated in fosterage transactions are enforceable only so long as a foster child maintains active status as a member of the fostering household. Any of the parties involved may initiate a termination of the arrangement. The relationship invariably terminates when a foster child establishes his own household after marriage.

There is a close correspondence between the kinship relations of natural and foster parents and the circumstances and motivations that lead to fosterage. Three types of relationship account for 84 percent of current Rotanese fosterage: (1) a natural and a foster parent are siblings; (2) a natural parent is an offspring of a foster parent and married; and (3) a natural parent is an offspring of a foster parent and unmarried. The distribution of each of these is summarized in table 24.[7]

While apparently not the most common case in which fosterage arrangements arise, the situation wherein a natural and a foster parent are siblings was the most common example of fosterage described by informants. Two motivations were cited in these examples. In the first instance, an individual would express a desire to alleviate a sibling's economic burden by fostering one or more of his offspring. In the second case, an individual would express a desire to have children in an otherwise childless household and would ask a sibling to give up one or more children for fosterage.

Rotanese grandparents were characterized by informants (including grandparents) as desiring to foster grandchildren. Often, an 'old Chamorro custom' was cited in which grandparents had the right to raise a first grandchild as their own. All of my informants agreed that this custom had long since died out, but they felt, nevertheless, that allowing one's child to be fostered by

TABLE 24. Closest Kin Relationship of Natural Parents to Foster Parents

Relationship	Number of Foster Children
Sibling	8
Offspring—Married	15
Offspring—Unmarried	9
Other	6
TOTAL	38

SOURCE: Author's field notes, 1970–1971.

the child's grandparents was an appropriate obligation of kinship. Among the twenty residual nuclear households on Rota, six contained foster grandchildren.

The notion that fostering grandchildren expresses family solidarity and continuity is further borne out by the presence of more than one-half of the grandchildren in my sample in established nuclear households. Typically, if a couple decides to emigrate to Guam or Saipan, grandparents will ask to foster one or more grandchildren as a *rekwetdo* 'keepsake' of the departing couple, even though a number of their own children may still be resident in the household.

The discussion so far applies primarily to the legitimate children of a married couple. Illegitimacy presents a different set of problems. I was unable to gather accurate data on Rotanese illegitimacy, but the impression I gained from informants in this Catholic community was that bastardy, while held to be morally unjustifiable, did not warrant strong rebuke for either parents or offspring. Illegitimate children are generally raised by the mother in the mother's natal household. The fostering of an illegitimate child by his grandparents becomes an obligation of kinship when the natural mother does not reside on Rota and cannot establish a viable household in her off-island circumstances, as might be the case if she were going to school or working and living alone.

Two principles emerged from these data as normative rules in the conduct of fosterage arrangements. First, any such arrangement can only be initiated by the future foster parent. Informants stressed the inappropriateness of offering up one's child for fosterage. This would be viewed as an admission of inadequacy on the part of the natural parent and an unwarranted exploitation of the supportive obligations of kinship. Second, any of the parties to the arrangement, including the child in question, may initiate its termination.

The operation of these principles has interesting consequences. Although they are not construed as demands, Rotanese do not expect requests to foster children to be denied. This is generally true of all requests made by kinsmen of one another. Subtle and sometimes lengthy assessments of relevant circumstances must be carried out before such a state of positive anticipation can be achieved. An individual will ordinarily be quite certain that a particular child is available for fosterage before actually confronting the parents with a fosterage request. On the other hand, parents (and children themselves) who seek out foster parents among their relatives are expected to create covert circumstances and situations that allow a potential foster parent to anticipate a positive response to his fosterage request.

That fosterage termination is completely optional is most convincingly illustrated in the case of fostered grandchildren. Informants were quick to point out the self-centered strategies of fostered grandchildren who command favored treatment as a price for continued residence with the grandparents. Young school-age informants readily volunteered information on an assortment of ploys used to work their will with grandparents, the most common of which was an implied threat to return to their natal household. Conversely, parents may terminate such an arrangement if they feel their child is enjoying too lax an up-bringing, and grandparents may return fostered grandchildren who fail to show proper respect for their elders.

It is evident that Rotanese fosterage functions to express and strengthen ties of kinship, at least to the extent that fosterage arrangements are ". . . behaviors exclusive to the relations among kinsmen" (Lieber 1970:159). Fosterage also supports and is part of a system of reciprocal kin relations wherein disputes over the sharing of resources and services are minimized by delaying actual requests until situations are structured to assure positive responses.

Because parents do not offer their offspring as foster children, the fosterage system does not function as a reciprocal demand on kinship obligations. In this sense, its impact as an integrative force is weakened. For instance, I have mentioned a trend toward emigration. If parents could be expected to call upon individuals, particularly siblings, to act as foster parents, the flow of families away from Rota might be more restricted as a result. This would be the case because fostering a child carries with it the secondary obligation of raising that child on Rota as a Rotanese. Thus, fosterage has the effect of binding the fostering household to the island for the duration of the arrangement. However, since parents do not ask kin-related (or any other) households to foster their children, fosterage does not serve as an overt check on the flow of emigrating households.

While adoption functions widely in Oceania as a procedure for the redistribution of property, it specifically does not serve this function on Rota. Foster children are potential heirs to their foster parent's estate only by virtue of a pre-existing kinship relation, not as a result of the fosterage arrangement itself. It cannot be denied that the selection of foster children implies a preference that might be extended to inheritance, but the claims of an individual's spouse and natural offspring generally exclude those of other kinsmen (Smith 1972:143–144).

The economic functions served by Rotanese fosterage are limited to the daily cycle of socioeconomic activities in households. Considering the increasing dependence on imported goods and the rising standards of health and education, the financial responsibilities of raising children are great. The distribution of children within households has considerable impact on the economics of these households. In a community where more than one-half of the households depend on government employment for cash income, the cost of raising children is no longer balanced by their labor input in housekeeping and minor agricultural chores. It may be concluded, then, that Rotanese fosterage functions primarily to relieve economically burdened households by relocating children in more prosperous households. It does not function as a means of property redistribution.

ALTERNATE STRATEGIES

As mentioned above, the incidence of fosterage in Rotanese households is lower than in any community cited in Carroll's volume (1970a). Such observed differences in the functional significance of adoption may be partially accounted for, or at least described more precisely, by a consideration of alternate strategies that serve the same or similar functions.

This is not to say that a consideration of alternate strategies will provide an adequate explanation for their differential significance. In general, I concur with the critiques of functionalist explanations as being teleological and assuming an unwarranted degree of institutional integration and equilibrium for sociocultural systems (Jarvie 1965; Merton 1957). However, functional propositions are valuable as heuristics. In particular, I want to develop the second part of the "theorem" that "... *just as the same item may have multiple functions, so may the same function be diversely fulfilled by alternate items*" (Merton 1957:33–34).

Specifically, I suggest the hypothesis that *if a function is served by a number of alternate strategies, then any one of those strategies will tend to be utilized in inverse proportion to the utilization of the others*. This hypothesis does not concern an explanation of why certain strategies dominate others or how it came to be that alternate strategies developed in the first place. It is rather a statement of relationships that requires explicit and systematic description.

Rotanese fosterage functions as an expression of kinship solidarity. Since fosterage transactions are restricted to kinsmen, they call into play a variety of rights and duties associated with kinship, but so do a number of other strategies, such as those entailed in marriage, land tenure, and household formation. Fosterage on Rota is relatively insignificant compared to these other strategies.

Clearly, the hypothesis of alternate strategies cannot be considered in isolation. At a higher level, kinship systems serve additional functions, including the expression and maintenance of social integration. Where kinship systems are confronted with other strategies of social integration, variations in the relative significance of strategies supporting kinship emerge. The strategies that decline in this process will be those that serve the most restricted sets of functions in the sociocultural system. Adoption is one of these as compared, say, to marriage, land tenure, and household recruitment through birth.

In the Rotanese case, I have mentioned several social units not based on kinship that contribute significantly to the social integration of the community. Rotanese households nowadays tend to maximize autonomy as socioeconomic units. They are not necessarily constrained by the fortunes or failures of other households. The impact of these trends on fosterage is much greater than on other kin-based institutions, primarily because many of the others continue to serve a broader range of functions in the face of a declining role for kinship in the community.

More to the point, perhaps, is the fact that a number of kin-based strategies on Rota operate at least as effectively as fosterage to alleviate the economic burden of children on households, and thus they fulfill many of the same economic functions as fosterage. One such strategy is the amalgamation of households. Married couples often remain with one or the other set of parents even after they have children of their own. It is not uncommon for families in young nuclear households to return to their original extended households in times of economic difficulty. Similarly, the generalized sharing of local produce and labor services among kinsmen undermines at least the economic need for actually removing children from burgeoning households. This does not preclude, of course, the sharing of children as resources among kinsmen for purely affective or symbolic reasons (see Marshall, chapter 2).

Land tenure and adoption practices are intimately related in many Oceanic communities, although this does not appear to be the case on Rota. Rotanese land tenure is only partially constrained by kinship. Inheritance is, of course, a major system of real property transfer, but kinsmen otherwise play a minor role in the overall acquisition and use of land. The availability of land through cash purchase, the homestead program, and government leasing of grazing parcels, in combination with the existing surplus of arable land, tend to check the role of fosterage and other kinship institutions with regard to the distribution of real property.

An aspect of the inheritance system with particular relevance to fosterage is the practice of passing land to offspring as a corporate whole in cases where it is felt that dividing the land would result in parcels of insufficient size (Smith 1972:162–165). In addition to being one of several traditional expressions of kinship solidarity, this practice precludes much of the necessity for redistributing children with regard to landholdings; it thereby mitigates widespread adoption and fosterage transactions as psychological or ecological responses to land hunger (see Brady, chapter 7).

The socioeconomic situation on Rota today promotes the functional interplay of a number of alternate strategies not based on kinship that serve the same economic functions as fosterage. Perhaps the most significant of these compared to fosterage is the option for families to emigrate to Guam or Saipan in search of economic opportunity. In some cases, such a move may stimulate the initiation of a fosterage transaction, especially between a child and his grandparents as discussed above. In this instance, however, fosterage functions more as an expression of kinship solidarity than as a release from economic hardship. Most emigrating families move into better, not worse, economic circumstances and hence acquire a greater capacity to hold on to their members.

These examples illustrate the presence of alternate strategies to fosterage in the Rotanese sociocultural system. In their collective capacity to serve similar functions, these alternate strategies must be taken into account when considering the relative significance of Rotanese fosterage. In the remaining discussion, the concept of *activity system* is taken up as a means of more explicitly describing the variable significance of alternate strategies.

ALTERNATE STRATEGIES AS ACTIVITY SYSTEMS

The concept of activity system has been developed in detail by Howard (1963, 1970) in the context of decision-making analyses. He begins by questioning the notion of social structure:

> Instead of conceiving of a society as having a social structure, I would suggest we conceive of a social behavior as being structured by participating in given activities within which behavioral choices (decisions) are regular and predictable. Our 'systems' would then be best regarded as *activity systems*, the relevant units being the principles ... that are predictive of choice among behavioral alternatives (Howard 1963:410).

In this sense, the strategies discussed above may be considered as activity systems. Where Howard has focused on decision-making principles as internal elements of activity systems, I have concentrated on relations among activity systems that are functional equivalents.

In a later paper, Howard discusses activity systems in terms of the kinds of decisions that constitute them:

> Not all behavioral decisions are subject to normative evaluation. Some choices that confront people involve several equally respectable possibilities, such as the choice of occupation in our society. Under such circumstances individual motivation is a significant determining factor, and in order to account for such behavior we need to take into

account psychological variables as well as cultural principles. I refer to these as *strategic* decisions. Decisions that allow no alternatives to what is agreed upon as being correct I refer to as *normative* decisions. One's 'choice' under these latter conditions is between doing the right thing and doing something deviant (Howard 1970:346).

At one level, the presence of alternate strategies is partially determined by the possibility of strategic decisions. But what is more illuminating to the issue of relative functional significance is the combination of strategic *and* normative decision principles as internal components of particular strategies or activity systems.

I suggest as a corollary to the hypothesis I presented above that *the significance of a given alternate activity system is directly related to the ratio of normative to strategic decision principles within that system.* Thus, Rotanese fosterage is constrained by only a few normative decision principles that restrict its operation to kinsmen and require that transactions be initiated only by future foster parents. On the other hand, the number of strategic decision principles pertaining to fosterage is quite large, including a full range of personal motivations affecting the parties involved, a flexible set of time and space components relating to the initiation, maintenance, and termination of fosterage transactions, and the potential of all parties involved to alter or terminate the fosterage arrangement once it is established.

With reference to the expression of kinship solidarity, marriage involves a host of normative decision principles concerning such matters as exogamy, the conduct of courtship, and ideal kinship behavior. Regarding other activity systems that serve the same economic functions as fosterage, consider the passing of land to offspring as a corporate whole. The normative decision principles in this case concern the rights of the spouse, the types and amounts of land available, the rights and duties of the eldest child as head of the corporation, and the allocation of usufruct rights within the corporation, to name the more important elements.

For both marriage and corporate inheritance, assume for the sake of argument that the greater number of normative decision principles compared to fosterage does not affect the number of strategic decision principles involved. In fact, the number of strategic principles might decline, but it would certainly not increase. Marriage and corporate inheritance may then be ranked over fosterage in absolute terms relative to the number of normative decision principles constraining these three alternate activity systems. This being the case, the corollary is supported to the extent that the relatively greater functional significance of marriage and corporate inheritance compared to fosterage has been demonstrated in previous discussion.

SUMMARY AND CONCLUSIONS

Viewed as recruitment strategies, adoption practices in Oceania have been explained functionally as expressions of kinship solidarity and as procedures for the redistribution of property. A review of recent literature indicates that these functional explanations are valid, but that there is cross-cultural variation in the degree to which adoption serves these functions. Data on Rotanese fosterage both support these conclusions and constitute a counterexample of the generally high incidence of adoption in the Pacific.

The frequency of fosterage on Rota is about one-half that of the average adoption occurrences in a sample of Oceanic communities drawn from Carroll's volume (1970a). Rotanese fosterage also may be distinguished in terms of the small number of rights and duties transferred and the fragility of the arrangements. Being restricted to kinsmen, Rotanese fosterage expresses and strengthens the relations among kinsmen; by removing children from economically burdened households, it serves important economic functions.

A comparison of alternate strategies to fosterage on Rota suggests the following hypothesis concerning the relative significance of functional equivalents: If a function is served by a number of alternate strategies, then any one of those strategies will tend to be utilized in inverse proportion to the utilization of the others. A corollary to this hypothesis emerges when alternate strategies are treated as activity systems consisting of various ratios of normative and strategic decision principles: The significance of a given alternate activity system is directly related to the ratio of normative to strategic decision principles within that system.

The data from Rota support this hypothesis and its corollary, although the analysis has been necessarily brief. A real test of their validity must be cross-cultural. The basis for such controlled comparison has been established in Carroll's volume (1970a) and in the present chapters. Our understanding of adoption practices per se will surely be increased by an examination of their inter-relations with other adaptive strategies.

NOTES

Materials for this chapter were gathered during a twelve-month field study on Rota, Mariana Islands (July 1970 to June 1971). The support of a predoctoral grant (no. 2491) from the Wenner-Gren Foundation for Anthropological Research, Incorporated, is gratefully acknowledged.

1. The sample of Pacific communities is neither representative nor random. The communities are those in Carroll's volume (1970a) for which appropriate data are presented. Against the point I am making is the fact that of the two communities with the highest frequency of adoption, Nukuoro has the fewest household cases, making it the least desirable example in terms of magnitude, and the Romónum figure is based on a statement of the adoption rate rather than on a compilation of cases. Regarding support for the Romónum example, however, see Marshall (chapter 2) for another example from greater Trukese society in which a compilation of cases is given.

2. The exception is Martin Silverman (1970). Non-Banabans on Rambi Island can only gain an economic foothold through adoption. Why Banabans should adopt non-Banabans is not made clear, and all economic advantages of the arrangement seem to fall to the non-Banabans. However, ". . . in most child adoptions by Banabans of non-Banabans there is already a consanguineal or affinal link between the adopter and a parent of the adoptee . . ." (Silverman 1970:222).

3. It is interesting to compare this statement with those concerning the Tamana Islanders' use of adoption practices as a threat to withhold or deflect economic benefits from kinsmen (Lundsgaarde 1970:265). This, it seems to me, is an important manifestation of the economic functions of adoption on Tamana Island.

4. Ruth Goodenough associates the high incidence of adoption on Romónum with fertility rates: "The current adoption rate is high. Evidence suggests that the current high has peaked in a period of unevenly reduced fertility in women, most probably as a result of venereal infection" (1970:337). It should also be noted, however, that on Romónum "adoption is almost always a transaction between kinsmen, and usually close kinsmen" and that "adoption gives adopted children added social and economic options" (1970:337). For a different treatment of adoption in greater Trukese society, see Marshall (chapter 2).

5. Much of the ethnographic material presented here is discussed in greater detail in my doctoral dissertation (Smith 1972).

6. Laura Thompson includes the word *pinigsai* 'adopted child' in a list of "... practically obsolete kin terms" (1945:15). Spoehr does not mention the term for Saipanese 'adoption' (1954:142), and it was unfamiliar to numerous Rotanese teenagers, unless the subject of family members already had been established in our conversation. It is quite possible that the term *pineksai* is restricted to Rota and that it occurs infrequently in reference to specific foster children. The term was recognized immediately by adults interviewed, however, and they readily supplied it when I professed linguistic ignorance. No synonym was ever suggested.

7. The six cases listed as "other" in table 24 are truly disparate. One household has two foster children who are natural brothers unrelated to their foster parents. The elder, who is twenty-four years old, works for his foster parents in a family business and considers himself more a boarder than a foster child. In another case, the foster child is a mentally retarded illegitimate girl who has been rejected by her mother and is shuttled from one household to another. A fourth foster child is an infant godchild of the foster parents' son-in-law who lives on Guam. A fifth case involves a distantly related foster child. Finally, a wealthy childless couple has legally adopted an unrelated Saipanese girl under provisions of the Trust Territory Code.

12

ADAPTIVE ENGINEERING:
AN OVERVIEW OF
ADOPTION IN OCEANIA

Ivan Brady

INTRODUCTION

The data contained in this volume display adoption as a multi-functional institution that can be applied to many diverse needs and situations that people on islands encounter in the course of sustaining themselves and perpetuating their social systems. Amidst this diversity, however, is a general thesis asserted in various ways by the preceding chapters: by creating new or reinforcing existing kinship relations, adoption actualizes or extends the range of sociability, resource sharing, alliance, and population survival (see also Firth 1929; Monberg 1970; Carroll 1970a). A corollary thesis is that adoption is an adaptive mechanism for equitably distributing people relative to the variable require-ments for personnel that domestic and descent groups are likely to develop in exploiting their physical and cultural environments over time (see also Goodenough 1955; Fischer 1970; Keesing 1970, 1975). The purpose of this final chapter is to provide additional support for these generalizations and to develop some others that are closely related by: (1) reviewing the nature of adoption as a resource management strategy; and (2) assessing the functional importance of adoption as an alliance and internal reinforcement mechanism in groups with different problems for maintaining solidarity and structural continuity.

ADOPTION AS A RESOURCE MANAGEMENT STRATEGY

Managing strategic resources such as land, foodstuffs, political power, and personnel in a manner that selects for population survival and sociocultural persistence in changing environments is a basic adaptive problem faced by human societies. Such management frequently depends on an internal pooling and sharing of the fruits of domestic production in households, and on the exchange of strategic resources between households and other types of basic production and consumption units. Kinship theoretically provides an ideological charter for integrating individuals and groups in ways that are consistent with these interests. It is also often the idiom through which political demands are advanced, economic goals are maximized, and adaptive social alignments are arranged (see Keesing 1975:122). Adoption is a specific type of kinship phenomenon and resource management strategy that incorporates these attributes.

From the standpoint of the individuals involved in each transaction, adoption serves multiple and often disparate goals. From a broader analytic perspective, the basic dimension of these goals appears to be a reallocation or new arrangement of what is probably the most strategic resource of all in human societies: interpersonal relationships that are structured in a context of solidarity and perpetuity with other human beings. People themselves are the media of exchange in these instances, as in marriage and birth, and new or revised solidary relationships upon which individuals or groups can depend for concerted action and mutual assistance in times of need theoretically are engineered as products or outcomes in each event.

Like marriage, but unlike birth in some contexts, however, adoption is a conscious, goal-oriented, and volitional permutation of existing alignments of personnel and related resources (see chapter 1). All such transformations in interpersonal relations and their emergent patterns are governed by the rules and processes of kinship reciprocity in general—that is, all are constrained and regulated in part by institutionalized obligations to give, to receive, and to reciprocate for services rendered, goods transferred, and resources shared in various social contexts (see Mauss

1967; Sahlins 1965, 1972; Brady 1972; Laughlin 1974). The exchange of strategic resources of any type necessarily entails some compromise in specific resource control by each of the parties involved, although not necessarily in the sense of a zero-sum game in which one person's gain is another person's loss (see Buchler and Nutini 1969). Different demands may be satisfied and positive relations engineered in both directions through a single exchange event, or through the multiple and cumulative complexities of alternating exchanges over time (see Lévi-Strauss 1969; Prattis 1973). However, relative to the focus of adoption transactions on consciously engineered solidarity as outcomes in each event, it is important to recognize that the principle of generosity and the particular compromises involved " . . . can create conflict as well as contribute to solidarity, and can also be manipulated to secure an advantage over one's fellows" (Cook 1966:328–329; see also Sahlins 1960, 1963; Trivers 1971:35; Whitten and Whitten 1972:258).

Adoptions couched in the principle of generosity and aimed at resolving conflict on one level of interpersonal relations can easily provoke conflict on other levels. Recruiting adoptees to fill vacant domestic work roles in households, for example, may bring resentment from other members of those households who suddenly find themselves in close competition with the adoptees for such strategic resources as food, property, or parental affection. The jural and operational demands of pooling labor and other resources in the household context may mitigate some of these conflicts, but they occur, nevertheless. Similarly, relinquishing children for adoption may relieve economically disadvantaged groups of some of their members and set up new relations for supplementary income through reciprocity with the adopters. The same transaction may produce psychological conflict or stress from the donors' perspective because of their sentimental or affective demands for close association with the adoptees. Compromise is the inevitable common denominator of such transactions, and reciprocity is the rule that helps to determine the outcome.

The point of adoption as a resource management strategy is to mediate rather than to provoke conflict, of course, and such mediation may be especially important when it is applied to problems of differential access to personnel and certain types of interpersonal relationships that are perceived as basic for maintaining order and continuity in the society. From the standpoint of individual actors in the social system, conflict mediation of this sort may be manifested widely in continuing negotiations over the balance of power between the sexes and between the old and the young, the common interests of age-mates that crosscut the interests of members of the same kinship groups, the relative strength of ties between primary relatives such as husband and wife or brother and sister, and the juxtaposition of corporate groups in conflict over access to physical resources (Keesing 1975:142), among other possibilities. Social systems are sustained and perhaps altered in time as individuals and groups attempt to mediate these and related problems that impinge on their survivability. Adoption is only one of several types of exchange patterns that may develop and flourish under such circumstances; but it is nonetheless a prime example of sociocultural engineering that may be applied to problems of structural discontinuity, insufficient resources or other inequities that people must resolve in the course of perpetuating themselves and their societies.

Understanding the adaptive significance of adoption in a given social system thus requires, among other things, assessing the role of adoption in mediating specific conflicts under changing sociocultural and ecological conditions, and this, in turn, may require estimating the degree to which adoption is applied exclusively to such problems relative to other means available to the population for achieving the same ends. The problem of exclusiveness in this context begs some classic functional questions that may only be answered in depth by tracing the data through a mazeway of theoretical and empirical entanglements, none of which may be easily resolved. Functional propositions concerned with the relations between sociocultural forms under given structural and ecological conditions, as well as with the interaction of those forms over time, inevitably lead in broader analyses to a necessary distinction between efficient and ultimate causality, to presumptions of "open" versus "closed" systems, and perhaps to a reconciliation of what is meant by such analytic constructs as "homeostasis" in the light of empirical evidence for ongoing change and some disequilibrium as a natural feature of human social systems, among other considerations (see Jarvie 1965;

Leach 1965; Harris 1968). Without ignoring or underestimating the importance of these broad problems for studying function, structure and process in adoption, the goal in the remainder of this chapter is more narrowly conceived as a logical next step for ultimately sorting out the broader issues. Specifically, the goal in the following section is to obviate some potential misinterpretations of the functional propositions developed thereafter, and, in a more positive sense, to provide a preliminary framework in terms of which subsequent analyses of the adaptive functions of adoption—and the relationship of adoption to birth, marriage, and certain kinds of descent rules—may be evaluated.

ADOPTION, FUNCTIONALISM, AND THE PROBLEM OF "NEEDS" SERVED

In concrete and culturally specific terms, the functions of adoption as an adaptive problem-solving device are as diverse as the motivations of the persons who enter into such arrangements. This diversity applies to both individual and group interests with nearly equal scope in the societies described in this and in Carroll's (1970a) volume, thereby undermining many generalizations that might be proposed from a smaller sample and strengthening others because of the empirical diversity that may be included in them. But it is erroneous in any case to argue that the needs served by adoption are inherently psychological, biological, or social in Malinowski's (1939) universalistic and ad hoc sense, and it is tautological to assert that needs so conceived ultimately "cause" adoption to be developed and applied as a sociocultural feature of the system in which it appears. No such assumptions are made in this or in previous chapters in this volume. Even if such needs were universal and phrased in an appropriate theoretical context, it is fallacious to assume that any variable is caused either efficiently or ultimately by virtue of its relationship to a constant or set of constants. Furthermore, even if such needs are conceived as variables that fluctuate under specifiable conditions, adoption is clearly not a universal response to any adaptive pressures generated thereby.

It is reasonable to assert that the specific functions of and needs served by adoption are highly relative and situationally determined by the complex interactions of individual organisms—as members

of social groups—with particular physical and cultural environments as those environments change over time (see Laughlin and
d'Aquili 1974). It is also evident that ultimate explanations of the
development, decline, and broad-level functions of adoption or any
other sociocultural form must necessarily hinge on more than
functional propositions about the internal structuring of culture
(see Goodenough 1970a : 121 ff; Laughlin and Brady 1976). But,
in advance of more comprehensive analyses, the functional interrelationships between adoption and other cultural forms in
particular contexts can and should be specified without necessarily
invoking the tautological and teleological causal inferences that
observers like Malinowski once took for granted as acceptable.
Indeed, such specifications are often the first and most important
step to achieving a broader understanding of sociocultural phenomena.

   It is equally simplistic in this regard to view adoption as primarily a case of "culture stepping in where nature fails," or where it
has not had an opportunity to fail, as it were, in cases where
unmarried persons adopt children as their own for various purposes
(see Silverman 1970:231). Adoption may be used to mediate
demographic conflicts of various kinds, but it is not a universal
solution to such problems as random irregularities in birth rates or
placements of individuals by sex relative to the demands of
particular groups for heirs to their estates or for balance in the
division of labor in their households. Even in societies with high
adoption rates whose members make use of adoption on some
occasions to offset these particular problems, some people who do
not have children may fail to adopt any despite their demonstrable
needs for them, and other people who have a sufficient number of
children of the proper sex to provide heirs or to balance the division
of labor in their households may nevertheless adopt several
additional persons and incorporate them as active participants in
the group's activities. Obviously, variables other than demographic
needs or fluctuations in demographic processes must be taken into
account to understand the functions of adoption in such societies
(see especially Marshall, chapter 2), including some variables that
may be perceived as having no direct relationship to demographic,
ecological, or other "natural" processes that enter into the reaction
system of these populations over time.

A satisfactory analysis must also allow for adoption and related practices to surface in some efficient way as an instance of culture stepping in where "society" fails, for example, where society proposes an ideal charter for kinship relations and behavior from the standpoint of the individuals who are socialized in that system, and then fails to meet some of the variable demands that individuals and groups encounter as 'kinsmen' in an operational or actual sense. Silverman's interesting account of adoption among the Banabans deals with this problem generally, and a brief quotation from his account may suffice to make the point here:

> Adoption can . . . constitute the recognition of a state of affairs where expectations of the behavior of kinsmen as persons fall short of the ideals of kinship behavior (e.g., to ensure the care of one's child, or oneself); where the ideals of kinship behavior are enacted by people so enjoined to act but who are considered particularly liable not to (as in the case of stepparents); or where they are enacted by people not even enjoined to do so (as in some adoptions of non-kinsmen) (1970:231; see also Silverman 1971).

With these provisions and limitations in mind, and at the risk of overgeneralizing from the kaleidoscope of motivations, processes, and designs of adoption documented in this volume and elsewhere, three basic functions of adoption as a resource management strategy that apply primarily to group interests in Oceania appear to be: (1) strengthening or maintaining internal group solidarity; (2) supporting existing alliances between individuals and groups or developing new ones; and, (3) resolving certain structural conflicts or contradictions that may obtain in kinship, descent, or property group alignments. The following is a summary of these patterns and some of the analytic problems that pertain to their identification in variable contexts.

ADOPTION, ALLIANCE, AND STRUCTURAL CONTINUITY

The possibilities for strengthening *intragroup* relations by using adoption as a reinforcement or support system are everywhere complex and represented by a large number of situational determinants. One such use of adoption that has already been mentioned is as a process of recruitment to fill vacant domestic work roles in households, another is to provide childless couples with social offspring, still another is to transform expected or ideal kinship behavior into actual solidarity by adopting the child of a relative who would otherwise have remained distant, and so on. The possibilities for engineering new or strengthening existing *intergroup* alliances through adoption are as numerous as those engineered through marriage and in fact might be considered greater than the latter. Like marriage, adoption can link unrelated groups together in solidary relationships, but it can also cover a domain of intergroup alliance where marriage is prohibited. This point has special relevance for understanding the relationship of adoption to marriage in several Oceanic kinship systems, and it will be developed in greater detail below. For the moment, it is important to note that adoption is generally subordinate to marriage as a mechanism of alliance between groups that are otherwise unrelated to each other and that the relative importance of adoption as an internal support and alliance mechanism between groups of any type varies considerably from one society to the next.

Some island societies restrict the scope of formal changes in kinship identity and interpersonal relationships entailed by adoption to the adopters, the adoptees, and the immediate kin of the adoptees as individuals. Other societies mandate a broader level of integration of adoptive ties as a matter of course—that is, they systematically cultivate the wider networks of kin of each principal through jural expansion of the adoptive link. Still other societies appear to vacillate between these two poles according to the situation at hand. These are variations in the jural scope of adoption transactions that are usefully conceptualized as variations between the core of an adoptive context and its periphery.

The core of an adoptive context coincides with the universal practice of recruiting adoptees on a model of primary rather than secondary kinship identities and for this reason is inevitably associated with a domestic group alignment of one kind or another. It is structured at minimum by a triadic relationship that links the adoptee, the adopter(s), and the adoptee's primary jural parent(s) in adoptive child transactions and by a dyadic relationship between the adopter and the adoptee in adoptive sibling transactions (see chapter 1). It may or may not be expanded to include other persons.

The relative importance of adoption as an alliance mechanism, however, is not determined simply by the presence or absence of extensions of the core context to include other persons. Such extensions may affect the jural profile of the adoptive context in important ways, and the possibility of such extensions may, in fact, constitute an important motivation in some societies for entering into an adoption agreement in the first place. But the focal point of alliances negotiated through adoption lies with the principals of the core unit in every instance. Wider relations entailed by the transaction, if any, are necessarily adjunct or subordinate to those engineered and maintained by the core unit. Alliance functions through adoption are therefore keyed in the most immediate and strategic sense to members of the core unit as principal negotiators, and variations on this level depend directly on such things as the relative kinship distance between the principals and the degree of jural exclusivity entailed by the transaction.

The adoption of persons from closely related groups may minimize the singular importance of adoption as an alliance mechanism insofar as the principals may also calculate their interdependence and solidarity on other structural bonds that exist between them. The role of adoption as an alliance feature in such cases is thereby supplemental, and the primary effect of the transaction may be to strengthen or maintain the existing set of interpersonal relations within the adoptive core unit. But not all persons and groups with existing structural bonds are necessarily related to each other in precisely the same way, of course, or even on the same principles. So the relative importance of adoption as an alliance feature must be measured in part against the span of existing social distance traversed by each transaction, and in part against other vital contextual features such as the degree of jural exclusivity established and maintained as part of the transaction itself.

Greater or lesser emphasis may be placed on alliance functions through an adoptive bond according to the number and kind of alternative bonds available to persons in the same interactional sphere (see Smith, chapter 11) and according to the degree to which all such bonds can be situationally or structurally isolated from each other for social action purposes. Similarly, alliance functions may be minimized in adoptive child transaction where jural exclusivity of the adoptee's previous kinship identity is strongly developed (see Firth 1959:127). Jural inclusiveness theoretically promotes greater interdependence between the principals in such transactions by transferring some rights of jural parenthood to the adopters without arbitrarily cancelling the adoptee's previous kinship identity (see Goodenough 1970a:31) and perhaps by cultivating the role the principal negotiators may play as coparents of the child (see Brady, chapter 7). Jural exclusiveness tends to cancel out such interdependence as a matter of course, especially when the principal negotiators are not otherwise related. Furthermore, even where the principals are connected by their respective jural interests in the adoptee, the natural or former primary jural parents of the adoptee do not necessarily establish a formal and direct kinship link with the adoptive parents by virtue of the adoptive bond itself (see Rynkiewich, chapter 6).

Silverman's (1970) summary of adoption practices among the Banabans exemplifies those instances in which adoption is only of minimal importance as an alliance feature and is narrowly defined in jural scope. Despite a proliferation of types of adoption transactions and a relatively high frequency of occurrence, Banaban adoption "... is not a structural principle relating groups in the society, nor is it the regular expression of a continuing relationship between groups" (1970:231). Similarly, "The central idea or outcome [of adoption] need not be the strengthening of the solidarity of the kindred" (1970:218), although some adoptions evidently are undertaken with the explicit goal in mind of strengthening or maintaining some kinship relations that already exist (1970:219 ff). This is accomplished most readily through the adoption of consanguines. Moreover, when adoptive relations are extended for any purpose beyond the core context of the principal negotiators and adoptees (where these are different persons), the extension generally excludes binding property relations. For example, in Banaban sibling adoptions, the members of the adopter's 'near kindred' must give their approval and the 'real' siblings of the adopter subsequently consider the adoptee their 'sibling', but the adoptee is allowed to share only the portion of the siblings' land estate that is the adopter's rightful share as an individual. The adoptee does not acquire an equal share of the land controlled by all siblings in the adoptive land group (1970:229), despite the functional and symbolic importance of unity in the sibling set as a whole. Thus, a wide variety of interpersonal relationships and property alignments may be manipulated for adaptive ends through Banaban adoption, but the importance of adoption as an internal support and alliance system is quite narrowly defined.

The Banaban patterns contrast markedly with some forms of adoption and guardianship in the closely related but more highly-stratified societies of the northern Gilberts (see Lambert 1964, 1970; also cf. Lundsgaarde 1970) and in many other Oceanic societies described in this and in Carroll's (1970a) volume. None of this variation is especially surprising, insofar as the kinship, economic, and political systems of these groups also differ in important ways and given that adoption is a multifunctional institution that is easily applied to diverse situations, as previously mentioned. But a close inspection of adoption in some of the societies that contrast most with the Banaban case reveals some primary applications of adoption that transcend the level of strictly individual or domestic concerns and that might be overlooked by investigators concerned with adoption only from a domestic cycle or descent group perspective. Moreover, it appears that some of the variations in jural scope and relative importance of adoption as an alliance and internal support system coincide with major points of structural discontinuity or contradictions that are intrinsic to the operation of kinship and marriage practices in those societies and that adoption may play a strategic role in the resolution of such problems. One such pattern obtains among the South East Ambrymese of the New Hebrides (see Tonkinson, chapter 10).

The primary use of adoption among the South East Ambrymese is not a domestic one in the sense of filling vacant domestic work roles or balancing the division of labor in households, although these needs are served by Ambrymese adoption on occasion. Rather, the primary use of adoption appears to be to reallocate rights in persons of the proper sex as a support system for sister exchange marriages between patrilineages. The adoption of boys from related subgroups tends to strengthen the internal solidarity of the lineage as a whole through a series of overlapping and reciprocal prestations, thereby intensifying the obligations of fellow kinsmen to contribute to each other's needs in mustering bridewealth accumulations. Mustering substantial bridewealth, in turn, supports the lineage's ability to obtain wives for its sons. The adoption of girls provides a more direct link to the marital exchange system: they are the primary media of exchange in this case. Adoption provides a means for obtaining women for subgroups within the lineage who have no daughters of their own or who have an insufficient number of claims on people who stand in that relationship to them relative to the number of sons that must be provided with wives.

Adoption among the South East Ambrymese is thus an important and institutionalized alternative to birth as a mode of recruiting people to fill specific kinship identities within the marital exchange units. It is applied widely within lineages as a reciprocal and binding source of support, and it is closely interfaced with the exchange and alliance system of the wider society as one solution to the inevitable problems of sexual imbalance in social units that depend on sex-specific alignments with other like units for collective endurance. Adoption is only of minimal importance as a domestic group recruitment process in this society, however, since it rarely involves an actual change in residence for the adoptees. Moreover, it is not bound up with political considerations to any great extent since the system is basically egalitarian; it is not closely tied to land tenure considerations, as in some other Pacific societies discussed below; and adoptions among existing kin seldom mandate substantial changes in relations between the adopter and the adoptee's natal group as individuals. A less comprehensive analysis than Tonkinson's might easily conclude that adoption does not exist there. But the evidence is plain that adoption does exist in this society and that it is firmly integrated in the social system through carefully calculated alliance and internal support functions.

Shore's analysis of adoption in the highly stratified society of Samoa provides some interesting contrasts with the Banaban and the Ambrymese cases by examining adoption from the perspectives of both descent and alliance theory (see chapter 8). Samoan adoption provides for domestic level recruitment and serves at the same time as a vehicle for wider political alliances among groups. Transferring or assigning political power through descent links alone tends to preserve the vertical continuity and integrity of the descent line at the expense of horizontal alliance relations. Emphasizing the ties of adoption and marriage between groups, on the other hand, tends to strengthen horizontal political relations at the expense of descent line integrity. Adopting cognatic kin from other groups solves both problems at once by creating a horizontal political alliance that intersects with a prior bond of descent. This is an intersection of interests that could only be duplicated by incestuous marriage, so the role of adoption in this domain is especially strategic: it is a means for maximizing alliances that cannot be serviced directly by marriage. In other contexts, adoption is functionally equivalent to marriage: both are alliance mechanisms that will produce heirs, and both transform alliance relations into descent links. Adoption also represents a viable alternative or complement to birth as a domestic and descent group recruitment process. In any case, adoption serves important internal support and alliance functions in this society, and it contributes to the resolution of some structural problems that are intrinsic to the operation of the social and political system.

Samoan adoption patterns are similar to those that occur in other highly-stratified societies in Polynesia, despite many changes and some differential impact introduced in each of them through cross-cultural interference (see Hooper 1970; Howard et al. 1970; Levy 1970). But the relationship of adoption to land in these and many other cognatic systems contrasts with the Ambrymese pattern in fundamentental ways. In his belated consideration of cognatic systems, Lévi-Strauss suggests that they ". . . do not belong to the same typology as those which we call 'elementary structures of kinship'. Indeed, they introduce an additional dimension, for they no longer define, perpetuate and transform the method of social cohesion with regard to a stable system of descent, but to a system of land rights" (1969:105). Recognizing that unilineal systems also regulate land rights, cognatic systems nevertheless generate some problems of continuity and order in property relationships that are not likely either to occur at all or in the same form in elementary unilineal systems like that of the Ambrymese. One reason for this is that closure in corporate group membership in cognatic systems cannot be achieved with reference to descent ideology alone, as is theoretically possible in both elementary and complex unilineal systems. It is also usual for Oceanic cognatic systems to have wide prohibitions placed on cousin marriage, contrary to practices in most of the unilineal systems of the same region (see Murdock 1967:202, 206, 210), thereby obscuring or eliminating the possibility of using first or second cousin marriage as a means for systematically consolidating divided property in related descent groups. The role of adoption as an internal support and alliance mechanism may vary accordingly.

It is important to point out in this context, however, that some variations perceived in comparisons of alliance and internal support patterns of adoption in cognatic and unilineal systems may be more apparent than real. Where specific property rights are vested in unilineal descent groups and transmitted ordinarily by birthright, as in the matrilineal systems of Micronesia, the relationship of adoption to property group alignment and land transmission problems may be different in sociological fact but identical in principle to many patterns that obtain in cognatic systems. Property groups can be realigned, heirs to estates can be provided, and descent lines can be rescued from extinction through adoption in both cases. Alkire's study of socioeconomic relations on Lamotrek, Elato and Satawal provides a pertinent example from Micronesia:

> In a small population such as inhabits Lamotrek it is easy to see how natural processes can lead to the extinction of lineages. Disease, accidents, and natural disasters might lead to the disappearance of a lineage or even a clan in two or three generations. Land redistribution would be necessary because of this as well as because of any increase in the size of other lineages. And in the case of extinction, alternatives to matriliny are necessary if orderly redistribution is to occur. Adoption and patrilateral transmission of property are these alternatives (Alkire 1965:54; see also Marshall, chapter 2; Rynkiewich, chapter 6; Kirkpatrick and Broder, chapter 9).

Adoption may also be used to strengthen intergroup bonds in this society in a domain where marriage is prohibited, as in many cognatic systems. Although patrilateral and adoptive gifts of land are generally transferred across clan boundaries—that is, to persons and groups who are otherwise eligible for marriage, the adoption of persons from the same clan but different lineage or

descent line affiliations can strengthen alliance relations by reinforcing existing matrilateral and patrilateral kinship ties, especially
when the adoptee changes residence to the homestead of the
adoptive parents (Alkire 1965:60). Descent group exogamy normally prohibits marriage in this interlineage domain (but cf.
Alkire 1965:58–59).

Cognatic systems compensate in part for the vicissitudes of
natural disasters, disease, accidents, and other elements in the
environment that can lead to inequities in resource distribution
and problems of group continuity by calculating kinship and
descent ties widely at the outset, thereby eliminating some of the
particular problems of optional affiliation and property transmission faced by unilineal systems in similar environments. In fact, the
degree to which matrilineages in Micronesia rely on complementary filiation and adoption as alternative ways of aligning people
and resources may provide some important clues concerning the
inherent adaptability of cognatic kinship calculations in unstable
environments, all other things being equal. But the gain in inherent
structural flexibility in cognatic systems—at least in terms of
jural rules if not in actual practice—is also a loss in inherent
structural continuity, and the role of adoption as an internal
support and alliance mechanism may be especially important in
such systems as both an integrative and a disambiguating device
in kinship and property relations. A brief review of some data
from the Ellice Islands may suffice to illustrate the potential role
of adoption in this context (see also chapter 7).

A major problem of structural continuity in the Ellice Islands
is to maintain sibling solidarity and descent line integrity in the
context of cognatic descent, bilateral inheritance privileges, ambi-
local residence rules, and extensive prohibitions on cousin marriage. Kinship and property relations center on sibling solidarity
in several important respects, especially on male sibling solidarity
(see also Lieber 1970:160; Ottino 1970). Cognatic reckoning gives
every person a network of relatives who are combined in various
ways as ramage segments and corporate landholding units. A
sibling set that shares land and blood by birthright forms the focal
point of each land group. Brothers normally represent the dominant link in the sibling set because of a patrilateral bias in descent
reckoning that favors men over women in matters of rank,

inheritance, and authority. But inheritance is bilateral, and residence patterns at marriage generally displace some members of the sibling unit, sometimes displacing allegiance and encouraging fission in the natal group at the same time. This configuration of property rights and individual mobility poses a threat to the control that land groups must retain over their members and their joint property in order to preserve their integrity as a corporate and cooperative unit. The problem is aggravated further by widespread land hunger, since extensive fission in property groups over several generations can fragment individual landholdings to the point of making subsistence production difficult and inefficient. Moreover, there is tension between male siblings for control over the group's joint property, and such tension also contributes to fission rather than fusion in the sibling set as a whole.

Fission in Ellice sibling sets is thus an inherent structural problem with widespread ramifications throughout the social and economic system. Adoption may be used in combination with certain judicious applications of the patrilateral bias to mitigate some of these problems. The patrilateral bias can be maximized by giving sons more land than daughters, thereby insuring a greater dependence on men than on women for such things as subsistence production rights and authority. Sons may also be encouraged to bring their wives home to live with them at marriage. Both of these patterns select for male sibling interdependence and continuity as a unit. Adoption supplements these patterns in much the same way as first cousin marriage and intraclan adoption might in a unilineal system faced with similar problems (see McKinley 1973:736).

Adopting a real or classificatory sibling's child, for example, reinforces the existing bonds between the principals and serves as a reintegrative link against whatever measure of social, jural, affective, or physical distance separates them. If the principals are members of the same landholding unit, adoption decreases the likelihood of fission and property divisions within the group. If the principals are members of separate land groups as a result of previous divisions in their common ancestral estate, adoption may be especially important as a reintegrative mechanism: the mandatory allocation of land from the adopter to the adoptee reunites the descent line of the principals through the adoptee's property interests (see also Goody 1969:70). Jurally inclusive responsibilities for the adoptee further enhance the reintegrative process by formally activating what might have been only latent ties of shared jural parenthood prior to the transaction.

The mutual exchange of children as adoptees in the Ellice Islands, especially the exchange of sons between real or classificatory brothers, is an even stronger statement of mutual esteem, interest, and solidarity. Such exchanges tend to eliminate any asymmetry and inequality that might otherwise obtain in single child transactions at various points in the adoptive core. Either way, adoption mitigates some of the inherent structural liabilities of sibling group fission and discontinuity in property group alignments.

Ellice adoption also functions as a strategic alliance mechanism that is parallel to marriage in the event of adoptions between groups that are otherwise unrelated and as one that is complementary to marriage when applied to intergroup domains where marriage is prohibited, as in the Samoan case. Bilateral prohibitions on marriage between persons more closely related than fourth cousins place adoptions between real or classificatory siblings in the latter category. Combined with some of the data outlined above for other societies, these patterns support the suggestion that children might usefully be added to Lévi-Strauss' list of women, goods, food, services, and information as media of exchange and alliance in various kinship systems (see chapter 8). Compared to the Banaban case, where sibling solidarity problems obtain in a context of kinship and descent that is nearly identical to that of the Ellice Islanders, the Ellice data reaffirm the wisdom of not overestimating the singular importance of adoption in any combination of alliance and internal support functions. Other institutions, customs, and behaviors may carry a similar workload with comparable results, and they may do so, in fact, as support mechanisms for some of the liabilities and conflicts that may be produced as secondary effects of adoption itself.

SUMMARY AND CONCLUSIONS

Managing strategic resources in a manner that selects for population survival and sociocultural persistence is a fundamental problem faced by all human societies. Kinship and descent ideologies ideally provide a charter for integrating individuals and groups in ways that are consistent with these interests. Adoption is a specific type of kinship phenomenon that incorporates these attributes as a resource management strategy and exchange process. People are the media of exchange in adoption transactions, as in birth and marriage; and the basic resource at stake in each instance appears to be interpersonal relationships that are structured in a context of solidarity and perpetuity with other human beings and expressed as kinship identities.

As a form of adaptive engineering in interpersonal relationships, adoption is a sociological and symbolic means for manipulating and transferring kinship identities that are normally assigned by birthright to persons in culturally-posited 'congenital' matrices. Adoption candidates may include persons of any age and social status, and they may be recruited to fill kinship identities that range from siblingship to childhood, parenthood, and grandparenthood. Adoptive kinship identities produced in this manner may be closely modeled on the sociological and symbolic content of their consanguineal counterparts, or they may be subdivided in such a way that they fit into the kinship system without exactly duplicating any of the social identities and relationships normally entailed by consanguinity. Compromise is the inevitable common denominator of such transactions, and reciprocity is the rule that helps to determine the outcomes in the short and the long run.

Adoption is a prime example of conscious, volitional engineering in social life—it is a means for resolving conflict, on the one hand, and it is a process that may create conflict, on the other. The point of adoption as a resource management strategy is conflict resolution, however, and it may be applied in this respect to various types of structural discontinuities or inequities and disorders in resource allocations that people encounter in the course of perpetuating themselves and their social systems. Adoption offers a solution to a broad range of social, economic, and political problems that are likely to develop in small populations attached to island environments, including the insurance of equitable distributions of people relative to the requirements domestic and descent groups may have for heirs, balanced divisions of labor, sibling solidarity, enhanced political power, property alignments, and continuance of the groups themselves as corporate and cooperative entities. By creating new or reinforcing existing kinship relations, adoption accentuates, actualizes, or extends the range of sociability, resource sharing, and alliance, and it may do so with nearly equal sociological force in various types of kinship and descent systems. For example, where specific property rights are vested in unilineal descent groups and transmitted primarily by birthright, as in the matrilineal systems of Micronesia, the relationship of adoption to property group alignment and land transmission problems may be different in fact but identical in principle to many uses of adoption in cognatic systems: property groups can be realigned, heirs to estates can be provided, and descent lines can be rescued from extinction in each case. But a close inspection of the relationship between adoption and marriage as internal support and alliance mechanisms in such systems reveals some important differences as well as similarities.

Adoption parallels birth as a group recruitment process, and it is comparable in complexity and importance to marriage in the types of alliance and internal support functions it may serve. In some contexts, adoption is functionally equivalent to marriage: both transform alliance relations into descent links, and both can ally unrelated groups in new and solidary relationships. One important difference, however, is that adoption can also cover a domain of intergroup alliance where marriage is prohibited, that is, it can be used to reintegrate or ally descent lines or groups within the bounds of an exogamous unit.

Moreover, despite the frequent application of adoption to such domains by both unilineal and cognatic systems in Oceania, the range of persons to whom adoption can be applied as an alliance mechanism exclusive of marriage may be greater in cognatic than in unilineal systems because of associated differences in marriage rules. Wide prohibitions on cousin marriage theoretically expand the domain to which adoption can be applied in this capacity, and such prohibitions also eliminate the possibility of using first or second cousin marriage as a means for consolidating divided property or ruptured solidarity in related descent groups, even though the need for such consolidation may be great. The net effect is to increase the potential structural importance of adoption transactions in alliance relations and subsequent alignments of strategic resources. The implication here, of course, is that *adoption of kins-men in cognatic systems with extensive prohibitions on marriage may fulfill many of the same internal group support and alliance functions that close cross-cousin marriage does in unilineal systems,* which is an important hypothesis in its own right (see also McKinley 1973: 736).

Furthermore, marriage in Oceanic societies generally occurs either among 'non-kinsmen' in cognatic systems or between specially designated categories of 'kinsmen' such as first or second cross cousins in unilineal systems, whereas adoption in the same societies occurs among a broad segment of existing 'kin' most of the time and only rarely among 'non-kinsmen'. The way in which these two potential alliance mechanisms are applied to the universe of persons in each society is thus a matter of emphasis. It is, roughly speaking, a matter of complementary distribution.

Given these distribution patterns, and that alliance refers to solidary bonds formally established across group boundaries (in-cluding the internal segments of an exogamous unit) on the basis of common interests in people and other strategic resources, the relationship posited here between adoption and marriage can be restated in the form of a proposition: *the frequency and structural importance of alliance relations through adoption will be greater in cognatic systems than in unilineal ones in direct proportion to the extent of prohibitions on cousin marriage that obtain there;* or, as a corollary that is free of direct assumptions about the intersection of marital and descent rules: *if close cross-cousin marriage is allowed, adoption will play only a minor role in alliance between such units,* whereas *if cross-cousin marriage is widely prohibited, the role of adoption as an alliance mechanism will increase in frequency and struc-tural importance in that system,* all other things being equal, such as the number, size, and proclivity to fission in the alliance units, and the overall demand for widespread social integration posed by environmental pressure on strategic resources.

But what of the high frequencies of adoption in Oceania gener-ally and the tendencies to restrict adoption to relations among existing 'kin' in both unilineal and cognatic systems? The view of adoption as a strategy for managing or aligning vital resources and further investigations of the complementarity of adoption, birth, and certain kinds of marriage rules may help to shed some new light on these questions.

Some of the impetus to adopt existing 'kin' may derive directly from the potential use of adoption in aggregating strategic resources where they are most likely to dissipate visibly, that is, through the normal processes of fission, segmentation, and migration in domestic and descent groups. It is also possible that the same preferences may be more epiphenomenal than direct concerns in some contexts. Adoption may be played off as a by-product of obligations incurred in other kinds of exchange relations among kinsmen, including the myriad obligations and counter-prestations that are likely to obtain among classificatory siblings whose institutionalized roles include latent or secondary jural parenthood responsibilities for each other's children. Additional preferences for adopting existing 'kin' may be promoted by the knowledge that adoption bonds contracted in the absence of other supporting bonds are inherently less durable than those grounded first in the normative entailments of 'consanguinity' in that society, at least where solidarity in the long run is a major concern (cf. Carroll 1970c). It is obvious that other variables must be taken into account in attempts to explain the derivation and distribution of these preferences generally. But the points listed here are supported by ethnographic data to the extent that they must be included as important considerations in any such broader level explanations.

The relatively high frequencies and particular placements of adoption in the Pacific are also derived from multiple and complex processes, but they may be stimulated in part by: (1) instability or ambiguity in personnel or other strategic resource alignments where greater stability and intensity of social relations are required to cope with environmental fluctuations in a manner that produces optimal use of available resources; and, conversely, (2) parochial constraints imposed on personnel and other strategic resource alignments by ideal charters for kinship and marriage where greater flexibility in social action is required to produce optimal use of available resources in the face of similar environmental fluctuations. Each of these circumstances is in some measure the antithesis of the other, and each, moreover, has been identified as more likely to arise in societies with particular kinds of descent rules—cognatic in the former case and unilineal in the latter. But the inference here is more one of central tendency than absolute exclusivity in such systems, for some of the problems that occur in each kind of system may also appear in similar form or principle in the other. The crucial point is that adoption can function as an adaptive mechanism in both instances.

Perhaps the most determinant set of variables to be considered in explaining adoption frequencies and placement is the relationship of indigenous social forms (such as marriage, descent, inheritance, residence, and adoption itself) to the problems of environmental stress experienced over time. Tsunami, tropical cyclones, diseases, droughts, and other disruptive forces such as cross-cultural assimilation through colonialism or missionization may produce intense social displacement, demographic upheaval, and other kinds of strategic resource deprivation, especially in the small and relatively isolated social arenas that characterize most societies in the insular Pacific. The adaptive functions of adoption may be most visible under these circumstances, and the relatively high frequencies of adoption and related practices in Oceania may in fact reflect such concerns, both as surety against the intensity of future disruptions where the environmental forces are perceived as recurrent, and as wherewithal for survival or optimal repairs in the wake of such disruptions (see Laughlin and Brady 1976).[1]

Furthermore, since birth and marriage are ideally managed in a manner consistent with population survival and sociocultural persistence under variable environmental conditions, there is no reason to expect that adoption (or its functional equivalent) will not be exploited to its fullest capacity under the same conditions, especially where the actors in the system perceive adoption as applicable to social domains and demands not otherwise serviced —or serviceable at the time—by birth and marriage. Survival generally depends on a population's concerted ability to equilibrate these and other parts of its social action system through various kinds of sociocultural and ecological stress. Adoption is a multifunctional institution that can be and often is applied to diverse action contexts as a means for mediating such stress in Oceania. It has primary adaptive value.

PROSPECTUS

The accomplishments of this and Carroll's (1970a) volume do not pretend to be exhaustive of the nature and permutations of adoption everywhere. But we do have at hand a solid beginning for tracing adoption in fact and theory through the matrix of symbols, rules, choice, action, and adaptation in other societies and environments beyond Oceania. A systematic investigation of the propositions developed in these two volumes may represent an important next step for proceeding in such directions. To do so can only enhance our understanding of the meaning of kinship in particular societies, our knowledge of the ways in which kinship relationships can be manipulated to accommodate human adaptation, and our appreciation of the place of adoption in kinship studies as a whole.

NOTES

I am indebted to Charles Laughlin, Jr., DeWight Middleton, and especially to Mac Marshall for their help in clarifying many of the ideas developed in this chapter. None of them, of course, are responsible for any liabilities that remain. A special note of thanks is owed Dan Baker of the University Press of Hawaii for his cooperation and expert editorial assistance throughout the project.

1. The emphasis placed on social forms in this context is not meant to undermine the importance of technoeconomic preparedness for environmental flux in such societies. But it is worth observing that technoeconomic capacities themselves are transacted and channeled largely through the social exchange, alliance, and kinship networks of the indigenous cultures of the Pacific, and that the key to understanding the role of adoption in adaptation lies squarely in the latter domain.

REFERENCES

Alkire, William H.
1965   *Lamotrek Atoll and Inter-Island Socioeconomic Ties.* Illinois Studies in Anthropology No. 5. Urbana: University of Illinois Press.

Aoyagi, Machiko
1966   "Kinship organization and behavior in a contemporary Tongan village." *Journal of the Polynesian Society* 75:141–176.

Atkins, John R.
1974   "On the fundamental consanguineal numbers and their structural basis." *American Ethnologist* 1:1–31.

Barnes, J.A.
1971   *Three Styles in the Study of Kinship.* Berkeley and Los Angeles: University of California Press.

Barnett, Homer G.
1965   "Laws of sociocultural change." *International Journal of Comparative Sociology* 6:207–230.

Barth, Frederick
1966   *Models of Social Organization.* Royal Anthropological Institute Occasional Paper No. 23. London: Royal Anthropological Institute.

Beattie, J.H.M.
1964   "Kinship and social anthropology." *Man* 64:101–103.
1971   "Cutting kinship in Bunyoro." *Ethnology* 10:211–214.

Bowers, Neal M.
1950   "Problems of resettlement on Saipan, Tinian and Rota, Mariana Islands." Ph.D. dissertation, University of Michigan.

Brady, Ivan A.
1972   "Kinship reciprocity in the Ellice Islands: an evaluation of Sahlins' model of the sociology of primitive exchange." *Journal of the Polynesian Society* 81:290–316.

1973   Review of *Adoption in Eastern Oceania*, edited by Vern Carroll. *American Anthropologist* 75:436–439.

1974   "Land tenure in the Ellice Islands: a changing profile." In *Land Tenure in Oceania*, edited by Henry Lundsgaarde. ASAO Monograph No. 2. Honolulu: University Press of Hawaii.

1975   "Christians, pagans and government men: culture change in the Ellice Islands." In *A Reader in Culture Change: Volume II, Case Studies*, edited by Ivan A. Brady and Barry L. Isaac. Cambridge: Schenkman Publishing Co.

Brown, Robert
1963   *Explanation in Social Science*. Chicago: Aldine.

Bryan, Edwin H., Jr.
1946   *A Geographic Summary of Micronesia and Notes on the Climate of Micronesia*. Honolulu: United States Commercial Co.

Buchler, Ira R., and Henry A. Selby
1968   *Kinship and Social Organization: An Introduction to Theory and Method*. New York: Macmillan.

Buchler, Ira R., and Hugo G. Nutini (eds.)
1969   *Game Theory in the Behavorial Sciences*. Pittsburgh: University of Pittsburgh Press.

Carroll, Vern
1970a   *Adoption in Eastern Oceania*, edited by Vern Carroll. ASAO Monograph No. 1. Honolulu: University of Hawaii Press.

1970b   "Introduction: what does 'adoption' mean?" In *Adoption in Eastern Oceania*, edited by Vern Carroll. ASAO Monograph No. 1. Honolulu: University of Hawaii Press.

1970c   "Adoption on Nukuoro." In *Adoption in Eastern Oceania*, edited by Vern Carroll. ASAO Monograph No. 1. Honolulu: University of Hawaii Press.

n.d.   "Incest prohibitions in Polynesia and Micronesia." *Journal of the Polynesian Society*, in press.

Chock, Phyllis P.
1974   "Time, nature and spirit: a symbolic analysis of Greek-American kinship." *American Ethnologist* 1:33–48.

Churchward, C. Maxwell
1959   *Tongan Dictionary*. London: Oxford University Press.

Cook, Scott
1966   "The obsolete 'anti-market' mentality: a critique of the substantive approach to economic anthropology." *American Anthropologist* 68:323–343.

Defngin, Francis
1958   "Yapese names." In *The Use of Names in Micronesia*, edited by John E. de Young. Anthropological Working Papers No. 3. Agana, Guam: Office of the High Commissioner, Trust Territory of the Pacific Islands.

Dillingham, Beth, and Barry L. Isaac

1975 "Defining marriage cross-culturally." In *Being Female: Reproduction, Power, and Change*, edited by Dana Raphael. World Anthropology Series. The Hague: Mouton.

Douglas, Mary

1966 *Purity and Danger*. Baltimore: Penguin Books.

Eggan, Fred

1972 "Lewis Henry Morgan's *Systems:* a reevaluation." In *Kinship Studies in the Morgan Centennial Year*, edited by Priscilla Reining. Washington, D.C.: The Anthropological Society of Washington.

Evans-Pritchard, E.E.

1962 "Zande blood brotherhood." In *Social Anthropology and Other Essays*, by E.E. Evans-Pritchard. Glencoe: Free Press.

Finney, Ben R.

1964 "Notes on bond-friendship in Tahiti." *Journal of the Polynesian Society* 73:431–435.

1965 "Polynesian peasants and proletarians." *Journal of the Polynesian Society* 74:269–328.

Firth, Raymond

1929 *Economics of the New Zealand Maori*. Wellington: R.E. Owen, Government Printer (second edition 1959).

1936 *We, the Tikopia*. London: George Allen and Unwin (Beacon Press edition, 1965).

1957 "A note on descent groups in Polynesia." *Man* 57:4–8.

1963 "Bilateral descent groups: an operational viewpoint." In *Studies in Kinship and Marriage*, edited by I. Schapera. Royal Anthropological Institute Occasional Paper No. 16. London: Royal Anthropological Institute of Great Britain and Ireland. Reprinted in *Polynesia: Readings on a Culture Area*, edited by Alan Howard. Scranton: Chandler Publishing Co., 1971.

Fischer, Ann

1963 "Reproduction in Truk." *Ethnology* 2:526–540.

Fischer, John L.

1970 "Adoption on Ponape." In *Adoption in Eastern Oceania*, edited by Vern Carroll. ASAO Monograph No. 1. Honolulu: University of Hawaii Press.

Fortes, Meyer

1962 *Marriage in Tribal Societies*. Cambridge Papers in Social Anthropology No. 3. Cambridge: Cambridge University Press.

1969 *Kinship and the Social Order: The Legacy of Lewis Henry Morgan*. Chicago: Aldine.

Foster, Stephen

1972 Review of *Adoption in Eastern Oceania*, edited by Vern Carroll. *Journal of the Polynesian Society* 81:268–270.

Freed, Stanley A.

1963 "Fictive kinship in a North Indian village." *Ethnology* 2:86–103.

Freeman, Derek
1964   "Some observations on kinship and political authority in Samoa."
       American Anthropologist 66:553–568.

Furness, William Henry, III
1910   *The Island of Stone Money.* Philadelphia: Lippincott.

Gellner, Ernest
1957   "Ideal language and kinship structure." *Philosophy of Science*
       24:235–242.
1960   "The concept of kinship." *Philosophy of Science* 27:187–204.

Gifford, L.W.
1929   *Tongan Society.* Bernice P. Bishop Museum Bulletin No. 61.
       Honolulu: Bishop Museum Press.

Gilson, Richard P.
1963   "Samoan descent groups: a structural outline." *Journal of the Poly-
       nesian Society* 72:372–377.
1970   *Samoa 1830–1900: the Politics of a Multi-Cultural Community.*
       Melbourne: Oxford University Press.

Goodenough, Ruth Gallagher
1970   "Adoption on Romónum, Truk." In *Adoption in Eastern Oceania,*
       edited by Vern Carroll. ASAO Monograph No. 1. Honolulu:
       University of Hawaii Press.

Goodenough, Ward H.
1951   *Property, Kin, and Community on Truk.* Yale University Publications
       in Anthropology No. 46. New Haven: Department of Anthropology,
       Yale University.
1955   "A problem in Malayo-Polynesian social organization." *American
       Anthropologist* 57:71–83.
1965   "Rethinking 'status' and 'role': towards a general model of the
       cultural organization of social relationships." In *The Relevance of
       Models for Social Anthropology,* edited by Michael Banton. ASA
       Monograph No. 1. New York: Praeger.
1970a *Description and Comparison in Cultural Anthropology.* Chicago:
       Aldine.
1970b "Epilogue: transactions in parenthood." In *Adoption in Eastern
       Oceania,* edited by V. Carroll. ASAO Monograph No. 1. Honolulu:
       University of Hawaii Press.

Goody, Jack
1969   "Adoption in cross-cultural perspective." In *Comparative Studies in
       Society and History* 11:55–78.

Gough, Kathleen
1959   "The Nayars and the definition of marriage." *Journal of the Royal
       Anthropological Institute* 89:23–34.

Greenberg, Joseph H.
1966   "Language universals." In *Current Trends in Linguistics,* Vol. 3,
       edited by Thomas A. Seboek. The Hague: Mouton.

Hainline, Jane [see Underwood, Jane Hainline]
1965   "Culture and biological adaptation." *American Anthropologist* 67:1174–1197.
Hanson, Alan
1970   *Rapan Lifeways.* Boston: Little, Brown and Co.
Harris, Marvin
1968   *The Rise of Anthropological Theory.* New York: Thomas Y. Crowell Co.
Hogbin, Ian
1935–   "Adoption in Wogeo." *Journal of the Polynesian Society* 44:208–215;
1936   45:17–38.
1971   Review of *Adoption in Eastern Oceania,* edited by Vern Carroll. *Mankind* 8:76–77.
Hooper, Antony
1970   "Adoption in the Society Islands." In *Adoption in Eastern Oceania,* edited by Vern Carroll. ASAO Monograph No. 1. Honolulu: University of Hawaii Press.
Howard, Alan
1963   "Land, activity systems, and decision-making models in Rotuma." *Ethnology* 2:407–440.
1970   "Adoption on Rotuma." In *Adoption in Eastern Oceania,* edited by Vern Carroll. ASAO Monograph No. 1. Honolulu: University of Hawaii Press.
Howard, Alan, Robert H. Heighton, Jr., Cathie E. Jordan, and Ronald G. Gallimore
1970   "Traditional and modern adoption patterns in Hawaii." In *Adoption in Eastern Oceania,* edited by Vern Carroll. ASAO Monograph No. 1. Honolulu: University of Hawaii Press.
Hunt, Edward E., Jr., Nathaniel R. Kidder, and David M. Schneider
1954   "The depopulation of Yap." *Human Biology* 26:21–51.
Jakobson, Roman
1957   "Shifters, verbal categories and the Russian verb." Article published by the Russian Language Project, Harvard University. Cambridge: Harvard University Press.
Jarvie, I.C.
1965   "Limits of functionalism and alternatives to it in anthropology." In *Functionalism and the Social Sciences: The Strength and Limits of Functionalism in Anthropology, Economics, Political Science, and Sociology,* edited by Don Martindale. Philadelphia: The American Academy of Political and Social Science.
Kaeppler, Adrienne L.
1971   "Rank in Tonga." *Ethnology* 10:174–193.
Kay, Paul
1963   "Aspects of social structure in a Tahitian urban neighborhood." *Journal of the Polynesian Society* 72:325–371.

Keesing, Roger M.

1967 "Statistical models and decision-models of social structure." *Ethnology* 6:1–16.

1970 "Kwaio fosterage." *American Anthropologist* 72:991–1019.

1971 "Formalization and the construction of ethnographies." In *Explorations in Mathematical Anthropology*, edited by Paul Kay. Cambridge: MIT Press.

1972 "Simple models of complexity: the lure of kinship." In *Kinship Studies in the Morgan Centennial Year*, edited by Priscilla Reining. Washington, D.C.: The Anthropological Society of Washington.

1975 *Kin Groups and Social Structure.* New York: Holt, Rinehart and Winston.

Kirkpatrick, John T.

1973 "Personal names on Yap." Master's thesis, University of Chicago.

Kiste, Robert C.

1968 *Kili Island: a Study of the Relocation of the ex-Bikini Marshallese.* Eugene, Oregon: Department of Anthropology, University of Oregon.

Kennedy, Donald G.

1931 *Field Notes on the Culture of Vaitupu.* Polynesian Society Memoir No. 9. Wellington: The Polynesian Society.

1953 "Land tenure in the Ellice Islands." *Journal of the Polynesian Society* 64:348–358.

Kennedy, R.

1937 "A survey of Indonesian civilization." In *Studies in the Science of Society*, edited by George P. Murdock. New Haven: Yale University Press.

Koch, Gerd

1963 "Notizen über Verwandtschaft, Adoption und Freundschaft im Ellice-Archipel (Westpolynesian)." *Baessler Archiv* N.S. 11:107–114.

Krämer, Augustin

1902 *Die Samoa-Inseln.* 2 Vols. Stuttgart: E. Naegele.

Labby, David

1971 "Incest as cannibalism: the Yapese analysis." Ms. (privately circulated).

1972 "The anthropology of others: an analysis of the traditional ideology of Yap, Western Caroline Islands." Ph.D. dissertation, University of Chicago.

Lévi-Strauss, Claude

1963 "The bear and the barber." *Journal of the Royal Anthropological Institute* 93:1–11.

1967a *Structural Anthropology.* Garden City, New York: Anchor Books.

1967b "Language and the analysis of social laws." In *Structural Anthropology.* Garden City, New York: Anchor Books.

1969 *The Elementary Structures of Kinship.* Boston: Beacon Press.

Levy, Robert I.
1970   "Tahitian adoption as a psychological message." In *Adoption in Eastern Oceania*, edited by Vern Carroll. ASAO Monograph No. 1. Honolulu: University of Hawaii Press.

Lieber, Michael D.
1970   "Adoption on Kapingamarangi." In *Adoption in Eastern Oceania*, edited by Vern Carroll. ASAO Monograph No. 1. Honolulu: University of Hawaii Press.
1974   "Land tenure on Kapingamarangi." In *Land Tenure in Oceania*, edited by Henry Lundsgaarde. ASAO Monograph No. 2. Honolulu: University Press of Hawaii.

Lambert, Bernd
1964   "Fosterage in the Northern Gilbert Islands." *Ethnology* 3:232–258.
1970   "Adoption, guardianship, and social stratification in the Northern Gilbert Islands." In *Adoption in Eastern Oceania*, edited by Vern Carroll. ASAO Monograph No. 1. Honolulu: University of Hawaii Press.

Laughlin, Charles D., Jr.
1974   "Deprivation and reciprocity." *Man* 9:380–396.

Laughlin, Charles D., Jr., and Ivan A. Brady
1976   "Extinction and survival in human populations: diaphasis and change in adaptive infrastructures." Ms. (privately circulated).

Laughlin, Charles D., Jr., and Eugene D'Aquili
1974   *Biogenetic Structuralism*. New York: Columbia University Press.

Leach, Edmund
1955   "Polyandry, inheritance and the definition of marriage." *Man* 55:182–186.
1958   "Concerning Trobriand clans and the kinship category *tabu*." In *The Developmental Cycle in Domestic Groups*, edited by Jack Goody. Cambridge Papers in Social Anthropology No. 1. Cambridge: Cambridge University Press.
1961   "Rethinking anthropology." In *Rethinking Anthropology*, by Edmund Leach. London: Athlone Press.
1964   "Animal categories and verbal abuse." In *New Directions in the Study of Language*, edited by Erich H. Lenneberg. Cambridge: MIT Press.
1965   "On the 'founding fathers'." *Encounter* 25:24–36.

Lingenfelter, Sherwood
1971   "Political leadership and culture change in Yap." Ph.D. dissertation, University of Pittsburgh.

Lowie, Robert
1930   "Adoption—Primitive." In *Encyclopedia of the Social Sciences*, edited by K.A. Seligman. New York: Macmillan.

Lundsgaarde, Henry P.
1970   "Some legal aspects of Gilbertese adoption." In *Adoption in Eastern Oceania*, edited by Vern Carroll. ASAO Monograph No. 1. Honolulu: University of Hawaii Press.

302 REFERENCES

Lundsgaarde, Henry P., and Martin G. Silverman
1972 "Category and group in Gilbertese kinship: an updating of Good-enough's analysis." *Ethnology* 11:95–110.

Mahoney, Francis
1958 "Land tenure patterns on Yap Island." In *Land Tenure Patterns: Trust Territory of the Pacific Islands*, edited by John E. de Young. Agana, Guam: Office of the High Commissioner, Trust Territory of the Pacific Islands.

Malinowski, Bronislaw
1939 "The group and the individual in functional analysis." *American Journal of Sociology* 44:938–964.

Marsack, C.C.
1958 *Notes on the Practices of the Court and the Principles in the Hearing of Cases.* . . . Apia: Lands and Titles Court of Western Samoa.

Marshall, Keith ("Mac")
1971 "Incest and endogamy on Namoluk Atoll." Ms (privately circulated).
1972 "The structure of solidarity and alliance on Namoluk Atoll." Ph.D. dissertation, University of Washington.

Mauss, Marcel
1967 *The Gift.* New York: W.W. Norton and Co. (first published 1925).

McArthur, Norma, and J.F. Yaxley
1968 *Condominium of the New Hebrides: A Report on the First Census of the Population, 1967.* Sydney: Government Printer.

McKinley, Robert
1973 Review of *Adoption in Eastern Oceania*, edited by Vern Carroll. *Journal of Asian Studies* 32:734–737.

Mead, Margaret
1928 *Coming of Age in Samoa.* New York: Morrow.
1930 *The Social Organization of Manu'a.* Bernice P. Bishop Museum Bulletin No. 76. Honolulu: Bishop Museum Press.

Meggitt, Mervyn J.
1962 "The growth and decline of agnatic descent groups among the Mae Enga of the New Guinea Highlands." *Ethnology* 1:158–165.

Merton, Robert K.
1957 *Social Theory and Social Structure.* Glencoe, Illinois: The Free Press (revised and enlarged edition).

Metge, Joan
1971 Review of *Adoption in Eastern Oceania*, edited by Vern Carroll. *Man* 6:518.

Monberg, Torben
1970 "Determinants of choice in adoption and fosterage on Bellona Island." *Ethnology* 2:99–136.

Morton, Keith L.
1972 "Kinship, economics, and exchange in a Tongan village." Ph.D. dissertation, University of Oregon.

Müller, Wilhelm
    1918   *Yap*. Ergebnisse der Südsee-Expedition, Series 2B, Vol. 2, edited by G. Thilenius. Hamburg: L. Friederichsen & Co.
Murdock, George P.
    1967   "Ethnographic atlas: a summary." *Ethnology* 6.
Office of the District Administrator
    1972   "Statistical questionnaire for preparations of the United Nations report." Colonia, Yap: Office of the District Administrator.
Ottino, Paul
    1970   "Adoption on Rangiroa Atoll, Tuamotu Archipelago." In *Adoption in Eastern Oceania*, edited by Vern Carroll. ASAO Monograph No. 1. Honolulu: University of Hawaii Press.
Pollock, Nancy
    1970   "Breadfruit and breadwinning on Namu Atoll, Marshall Islands." Ph.D. dissertation, University of Hawaii.
Prattis, J. Ian
    1973   "Strategising man." *Man* 8:46–58.
Roberts, H.S.
    1970   *Report of the Department of Justice for the year 1970*. Government of Tonga. Nuku'alofa: Government Printing Office.
Rynkiewich, Michael A.
    1972   "Land Tenure among Arno Marshallese." Ph.D. dissertation, University of Minnesota.
    1974   "Coming home to Bokelab." In *Conformity and Conflict: Readings in Cultural Anthropology*, edited by James P. Spradley and David W. McCurdy. 2nd edition. Boston: Little, Brown and Co.
Sā Tamasese
    n.d.   "Claim of the *Sulis* for the *Tamasese* title." Files of the Land and Titles Court, 1965. Apia, Western Samoa.
Sahlins, Marshall D.
    1960   "Production, distribution and power in primitive society." In *Men and Cultures: Selected Papers of the Fifth International Congress of Anthropological and Ethnological Sciences*, edited by Anthony F.C. Wallace. Philadelphia: University of Pennsylvania Press.
    1963   "Poor man, rich man, big-man, chief: political types in Melanesia and Polynesia." *Comparative Studies in Society and History* 5:285–303.
    1965   "On the sociology of primitive exchange." In *The Relevance of Models for Social Anthropology*, edited by Michael Banton. ASA Monograph No. 1. New York: Praeger.
    1972   *Stone Age Economics*. Chicago: Aldine.
Scheffler, Harold W.
    1966   "Ancestor worship in anthropology: Or observations on descent and descent groups." *Current Anthropology* 7:541–551.
    1970   "Kinship and adoption in the northern New Hebrides." In *Adoption*

in Eastern Oceania, edited by Vern Carroll. ASAO Monograph No. 1. Honolulu: University of Hawaii Press.

1972a   "Kinship semantics." In *Annual Review of Anthropology*, Vol. 1, edited by Bernard J. Siegel. Palo Alto, California: Annual Reviews, Inc.

1972b   Review of *Disconcerting Issue* by Martin G. Silverman. *Journal of Pacific History* 7:233–234.

1972c   "Baniata kin classification: the case for extensions." *Southwestern Journal of Anthropology* 4:350–381.

1973   "Kinship, descent and alliance." In *Handbook of Social and Cultural Anthropology*, edited by John J. Honigmann. Chicago: Rand McNally.

Scheffler, Harold W., and Floyd G. Lounsbury

1972   *A Study in Structural Semantics: The Siriono Kinship System*. Englewood Cliffs, New Jersey: Prentice Hall.

Schneider, David M.

1953   "Yap kinship terminology and kin groups." *American Anthropologist* 55:215–236.

1955   "Abortion and depopulation on Yap." In *Health, Culture and Community*, edited by Benjamin Paul. New York: Russell Sage Foundation.

1957   "Political organization, supernatural sanctions and the punishment for incest on Yap." *American Anthropologist* 59:791–800.

1962   "Double descent on Yap." *Journal of the Polynesian Society* 71:1–24.

1964   "The nature of kinship." *Man* 64:180–181.

1965a   "Some muddles in the models: or, how the system really works." In *The Relevance of Models for Social Anthropology*, edited by Michael Banton. ASA Monograph No. 1. New York: Praeger.

1965b   "Kinship and biology." In *Aspects of the Analysis of Family Structure*, edited by A.J. Coale. Princeton: Princeton University Press.

1967   "Descent and filiation as cultural constructs." *Southwestern Journal of Anthropology* 23:65–73.

1968a   *American Kinship: A Cultural Account*. Englewood Cliffs, New Jersey: Prentice-Hall.

1968b   "Virgin birth." *Man* 3:126–129.

1969   "Kinship, nationality and religion in American culture: toward a definition of kinship." In *Forms of Symbolic Action*, edited by Robert F. Spencer. Proceedings of the 1969 Annual Spring Meeting of the American Ethnological Society. Seattle: University of Washington Press.

1970   "American kin categories." In *Échanges et Communications: Mélanges Offerts à Claude Lévi-Strauss...*, edited by Jean Pouillon and Pierre Maranda. The Hague: Mouton.

1972   "What is kinship all about?" In *Kinship Studies in the Morgan Centennial Year*, edited by Priscilla Reining. Washington, D.C.: The Anthropological Society of Washington.

Shore, Bradd
1971   "Incest, power and exogamy in Samoa." Ms. (privately circulated).
Silverman, Martin G.
1970   "Banaban adoption." In *Adoption in Eastern Oceania*, edited by Vern Carroll. ASAO Monograph No. 1. Honolulu: University of Hawaii Press.
1971   *Disconcerting Issue: Meaning and Struggle in a Resettled Pacific Community*. Chicago: University of Chicago Press.
Smith, J. Jerome
1972   "Intergenerational land transactions on Rota, Mariana Islands: a study of ethnographic theory." Ph.D. dissertation, University of Arizona.
Spoehr, Alexander
1949   *Majuro, A Village in the Marshall Islands*. Fieldiana: Anthropology, Vol. 39. Chicago: Chicago Natural History Museum.
1954   *Saipan: The Ethnography of a War-devastated Island*. Fieldiana: Anthropology, Vol. 41. Chicago: Chicago Natural History Museum.
Swartz, Marc J.
1960   "Situational determinants of kinship terminology." *Southwestern Journal of Anthropology* 16:393–397.
Thompson, Laura
1945   *The Native Culture of the Mariana Islands*. Bernice P. Bishop Museum Bulletin No. 185. Honolulu: Bishop Museum Press.
Tobin, Jack A.
1967   "The resettlement of the Enewetak people: a study of a displaced community in the Marshall Islands." Ph.D. dissertation, University of California, Berkeley.
Tonkinson, Robert
1968   *Maat Village, Efate: A Relocated Community in the New Hebrides*. Eugene, Oregon: Department of Anthropology, University of Oregon.
1974   *The Jigalong Mob: Aboriginal Victors of the Desert Crusade*. Menlo Park, California: Cummings Publishing Co.
Trivers, Robert L.
1971   "The evolution of reciprocal altruism." *Quarterly Review of Biology* 46:35–57.
Turnbull, Colin
1972   *The Mountain People*. New York: Simon and Schuster.
Turner, G. A.
1884   *Samoa a Hundred Years Ago and Long Before*. London: Macmillan.
Underwood, Jane Hainline.
1973   "The demography of a myth: abortion on Yap." *Human Biology in Oceania* 2:115–127.
United States Trust Territory of the Pacific Islands
1960   *Handbook for District and Community Court Judges, Clerks of Court*

306   REFERENCES

> *and Trial Assistants.* Moen, Truk, Caroline Islands: Chambers of
> the Chief Justice.

Weckler, Joseph E.

   1953   "Adoption on Mokil." *American Anthropologist* 55:555–568.

Whitten, Norman E., Jr., and Dorothea S. Whitten

   1972   "Social strategies and social relationships." In *Annual Review of Anthropology*, Vol. 1, edited by Bernard J. Siegel. Palo Alto: Annual Reviews, Inc.

Wilson, Walter Scott

   1968   "Land, activity and social organization of Lelu, Kusaie." Ph.D. dissertation, University of Pennsylvania.

   1971   Review of *Adoption in Eastern Oceania*, edited by Vern Carroll. *Micronesica* 7:244–245.

Wolf, Eric R.

   1966   "Kinship, friendship, and patron-client relations in complex societies." In *The Social Anthropology of Complex Societies*, edited by Michael Banton. ASA Monograph No. 4. New York: Praeger.

CONTRIBUTORS

IVAN BRADY is associate professor and coordinator for anthropology at the State University of New York College, Oswego. He completed his undergraduate work at Northern Arizona University in 1966 and received his Ph.D. from the University of Oregon in 1970. He was assistant professor of anthropology at the University of Cincinnati from 1970 to 1973. His fieldwork includes fifteen months of research on the Ellice Islands in 1968, 1969, and 1971.

CHARLES R. BRODER received his M.A. in anthropology in 1972 from the University of Chicago and has worked as a research associate for the State of Hawaii. He conducted research on the island of Yap in 1969 and 1972.

CANDACE CARLETON BROOKS is assistant professor of anthropology at San Jose State University. She received her Ph.D. from Stanford in 1969. She has spent sixteen months (1966, 1967, and 1970) doing field research in French Polynesia.

JOHN T. KIRKPATRICK received his M.A. from the University of Chicago in 1973. He conducted field research on Yap, Western Caroline Islands, for eight months in 1972 and 1973, and is currently doing research in French Polynesia. He has taught at Governor's State University and Northeastern Illinois University.

MAC MARSHALL is assistant professor of anthropology at the University of Iowa. He completed his undergraduate studies at Grinnell College (B.A. 1965), and did graduate work at the University of Washington (M.A. 1967, Ph.D. 1972). He conducted field research for eighteen months on Namoluk Atoll and with Namoluk people on Moen, Truk, from 1969 to 1971. He returned to Namoluk in 1976 for additional research.

KEITH L. MORTON is assistant professor of anthropology at California State University, Northridge. He received his Ph.D. from the University of Oregon in 1972. His field research includes eleven months in Tonga (1970–1971).

MICHAEL RYNKIEWICH is assistant professor of anthropology at Macalester College. He received his B.A. from Bethel College in 1966, completing his M.A. in 1968 and his Ph.D. in anthropology in 1972 at the University of Minnesota. His field research includes sixteen months on Arno Atoll in the Marshall Islands.

BRADD SHORE holds a research position at the Center for South Pacific Studies and a teaching position in anthropology at the University of California, Santa Cruz. He completed his undergraduate work at the University of California, Berkeley, in 1967. His work in Western Samoa includes two years as a teacher for the Peace Corps and eighteen-months' fieldwork for his graduate degrees from 1971 to 1974. He expects to receive his Ph.D. from the University of Chicago in 1976.

ROBERT TONKINSON did his undergraduate work and subsequently completed his M.A. (1966) in social anthropology at the University of Western Australia. He has done fieldwork in Australia and in the New Hebrides. He received his Ph.D. from the University of British Columbia in 1972 and is currently assistant professor of anthropology at the University of Oregon.

J. JEROME SMITH did his graduate work in anthropology at the University of Arizona, completing his M.A. in 1969 and his Ph.D. in 1972. His doctoral research involved twelve months of fieldwork on Rota, Mariana Islands, in 1971 and 1972; he returned for an additional nine months' work in 1974 and 1975. He is presently assistant professor of anthropology at the University of South Florida.

WALTER SCOTT WILSON was professor of anthropology and the chairman of the behavioral science faculty at the University of Guam. He received an M.A. in sociology from the University of Buffalo in 1959 and a Ph.D. in anthropology from the University of Pennsylvania in 1968. He did fieldwork on Kusaie from 1960 to 1961 and in the summers of 1964, 1966, 1973, and 1974. He passed away in November 1975.

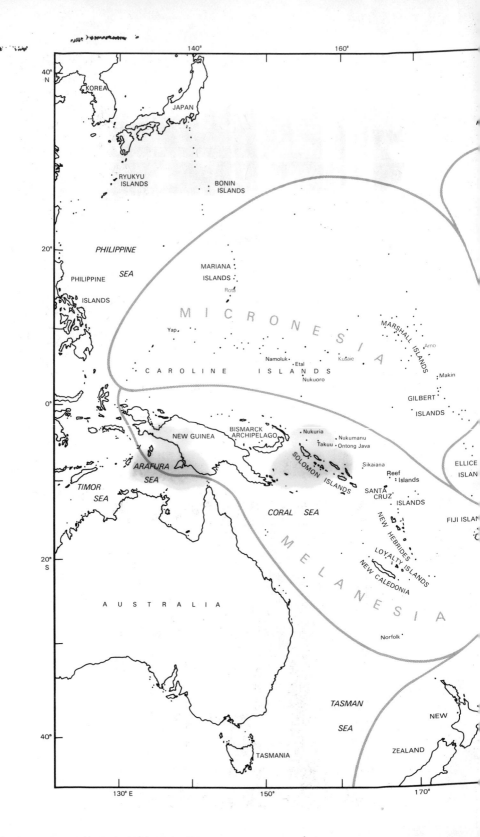